E-LEARNING
Uncovered ℠

Adobe©
Captivate© 2017

Diane Elkins
Desirée Pinder

E-Learning Uncovered: Adobe Captivate 2017

By Diane Elkins and Desirée Pinder

Copyright © 2017 by E-Learning Uncovered, Inc.

E-Learning Uncovered, Inc.

52 Tuscan Way, Suite 202-379

St. Augustine, FL 32092

www.elearninguncovered.com

Trademarks

Adobe Captivate is a registered trademark of Adobe Systems Incorporated. Microsoft is a registered trademark of Microsoft Corporation. iPad and iPhone are trademarks of Apple Inc., registered in the U.S. and other countries.

Other product and company names mentioned herein may be trademarks of their respective owners. Use of trademarks or product names is not intended to convey endorsement or affiliation in this book.

Warning and Disclaimer

The information provided is on an "as is" basis. Every effort has been made to make this book as complete and as accurate as possible, but no warranty or fitness is implied. The authors and the publisher shall have neither liability nor responsibility to any person or entity with respect to any loss or damages arising from the information contained in this book.

Chapter Table of Contents

Detailed Table of Contents

Detailed Table of Contents

Detailed Table of Contents

Detailed Table of Contents

Detailed Table of Contents

Detailed Table of Contents

Detailed Table of Contents

Detailed Table of Contents

Detailed Table of Contents

Introduction

I started using Captivate (well, its earlier version, RoboDemo) almost 15 years ago. The industry and the software have come a long way since then. Captivate continues to be a pioneer in advancing mobile technology, with everything from gesture navigation and geolocation, to even a game that uses a phone's accelerometer.

This release is no different. With the introduction of fluid boxes, Captivate 2017 strikes a balance between giving you design control with on resonsive projects (versus a fully templated approach) and reducing the amount of manual work needed (versus the previous breakpoints approach).

I'll be honest...they take a little getting used to. But once you get the hang of it, there's a lot you can really do with them. Enjoy trying them out!

Acknowledgments

Desiree and I would like to extend our special thanks to some of the many people who made this book possible. We'd like to thank Leslie Harrison for reviewing the book and helping us to keep it organized and free of unsightly typos.

Plus we'd like to thank the folks at Adobe, especially Pooja Jaisingh and Allen Partridge, for always being so willing to answer my questions!

Diane Elkins

Getting the Most Out of This Book

This book assumes you are a functional user of Windows software. If you are familiar with how to use dialog boxes, drop-down menus, and other standard Windows conventions, then you'll be fine. The book is written for the PC version of Captivate. If you are using Captivate for Mac, you'll still get a lot out of this book, but you may find some differences in some of the procedures. The Appendix has a few quick tips for Mac users.

Use the detailed table of contents and comprehensive index to help you find what you are looking for. In addition to procedures, look for all the hints, tips, and cautions that can help you save time, avoid problems, and make your courses more engaging.

 DESIGN TIP

Design Tips give you insight on how to implement the different features and include everything from graphic design to instructional design to usability.

 CAUTION

Pay special attention to the Cautions (which are full of "lessons learned the hard way") so you can avoid some common problems.

 BRIGHT IDEA

Bright Ideas are special explanations and ideas for getting more out of the software.

 POWER TIP

Power Tips are advanced tips and secrets that can help you take your production to the next level.

 TIME SAVER

Time Savers...well...save you time. These tips include software shortcuts and ways to streamline your production efforts.

 This symbol indicates a cross-reference to another part of the book.

Put your new skills to work by visiting the companion site at:

www.elearninguncovered.com

➤ Access practice files.

➤ Download free resources.

➤ Subscribe to our blog.

➤ Ask about bulk purchases.

➤ Explore the other books in the series.

Notes

Getting to Know Captivate

Introduction

Adobe Captivate 2017 is a rapid development authoring tool that lets you create engaging, interactive e-learning courses without programming knowledge. With Captivate, you can create courses that include text, graphics, animations, audio, video, screen simulations, interactions, branching, questions, and more.

Captivate also lets you create mobile-responsive content, letting you create courses that can be viewed on many types of devices.

Once your course is complete, Captivate offers several options to publish and distribute your course. You can publish to Flash or HTML5, CD-ROMs, learning management systems, or mobile devices.

In This Chapter

- The Captivate Interface
- The Properties Panel
- Objects and the Timeline
- File Management

Notes

The Captivate Interface

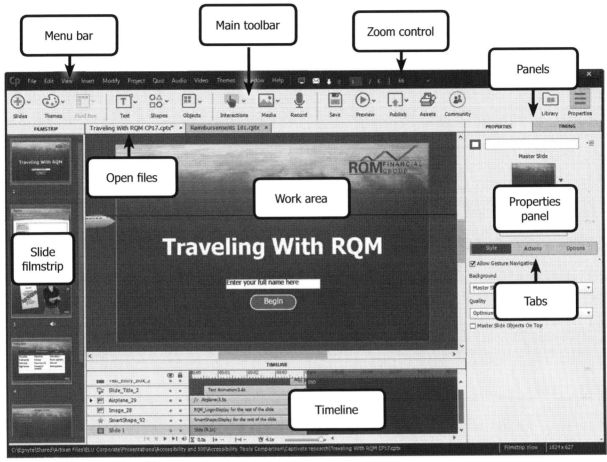

Appendix: Mac Interface, p. 293

Main Toolbar

The main toolbar is where many of the options are located for inserting new slides and objects, as well as previewing and publishing your project. Many of the buttons have drop-down menus with additional options.

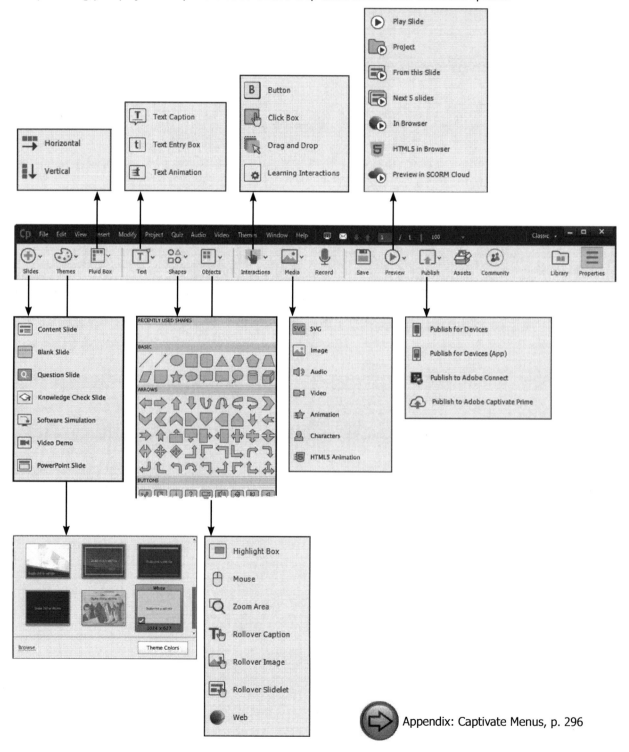

Appendix: Captivate Menus, p. 296

Customize the Interface

You can customize the Captivate interface to best fit your needs and working styles.

To show or hide a toolbar or panel:
1. Go to the **Window** menu.
2. Select or de-select the element you want to show or hide.

To show the Library or Properties pane:
1. Click the **Library** or **Properties** button on the toolbar. **(A)**

To collapse the contents of a panel:
1. Double-click the name of the panel. **(B)**

To expand the contents of a panel:
1. Click the name of the panel. **(B)**

To change the order of panels in a given group:
1. Click and drag the name of the panel to where you want it. **(C)**

To resize the Timeline panel:
1. Click and drag the top edge of the panel up or down. **(D)**

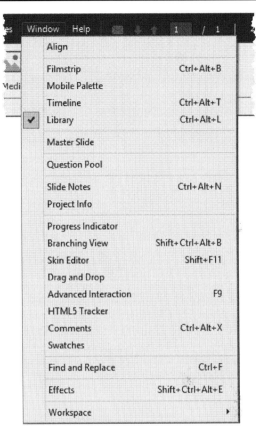

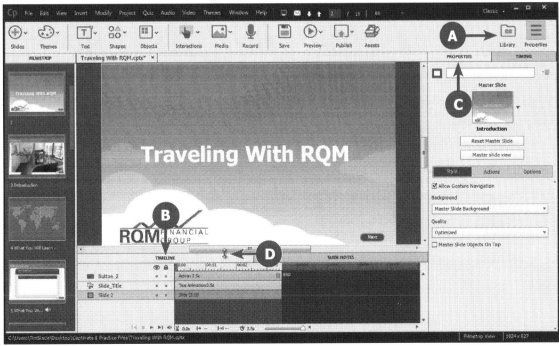

Customize the Interface (cont'd)

To change the size of the thumbnails in the filmstrip:

1. Right-click a thumbnail.
2. Select **Filmstrip**.
3. Select the size you want.

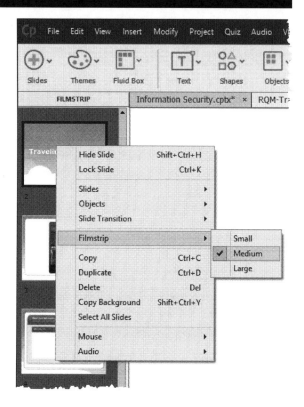

To change the magnification of the slide in the work area:

1. Click the zoom drop-down menu.
2. Select the magnification option you want.

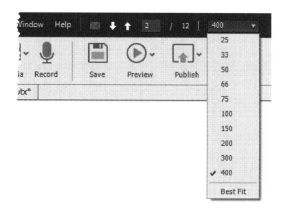

Creating Customized Workspaces

Workspaces are saved interface configurations. If you enable the setting, you can change the default views, rearrange the interface, and save that configuration. For example, you can create a workspace with the **Slide Notes** panel always showing if you plan to use closed captioning or you can put the **Library** panel below the **Properties** panel.

To enable workspace configuration:

1. Go to the **Edit** menu.
2. Select **Preferences**.
3. On the **General Settings** tab, check **Enable custom workspaces/panel undocking**.
4. Click the **OK** button.
5. Restart Captivate.

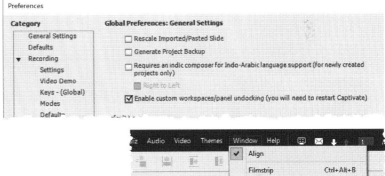

To configure your workspace:

- Use the **Window** menu to show and hide different features.
- Click and drag the name tab of different panels (such as **Timeline** or **Library**) to the location you want.

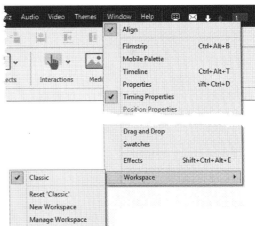

To save your own workspace:

1. Go to the **Window** menu.
2. Select **Workspace**.
3. Select **New Workspace**.
4. Enter a name for the workspace.
5. Click **OK**.

To apply an existing workspace:

1. Go to the **Window** menu.
2. Select **Workspace.**
3. Select the workspace you want.

Additional Workspace Options

Select **Manage Workspace** if you want to rename or delete any workspaces that you have created.

If you made changes to a workspace and want to go back to the original state, select the **Reset** option on the **Workspace** sub-menu.

You can access the same workspace options from the drop-down menu in the top-right corner of the interface.

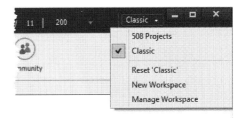

The Properties Panel

Your slides and every object on your slides have properties: images, captions, audio, etc. These properties are displayed and modified in the **Properties** panel. You will learn more about specific properties for each type of object in their respective chapters. Here are a few guidelines that apply to the **Properties** panel for any object type.

- If the **Properties** panel isn't showing, click the **Properties** button on the main toolbar. **(A)**
- Select an object in the work area or timeline to view and change its properties in the panel.
- Select more than one object to view and change certain shared properties.
- Click the various tabs to view more options. **(B)**
- Click triangle markers to expand and collapse individual sections, where available. **(C)**

The options in the **Properties** panel will vary based on the item or object you have selected.

 **TIME SAVER**

In blue, underlined number fields (known as hot text), either click and type a new number, or click and drag right to increase or left to decrease the number. **(D)**

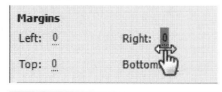

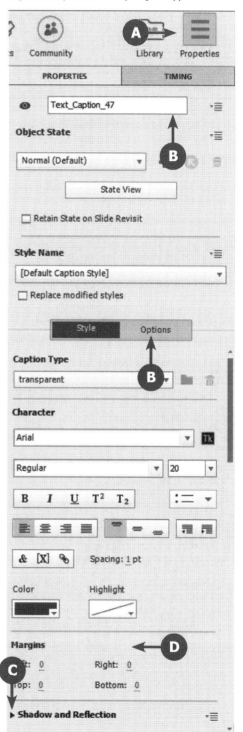

Objects and the Timeline

When you place an object on a slide, a corresponding line item is added to the timeline. Among other things, you can adjust:

- **Layering**: Objects at the top of the timeline appear in front of objects at the bottom of the timeline.
- **Visibility**: Click the dot next to an object under the "eyeball" icon to hide it from view while working. (This does not affect your published course, only what shows in the work area.)
- **Start Time and Length**: When the slide plays, objects appear when the bar for that object starts, and they disappear when the bar ends.

 Object Properties, ch. 6
Timing Slide Objects, p. 122

 **TIME SAVER**

Objects in the timeline are color-coded:
- Green: Interactive objects
- Blue: Standard content objects
- Beige: Placeholder objects

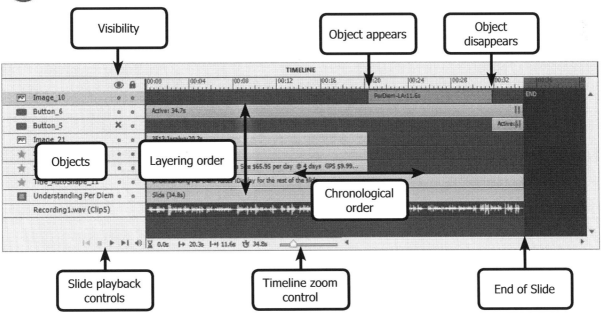

Visibility

Object appears

Object disappears

Objects

Layering order

Chronological order

Slide playback controls

Timeline zoom control

End of Slide

Select Objects

You can select objects in the work area or in the timeline.

Work Area

- Select a single object by clicking on it.
- Select multiple objects by holding the **Ctrl** or **Shift** key down while clicking on them or by dragging your mouse around the objects.

Timeline

- Select a single object by clicking it in the timeline.
- Select multiple objects by holding the **Ctrl** key down while clicking on them individually.
- Select consecutive items on the timeline by clicking the first object, holding down the **Shift** key, and then clicking the last object.

 **TIME SAVER**

Click anywhere in the work area and press **Ctrl** + **A** to select all objects on a slide.

File Management

Open an Existing Project

When you launch Captivate, the **Welcome** screen appears.

To open a project from the Welcome screen:

1. Click the **Recent** tab if it is not already selected.
2. Select the project you want.
3. Click the **Open** button.

—— or ——

1. Click the **Browse** button.
2. Find and select the file you want.
3. Click the **Open** button.

To open a project from the File menu:

1. Go to the **File** menu.
2. Select **Open Recent**.
3. Select the file you want.

—— or ——

1. Go to the **File** menu.
2. Select **Open**.
3. Find and select the file you want.
4. Click the **Open** button.

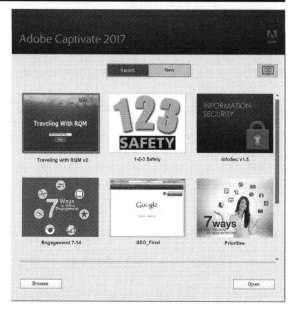

Moving Around a Project

Use any of the following methods to move around a project.

- Select a thumbnail in the filmstrip to go to that slide. **(A)**
- Use your **Page Up** and **Page Down** keys to move up or down one slide.
- Use the **Next Slide** and **Previous Slide** buttons to move up or down one slide. **(B)**
- Type a slide number in the field next to the arrows to jump to that slide. **(C)**

If you have more than one project open, move from project to project by clicking the tabs. **(D)**

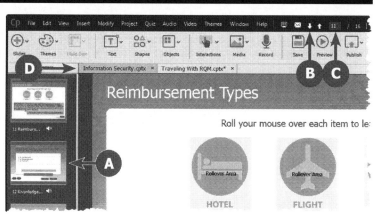

Save a Project

Options for saving a project:

- Go to the **File** menu, and select **Save**.
- Press **Ctrl + S**.

Other saving options:

- Go to the **File** menu, and select **Save As** to save the file under a different name or in a different location.
- Click **Save All** on the **File** menu to save all open projects.

CAUTION

- It is best to save your project on a local drive (such as your C drive) instead of a network drive or removable storage (such as a USB drive). Saving to something other than your local drive can cause problems with performance, saving, etc.

- Projects created in version 2017 cannot be opened in previous versions of Captivate.

Close a Project

Options for closing a project:

- Go to the **File** menu, and select **Close** to close the current project.
- Go to the **File** menu, and select **Close All** to close all open projects.
- Click the **X** in the tab to close a project but leave Captivate open. **(A)**
- Click the **X** in the top right corner of the window to close Captivate completely. **(B)**

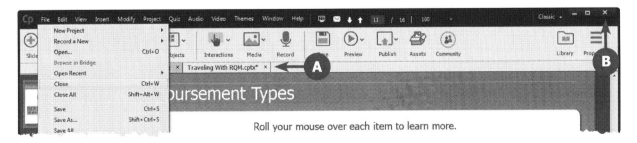

Preview a Project

To preview an individual slide:

1. Click the **Play** button in the timeline. **(A)**

———— or ————

1. Click the **Preview** drop-down button. **(B)**
2. Select **Play Slide**.

To preview more than one slide:

1. Click the **Preview** drop-down button.
2. Select the option you want.

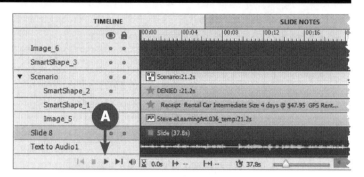

 # CAUTION

- When you preview a single slide, certain elements may not play properly, such as full-motion recordings or certain highlight boxes. Previewing more than one slide at a time gives you a more representative view of what your project will look like when published.

- When you select **In Browser**, the Flash version of the course previews. This version may not play on newer browsers, which might block Flash content playing from your computer instead of a web server.

 # BRIGHT IDEAS

- You can change the **Next 5 slides** option to a different number, such as the next 3 slides. Go to the **Edit** menu, select **Preferences**, and click the **Defaults** category to change this option. **(C)**

- Previewing in a browser has two advantages. It more closely simulates what your published course will look like if you are publishing to a browser. Since the preview appears in a browser window instead of a Captivate window, you can make changes to the Captivate file while you preview the project.

- If you will be publishing to HTML5, be sure to preview in that mode to make sure you are getting the results you want.

- Be sure to learn the keyboard shortcuts for previewing. They are big time savers!

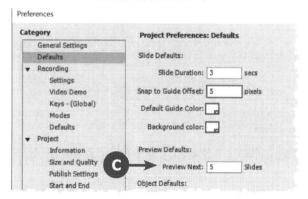

 Useful Keyboard Shortcuts, p. 298

Preview in SCORM Cloud

Adobe Captivate lets you preview your project in SCORM Cloud to verify how your course will run within a learning management system (LMS). Previewing in SCORM Cloud lets you identify and fix any LMS-related issues before publishing your content within your LMS.

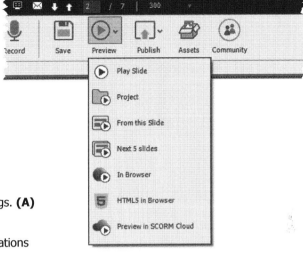

To preview in SCORM Cloud:

1. Click the **Preview** drop-down button.
2. Select **Preview in SCORM Cloud**.

To view the SCORM communication logs during preview:

1. Click the expand icon to view the communication logs. **(A)**

——— or ———

1. Click the download icon to download the communications logs as a **.txt** file. **(B)**

To view the SCORM Cloud preview results:

1. Click the **Close Window** button to exit the preview
2. Select **Get Results**.

 Publishing, ch. 12

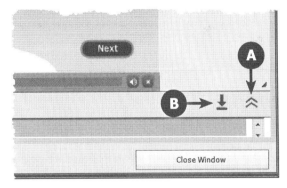

Result [Standard:SCORM1.2]

Course Details ❔	
course_id :	Course_ID1_ORG
course_title :	Captivate E-Learning Course
sco_id :	SCO_ID1
sco_title :	Course Object title
attempts :	1
suspended :	true
satisfied :	false
completion_status :	completed

Runtime data ❔	
success_status :	Unknown
entry :	Other
exit :	Suspend
location :	You%20Decide%3A%20Baggage
score_raw :	100.0
score_max :	100.0
score_scaled :	1.0

Notes

Creating New Projects

Introduction

Because Captivate is such a versatile tool, you can create many different types of projects, pulling from many different types of content. In this chapter, you will learn how to create the primary project types. In other chapters, you will learn about some of the more specialized project types.

Primary Project Types

Blank Project: Create a blank project when you want to build a lesson from scratch and add slides and elements individually. (You can also add blank slides to any project.)

Project From MS PowerPoint: Create a new project from an existing PowerPoint presentation, where each slide in PowerPoint becomes a slide in your Captivate project. (You can also add individual PowerPoint slides to any project.)

Image Slideshow: Create a new project from a series of images, where each image becomes a slide in your project. (You can also add individual image slides to any project.)

Software Simulation: Create a project by recording what you do on your computer, creating either a sit-back-and-watch demonstration or an interactive, try-it-yourself practice. (You can also add software simulations to any project.)

Video Demo: Create a full-motion video of what you do on your computer. (You can also add video demos to any project.)

Special Project Types

Responsive Project (Ch. 13): Create a new, blank project that reconfigures the view based on the type of device used by the student, such as computer vs. tablet vs. phone.

Project Template (Ch. 11): Create a template that includes slides, objects and object placeholders, settings, etc. to be used over and over again.

Project From Template (Ch. 11): Create a new project based on a saved template.

Project From Adobe Captivate Draft (Ch. 11): Create a new project based on content created in the Captivate Draft app for iPad.

Aggregator Project (Ch. 11): Create a new project that combines existing courses.

Multi-SCORM Packager (Ch. 11): Create a course from multiple projects that integrates with a learning management system (LMS).

In This Chapter

- Blank Projects
- PowerPoint Projects
- Image Slideshows
- Software Simulations
- Video Demos

Notes

Blank Projects

Create a New, Blank Project

To create a new, blank project:

1. On the **Welcome** screen, click the **New** tab.
2. Select **Blank Project**.
3. From the **Canvas** drop-down menu **(A)**, select the dimensions you want.
4. Click the **Create** button.

——— or ———

1. Go to the **File** menu.
2. Select **New Project**.
3. Select **Blank Project**.
4. Select the dimensions for your project from the drop-down menu or manually enter the dimensions.
5. Click the **OK** button.

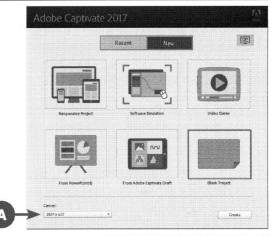

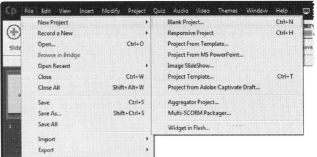

 DESIGN TIPS

- The drop-down menu with preset sizes includes resolutions that are optimized for iPad, iPhone, and YouTube.
- If you will be importing any PowerPoint slides, pick a slide size with the same aspect ratio. If you are using the widescreen format in PowerPoint, be sure to use a widescreen format in Captivate.

PowerPoint Projects

Rather than building your slides in Captivate, you can import existing content from PowerPoint. Slide notes, audio, and some animations carry over to the Captivate slide. Your PowerPoint slide notes go into the **Slide Notes** panel in Captivate, audio is added as an audio object in the timeline, and certain types of animations (both automatic and on-click) will work in Captivate as well. You can edit the PowerPoint slides directly from Captivate (assuming you have PowerPoint installed on your computer) and even link your project to the PowerPoint document to make sure you are working with the latest information.

You can either create a new project from PowerPoint or add individual slides to an existing project. In either case, one slide is created in Captivate for each imported slide from PowerPoint.

Create a New Project From PowerPoint

To create a new project from PowerPoint:

1. On the **Welcome** screen, click the **New** tab.
2. Select **From PowerPoint**.
3. Click the **Create** button.

——— or ———

1. Go to the **File** menu.
2. Select **New Project**.
3. Select **Project From MS PowerPoint**.

——— then ———

4. Find and select the file you want.
5. Click the **Open** button.
6. Enter the properties you want. (See below.)
7. Click the **OK** button.

Project Properties

This section is only available when creating a new project from PowerPoint. If you are importing slides into an existing project, then the project's properties will be used.

Name: The name of the PowerPoint file is used as the default name for the project. You can change the name here if you want to.

Width, Height, and Preset Sizes: Either select a preset size from the menu, or enter your own values for the size of the project. The default size is the size of your PowerPoint presentation.

Maintain Aspect Ratio: Check this box if you want the project to have the same proportions as the PowerPoint slides. This prevents the images from being stretched in one direction or the other.

Slide Thumbnails

Check or uncheck the box **(A)** for each slide to indicate which slides you want to import. To save time, use the **Select All** and **Clear All** buttons to select or de-select them all at once.

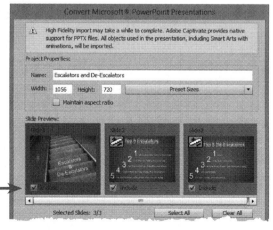

Create a New Project From PowerPoint (cont'd)

Project Properties (cont'd)

Advance Slide

Indicate if you want the slides to advance automatically on the timeline (like any other slide in your project) or advance on mouse click. If you select the mouse-click option, Captivate inserts a click box that covers each slide. When the student clicks anywhere on the slide, the slide advances, just like it would in PowerPoint.

High Fidelity (A)

The **High Fidelity** option proves better support for PowerPoint features found in **.pptx** files, such as SmartArt, hierarchical animations, certain text and object effects, etc. (In versions 5.5 and earlier, Captivate converted **.pptx** to **.ppt** as part of the import, removing some of these features.) If you have a **.pptx** file with any of these features, check the **High Fidelity** box to have them included in the import.

If you check **High Fidelity**, a **Slide Duration** check box appears. **(C)** Check this box if you want to retain any special timings you added in PowerPoint via **Rehearse Timings** or **Advance Slide** > **After**.

Linked (B)

When this box is checked, Captivate links to the PowerPoint file instead of embedding it into the presentation. This makes your project size smaller, but it also means you have to have access to the PowerPoint file to edit the project. In addition, if you link the file, any edits you make to the slide in Captivate are made to the original PowerPoint file as well—which you may or may not want.

Link when you want to...	**Embed** when you want to...
• Keep the file size small. • Update the PPT file when you update the Captivate slide.	• Work with the project even if you don't have access to the PowerPoint file. • Import a PPT file that is likely to change locations. • Make changes to the Captivate slide without changing the original PPT file.

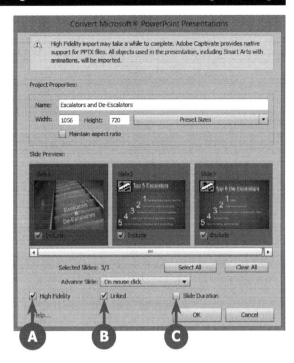

Insert Individual PowerPoint Slides, p. 35
Edit a PowerPoint Slide, p. 36
Update an Imported Slide, p. 37

CAUTION

• Students may not know they are supposed to click on the slide to trigger an animation or advance to the next slide. Make sure you include clear instructions.

• With a linked file, make sure the PPT file stays in the same location with the same file name. Otherwise, the link between the two will be broken.

• Avoid editing both versions of a slide at the same time (the Captivate slide and the linked PPT slide) as your edits might not be saved properly.

• During a high-fidelity import, make sure PowerPoint is closed, and do not do any copying or pasting until the importing is done.

Image Slideshows

There are three ways to add images to your projects:

Adding Image Slides, p. 38
Adding Images to a Slide, p. 61

- **New image slideshow**: Select a folder of images and create a new project with each selected image on its own slide. Use this to create a quick and easy slideshow.

- **Image slide**: Add a new slide with the image as the background.

- **Image on slide**: Place an image on any existing slide and either keep it as a slide object that can be moved, resized, and manipulated, or merge it to become part of the background.

Create a New Image Slideshow

To create a new image slideshow:

1. Go to the **File** menu.

2. Select **New Project**.

3. Select **Image SlideShow**.

4. Select a preset size from the menu or enter your own dimensions for the project.

5. Click the **OK** button.

6. Find and select the images you want to add.

7. Click the **OK** button.

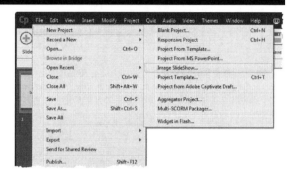

If your images are larger than the dimensions for the project, a dialog box appears after step 5 that gives you options for resizing the image as well as image-editing tools.

Resizing Options

Fit to Stage: This option shrinks the image to the largest size that will fit fully on the page. Since the image and the slide may have different aspect ratios (height/width proportions), you may end up with empty space either above and below or to the left and right of the image.

Crop: This option lets you crop the picture for a better fit. Drag the crop frame handles, and move the crop frame to select the part of the image you want to keep. The portion of the image selected will then appear as large as possible on the slide.

Constraint Proportion: If you are cropping the image, check this box to make the crop frame maintain the same aspect ratio as the slide. Uncheck it if you want to use a different aspect ratio.

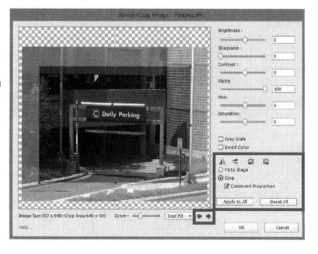

Apply to All: Click this button if you want to use the same sizing specifications for all pictures being imported. If you do not want to treat them all the same, click the arrows at the bottom of the screen to move from picture to picture, adjusting each one individually.

Editing Images, p. 61

Software Simulations

Software simulations, also known as screen recordings, let you capture whatever you are doing on your computer. You can create two different types of simulations: sit-back-and-watch demonstrations and interactive, try-it-yourself practices where the student gets to perform the steps and get feedback.

The standard Captivate software simulation is a series of static screen captures (one for every click, typing, etc., you perform) with an animated mouse movement on top. When published, it plays like a movie, even though it is more of a filmstrip behind the scenes. In addition, you can create a video demo—a full-motion recording of your actions (on a single slide), which plays back as a video.

Preparing for a Screen Recording Session

There are many things you'll need to plan and do before you even open Captivate, both in your computer settings and in the software you plan to capture. To help ensure you record a good, clean capture, use this checklist before you click the **Record** button.

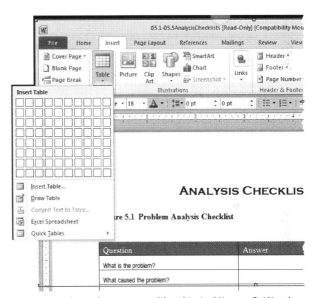

- ❑ Create sample files, scenarios, etc., to demonstrate during the capture. For example, to demonstrate how to approve a timesheet, you might first need to set up a supervisor, set up an employee, and create the timesheet to be approved.

- ❑ Walk through all the steps you plan to demonstrate. You'd be surprised at how many times this helps you realize you weren't sure about a step or that you need to do some more prep work.

- ❑ Undo anything you did during the walk-through. For example, if you walked through the steps for authorizing a timesheet, you might need to go back and unauthorize it or create a new one for the actual capture.

A drop-down menu like this in Microsoft Word that extends beyond your recording window can cause havoc during a recording session.

- ❑ Decide how big you want the application to be. Just because you have a monitor with a 1330 x 960 resolution doesn't mean you should record the application window that big. It is usually best to make the application window as small as possible without hiding features or having to scroll back and forth frequently.

- ❑ Position your application window so any drop-down menus stay within the recording area (designated by a red frame). Usually, moving the window to the edge of your monitor helps with this. It may force the drop-down menu to reposition itself.

- ❑ A camera shutter sound plays every time Captivate takes a capture. Turn up your volume so you can hear this sound.

- ❑ Turn off email, instant messenger, and any other application that might generate an unwanted pop-up window during your capture.

Record a Software Simulation

To record a software simulation:

1. On the **Welcome** screen, click the **New** tab.
2. Select **Software Simulation**.
3. Click the **Create** button.

———— or ————

1. Go to the **File** menu.
2. Select **Record a New**.
3. Select **Software Simulation**.

———— then ————

4. Configure the recording settings (covered in the remainder of this chapter). **(A)**
5. Adjust the red recording frame around the part of your screen you want to record. **(B)**
6. Click the **Record** button. **(C)**
7. Perform the steps of the procedure you are demonstrating.
8. Press the **End** button on your keyboard, or click the **Captivate** icon in your system tray.

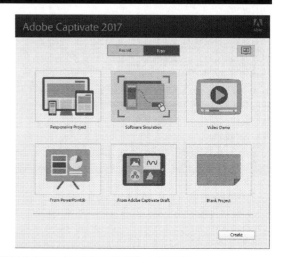

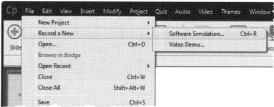

Recording Size Settings

When you set up your recording size, select **Screen Area** if you want to lock the pixel size of the red recording frame, and then manually size your application window. Select **Application** to have Captivate make adjustments to the red recording frame and the application together for a precise fit.

If you select **Screen Area**, you get the following options:

Window Selection menu: This menu is only active if you select **Application** instead of **Screen Area** as the recording type.

Custom Size: Enter the pixel dimensions you want your recording to be, or select one of the presets in the drop-down menu.

Full Screen: This option records everything on your entire monitor. If you have more than one monitor, you can choose the one you want to record.

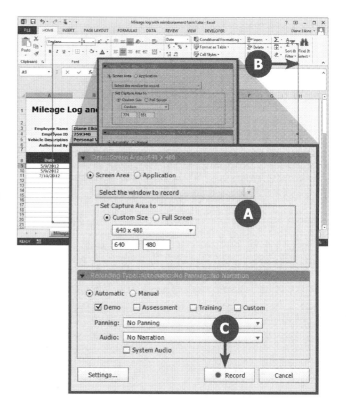

Recording Settings

Recording Size Settings (cont'd)

If you select **Application**, you get the following options:

Application Drop-Down Menu (A): Select the application you want to record. This menu shows all open applications.

Snap to: Application window: The recording frame snaps to the application at its current size.

Snap to: Application Region: The recording frame snaps to a specific region of the application, such as the toolbars across the top. Move your mouse around the application until the recording frame "finds" the region you want to record, and then click the mouse to set it there.

Snap to: Custom Size: You can enter a custom pixel dimension and have the application snap to fit those dimensions.

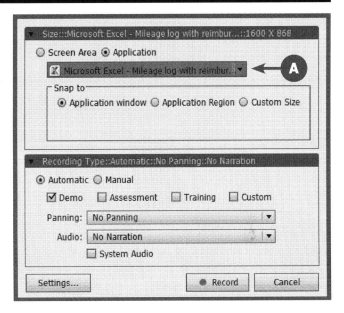

BRIGHT IDEA

What's the difference between **Screen Area: Custom Size** and **Snap to: Custom Size**? Both let you enter the specific dimensions you want. The difference is that with **Screen Area**, you need to manually size your application to fit within the red recording frame. With **Snap to**, Captivate resizes the application for you.

If you want to record the entire application (instead of part of it), then **Snap to** is usually a better choice. Captivate is likely to resize the window more precisely than you can manually, so you aren't likely to be off by a pixel or two. This is especially helpful if you have to go back later and take more captures, because both captures will be consistent.

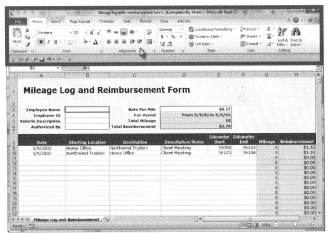

Red recording frame trying to "find" the application region you want, based on the location of your mouse

Recording Settings (cont'd)

Recording Type Settings

Automatic: Captivate automatically takes captures when you perform certain steps (such as mouse clicks and keystrokes) and when the system performs certain functions (such as displaying a warning).

You can record in up to four modes at once, based on which boxes are checked at the time of recording. You can customize each mode by clicking the **Settings** button, which is covered on the next page.

> **Demo**: Use this for a sit-back-and-watch lesson of the procedure, which is good for introducing the procedure and explaining all of the variations, hints, tips, etc.
>
> **Assessment**: Use this to test the students' knowledge as they perform every step themselves, with scoring for every step and the option to limit the number of attempts.
>
> **Training**: Use this to help students practice the procedure themselves, providing feedback but not grading their attempts.
>
> **Custom**: Use this method for completely custom recording settings.
>
> For this book, any simulation in which the student performs the steps (assessment, training, and some custom settings) will be called a practice.

Manual: All captures are done manually by you when you press the **Print Screen** key. You might use this if you just want an overview of the main screens, rather than showing every single step. (In **Automatic** mode, you can manually add a screen capture at any time with the **Print Screen** key on your keyboard.)

Panning: By default, panning is turned off, meaning the red recording frame is fixed in one place during the recording. You can also choose **Automatic Panning**, which moves the red recording frame around automatically if your mouse goes outside of the frame. **Manual Panning** lets you move the recording frame around manually during the recording.

Audio: By default, audio is not recorded during capture. If you want to record audio while you capture, select a microphone from the menu.

System Audio: In addition to recording audio from a microphone, you can capture audio from your system. For example, the software you are demonstrating might make alert noises. Check this box if you'd like to record the system audio.

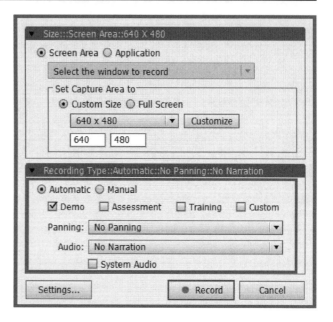

 DESIGN TIP

You can save time by recording in several modes at once. However, it is less challenging to the student if the practice exercise is exactly the same as the demonstration. Consider having a separate practice that has variations of the procedure. For example, if the demo is of someone entering a day of vacation on Tuesday, you may want a practice of someone entering a sick day on Wednesday.

With a wide application like this, it might be useful to use panning to move back and forth between the left and the right, rather than reduce the size to fit in the red recording frame.

Change Recording Preferences

To change recording preferences:

1. Click the **Settings** button in the recording window.
2. In the **Category** pane, select the category for the settings you want to modify.
3. Make the changes you want.
4. Click the **OK** button.

Recording Settings Category

Generate Captions In: If you are having Captivate automatically add captions, use this menu if you want to select a language other than English for those captions.

Audio Options

Narration: Check this if you want to record narration into a microphone during the capture.

System Audio: Check this to record any sounds generated by your computer during the capture.

Actions in Real Time: By default, each captured slide is the same length. Check this box if you want to base the slide length on how long it takes you to perform that step. This does not affect the path of the mouse.

Camera Sounds: During recording, a camera shutter sound plays every time a capture is taken, letting you know if you are getting the captures you need. Uncheck this box if you don't want those sounds. (The sounds are not included in the finished output.)

Keystrokes: When you type during a capture, Captivate captures each keystroke. Uncheck this box if you don't want individual keystrokes captured, but just want the whole typed passage to appear at once.

Hear Keyboard Tap Sounds: During recording, a tap sound plays for each key you type. Uncheck this box if you don't want to hear these sounds. (There is a separate option in **Publish Settings** for including keystroke sounds in the published output.)

Hide

Recording Window: Check this box if you don't want to see the red recording frame.

Task Icon and System Tray Icon: If you are recording your full screen, check these boxes to hide the Captivate icons. The task icon is what you use to move from program to program. The system tray icon is in the bottom-right corner of your screen.

Move New Windows Inside Recording Area: If another window opens during a capture, such as a dialog box, the pop-up window will be moved into the red recording area, unless you uncheck this box.

Smoothen movements for: During automatic recording, full-motion video is triggered every time you use a dragging action or the mouse wheel. Uncheck these boxes if you don't want this.

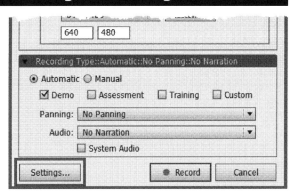

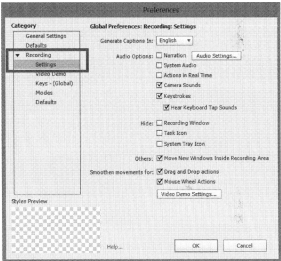

 Working with Audio, ch. 5

 CAUTION

If you are recording audio while you are capturing, be sure to turn off the options for camera sounds and keyboard tap sounds. Otherwise, your microphone might pick up the sounds.

 BRIGHT IDEAS

If you are recording narration and system audio, they are added as separate tracks in the timeline.

If you turn on the **System Audio** feature, other preferences, such as **Camera Sounds** are turned off to avoid conflicts.

Change Recording Preferences (cont'd)

Video Demo Category

Show Mouse in Video Demo Mode: By default, the mouse is included in any full-motion recording. Uncheck this box if you don't want the mouse recorded. For example, you might want a recording of some sort of animation and wouldn't want the mouse in the way.

Working Folder: This folder stores the temporary file of your full-motion recording after you save your project. Captivate decodes the files and stores them in this location to make it quicker to open and save files. This location can be changed by clicking the **Browse** button.

Video Color Mode: You can select the color setting for any full-motion video. **16 bit** creates a smaller file size, but the fewer number of available colors may affect your quality. **32 bit** gives you more colors, but will create a larger file.

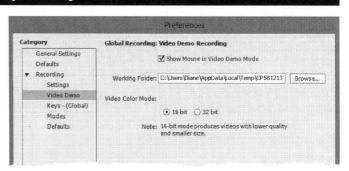

Keys Category

This category displays the various keyboard shortcuts that can be used during recording. If you want to change any of them, just click in a field and type the shortcut you want to use instead. For example, you may be taking a capture of an application that uses some of these function keys. In this case, you'd want to change the shortcut in Captivate so it doesn't create a conflict.

 Recording Shortcuts, p. 32

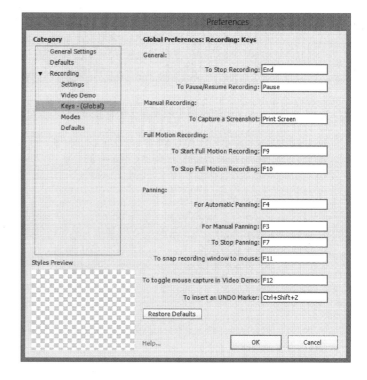

CAUTION

The **Print Screen** key is the default for manually capturing a screen in both Captivate and Snagit. If you have Snagit installed on your computer and press **Print Screen** during a capture, it may launch Snagit. You'll want to change the hotkey for manual captures in either Captivate or in Snagit to avoid a conflict during your capture session.

Change Recording Preferences (cont'd)

Modes Category

In the **Modes** category, you can configure settings for each of the automatic recording modes. First, select the mode you want to configure from the drop-down menu **(A)**, and then make any changes for that mode.

Captions

Add Text Captions: Captivate automatically adds captions to your steps (e.g., "Click the **OK** button").

Convert Tooltips to Rollover Captions: If your software has tooltips (small captions that show the name of the tool when you hover over it), Captivate creates a similar rollover caption for you.

Use Smart Shapes instead of Captions: If you are including captions or rollovers, you can choose to use Smart Shapes instead of traditional captions. To do this, check the box, and then select the type of shape you want: **Rectangle**, **Rounded Rectangle**, **Oval**, or **Cloud**.

Mouse

Show Mouse Location and Movement: Captivate shows the mouse moving along a streamlined path from one click to the next.

Add Highlight Boxes on Click: Captivate adds a highlight box around the item that you click. This provides visual emphasis and makes it easy to create job aids with the **Print** option on the **File** menu.

The default settings for **Demonstration** mode (shown below) include captions, mouse movement, and highlight boxes. The default settings for the two practice modes (**Assessment** and **Training**) do not include these objects, but instead, include the interactive elements covered on the next page.

CAUTION

This category in the **Preferences** dialog box only changes the *settings* for each mode, NOT which mode you will actually be recording in. That is determined by the recording window.

Recording Type Settings, p. 24

Smart Shapes, p. 66

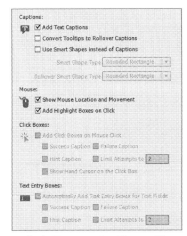

*Default **Demonstration** settings*

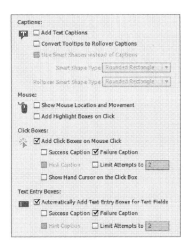

*Default **Assessment** settings*

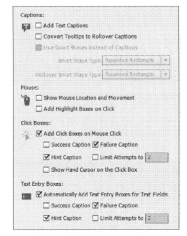

*Default **Training** settings*

Change Recording Preferences (cont'd)

Modes Category (cont'd)

Click Boxes

When this box is checked, Captivate converts every click you make while recording into a click box that the student must click during the practice playback.

Text Entry Boxes

When this box is checked, Captivate converts your typing during recording into a text entry box that the student must fill in during the practice playback.

Options

Success Caption: Check this box if you want to add a caption after each successful click or text entry to let the students know they were correct.

Failure Caption: By default, Captivate adds captions after each unsuccessful click or text entry to let students know they were incorrect. Uncheck this box if you don't want these captions.

Hint Caption: Check this box if you want to add a roll-over caption with a hint the students see when they roll over the click box or the text entry box.

Limit Attempts to X: By default, students cannot move forward in the practice until they complete the click or typing step correctly. You can check this box and indicate a specific number of attempts.

Show Hand Cursor on the Click Box: Check this box if you want the student's cursor to change to a hand cursor when it is over the click box area. Your students may recognize that this means they are over a hot spot.

Defaults Category

Before you record, you can set the styles to be used for captions, highlight boxes, and other elements added to your project.

To change the style, select an option from any of the drop-down menus. Each item has a number of preset styles already available. When you select one, you can see a preview in the **Styles Preview** pane in the bottom-left corner.

To add your own style, click the **Create New Style** button. New styles are then added to the appropriate drop-down lists. If you have a project open, the style changes apply only to that project. If you don't have a project open, the style changes apply to all future projects.

 Styles, p. 110

 CAUTION

Some anti-virus software blocks any application from recording keystrokes. If you have that type of protection, Captivate may not be able to record individual keystrokes to convert to a practice for students.

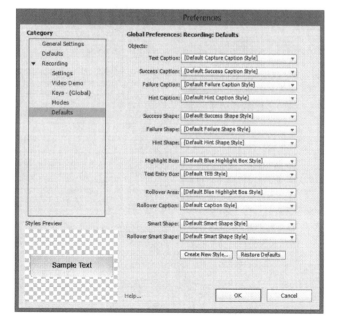

Video Demos

A video demo is a type of software simulation where you create a high-definition, full-motion recording of the steps you are performing. A new project is created with the recording as a single movie.

Record a Video Demo

To record in video demo mode:

1. On the **Welcome** screen, click the **New** tab.
2. Select **Video Demo**.
3. Click the **Create** button.

——— or ———

1. Go to the **File** menu.
2. Select **Record a New**.
3. Select **Video Demo**.

——— then ———

4. Configure the recording settings (covered on the previous pages).
5. Adjust the red recording frame that appears around the application being recorded, if needed.
6. Click the **Record** button.
7. Perform the steps of the procedure you are demonstrating.
8. Press the **End** button on your keyboard, or click the **Captivate** icon in your system tray.

 BRIGHT IDEAS

- Video demos are saved as a Captivate Video Composition file (**.cpvc**).
- Once you finish your recording, you can add captions and other objects, create zoom and pan effects, trim off portions of the beginning and end, etc.

 Managing Video Demos, p. 161

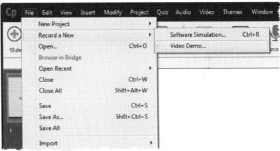

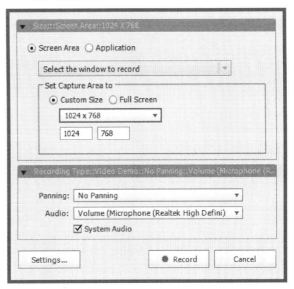

Capture Video Demo from iOS Device

Starting with Captivate 9 for Mac, you can record a video demo of content and apps running on an iOS device, such as an iPad. To use this feature, you must use Adobe Captivate 9 or above on a Mac running OSX version 10 or above and connect an iOS device (connected with a Lightning Cable) with iOS 8 and above.

Like regular video demos, iOS video demos are saved as a Captivate Video Compression file (**.cpvc**). Once you've captured your video demo on an iOS device, you can edit it just like a regular video demo.

Record a Video Demo from an iOS Device

To record a video demo from an iOS device:

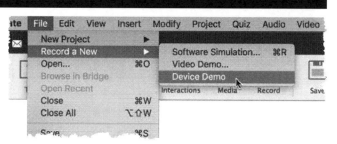

1. Connect your iOS device to your computer with a Lightning Cable.

2. Go to the **File** menu.

3. Select **Record a New**.

4. Select **Device Demo**.

5. Click the first drop-down menu on the toolbar. **(A)**

6. Select the device you want to record.

7. Click the second drop-down menu. **(B)**

8. Select the option to record device audio or no audio.

9. Click the **Record** button. **(C)**

10. Perform the steps of the procedure you are demonstrating.

11. Click the **Done** button when you are finished.

Manage Video Demo Projects, p. 161
Captivate for Mac Menus, p. 295

DESIGN TIPS

Here are some important instructional design and usability decisions to make when designing a practice.

- ❑ How will you communicate the task your students need to accomplish? Will an audio introduction tell them they are supposed to request a day of vacation in the system? Will it be a text box?

- ❑ Do you want to give them step-by-step instructions or just the general task? Will you tell them the first step is to click the **Request Leave** button, or do they need to remember that on their own?

- ❑ If you do include step-by-step instructions, where will they appear? In audio? In timed captions? In a text box down the side of the slide?

- ❑ Do you want to show a success caption for each step, or does the fact that the practice continues serve as adequate feedback?

- ❑ How many attempts should the student get? For a graded assessment, perhaps they should only get one. If the practice is for the student's benefit, perhaps they should have two. Will unlimited attempts cause the user to get frustrated and not be able to finish?

- ❑ Do you want to provide hints with hint captions and the hand cursor? For a graded assessment, you might not want to. Determine if they add value or not, as the student has to be on the hot spot to see the hints.

- ❑ How much help do you want to give students in a failure caption? Tell them simply to try again? Remind them what they are supposed to accomplish in general terms? Tell them the specific step? Point to the step?

BRIGHT IDEAS

Things to Do DURING Your Capture

Typing

Type carefully. If you fix a typo as you type, the mistake and your correction both show up in the final output. Yes, you can edit it later, but it is quicker to type carefully the first time.

If you are typing a longer passage, such as a sentence or two in a field about why the employee is requesting time off, consider just pasting it in rather than typing it. It can be cumbersome for a student to watch the typing of a long passage, and you are more likely to have a typo in a long passage. Pasting text already typed and ready in another document can be cleaner and easier for everyone.

If you do make a mistake with your typing, press the **Pause** key. Delete all of what you have typed. Press the **Pause** button again, and start typing from the beginning. This separates the incorrect typing on one slide and starts the new typing on another slide. During editing, delete the slide with the incorrect typing.

Scrolling and Dragging

Anytime you scroll or drag your mouse, full-motion recording is triggered, unless you have changed the defaults. The video increases your file size and is hard to edit, so it is often simpler if you reserve video for tasks that really need the moving video. Plan your steps carefully to avoid video when it is not needed. For example, if you need to scroll down to the bottom of the screen, click in the bottom of the scroll bar instead of dragging the slider down. If you need to select a word, double-click it instead of dragging across it with the cursor.

Tooltips

As you are capturing your steps, your mouse may be resting on a feature in your software long enough to make the tooltip appear. If it does, it might be visible in your capture. Pay attention to these tooltips when they appear, and, if needed, move your mouse and take another screen capture manually to get a clean shot without it.

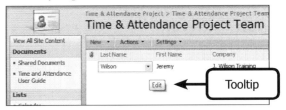

BRIGHT IDEAS

Useful Keyboard Shortcuts

Pause

Press the **Pause** key on your keyboard if you need to do anything during the capture that you don't want to record. For example:

- A window pops up, and you need to resize it or move it into the recording area.
- You get to a step and realize something isn't set up properly and needs to be fixed.
- You make a mistake and need to undo it.

While you are paused, the **Captivate** icon in your system tray has a very small dot, letting you know you are paused.

When you are done and ready to resume the capture, simply press the **Pause** key again.

Print Screen

During automatic recording, you can manually add an extra screen capture at any time by pressing the **Print Screen** key on your keyboard. For example, perhaps it took an extra second for a dialog box to load, and you aren't sure if the capture was taken before it fully appeared. It's easier to delete unneeded manual captures than to later recreate something you missed.

End

Press the **End** key to finish your capture.

Undo Marker

If you perform a step you don't want and will probably delete the slide, press **Ctrl** + **Shift** + **Z**. The screen is still captured, but it shows up as a hidden slide with a caption across it saying "Marked for Undo." You can unhide the slide and delete the caption later if you want to keep the slide after all.

Other Recording Shortcuts

There are many other keyboard shortcuts available, many of which can be customized. You can find them in **Preferences** on the **Keys** tab.

 Keys Category, p. 26
Useful Keyboard Shortcuts, p. 298

After Your Capture

You will most likely do a fair amount of editing to your project once you've captured it. For example, you may add or delete slides and captions, adjust mouse movements, etc. However, it doesn't make sense to spend time fine-tuning your capture if there is something wrong with it and it needs to be re-captured.

When you are finished with your capture, save it, and then walk through each of the slides to check for the following before you start editing:

- ❏ Are there any screens that were still loading when the screen shot was taken?
- ❏ Are there any typos in the on-screen typing?
- ❏ Is there anything showing that the student should not be seeing? A tooltip? An Outlook message indicator? Sensitive data?
- ❏ Are there any steps missing?

These are the big problems that are hard to resolve during editing. It is often quicker to just start the capture over again, rather than trying to fix these problems. Otherwise, you could spend 30–60 minutes trying to fix a problem that could have been eliminated if you took 5 minutes to take the capture over again.

Smaller problems, such as the mouse in the wrong place, are easier to fix during editing. As you become more familiar with taking captures, you'll learn what to look out for and which problems are best resolved with a re-capture.

Editing and Refining Your Captures

In the next several chapters, you'll learn ways to take your raw capture and turn it into a polished lesson or practice.

- Chapters 4 and 6 show you how to add and modify on-screen elements, such as text captions and highlight boxes.
- Chapter 5 shows you how to add audio narration.
- Chapter 7 shows you how to add or modify the interactive elements, such as an explanatory rollover caption or the click boxes and text entry boxes for a practice.
- Chapter 8 covers features specific to simulations, such as editing mouse movements.

Adding and Managing Slides

Introduction

Your slides are the backbone of your project. In some cases, your slides are set up when you first create your project. For example, if you are creating a software simulation, each individual screen capture is added as a slide. In the finished output, all of the slides are played together like a movie. If you are importing a PowerPoint presentation, then you'll have one Captivate slide for each of your PowerPoint slides. In other cases, you will want to add individual slides to a blank or existing project.

In this chapter, you'll learn how to add several slide types that correspond to the project types: blank slides, PowerPoint slides, and image slides. You'll also learn how to manage your slides effectively, whether changing the slide properties, creating master slides to maintain a consistent look, or rearranging and grouping slides to keep them organized.

In future chapters, you'll learn about additional slide types, such as text animation slides.

Slide Type	Chapter
Content slide	**3**
Blank slide	**3**
Question slide	10
Knowledge Check slide	10
Software Simulation slide	8
CPVC or Video Demo slide	8
PowerPoint slide	**3**
Image slide	**3**
Animation slide	4
Master slide	**3**
Placeholder slide	11

In This Chapter

- Inserting New Slides
  - Content and Blank Slides
  - PowerPoint Slides
  - Image Slides
- Slide Properties
- Slide Notes
- Master Slides
- Slide Themes
- Managing Slides

Notes

Inserting New Slides

Insert a Content or Blank Slide

To insert a content or blank slide:

1. Click the **Slides** drop-down button.
2. Select **Content Slide** or **Blank Slide**.

With **Content Slide**, the added slide uses the master slide and theme of the slide before it. With **Blank Slide**, the added slide is truly blank with no master or theme applied.

Themes, p. 47
Master Slides, p. 44

Insert a PowerPoint Slide

To insert individual PowerPoint slides:

1. Click the **Slides** drop-down button.
2. Select **PowerPoint Slide**.
3. Indicate where you want the slides to appear in your project. **(A)**
4. Click the **OK** button.
5. Find and select the file you want.
6. Click the **Open** button.
7. Select the slides and enter the properties you want. **(B)**
8. Click the **OK** button.

PowerPoint Import Properties, p. 18

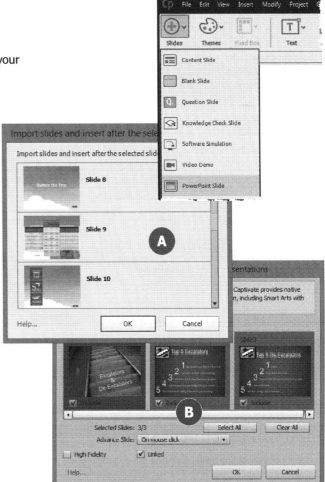

CAUTION

How many slides is too many? Adobe recommends a length of 50 to 60 slides, with a maximum of 150 slides.

Edit a PowerPoint Slide in Captivate

You can edit a PowerPoint slide from within Captivate. When you initiate editing, PowerPoint opens up within the Captivate interface, letting you access the capabilities of PowerPoint without having to leave Captivate.

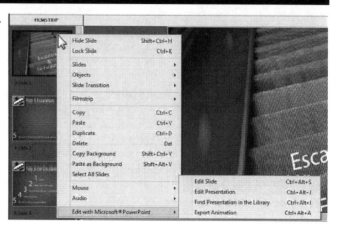

To edit an imported PowerPoint slide from within Captivate:

1. Right-click the slide.
2. Select **Edit with Microsoft® PowerPoint**.
3. Select the editing option you want. (See below.)
4. Make your changes to the slide, using the PowerPoint interface.
5. Click the **Save** button. **(A)**

Editing Options

Edit Slide: Only the selected slide will be opened for editing.

Edit Presentation: The entire presentation will be opened for editing.

Find Presentation in the Library: This highlights the presentation in the library. You can access more editing options from the library. (See next page.)

Export Animation: This option converts the selected slide to a **.swf** file. You can then save the **.swf** file and use it in other places, such as on a Web page or even in another Captivate project.

Imported PowerPoint slide being edited in Captivate

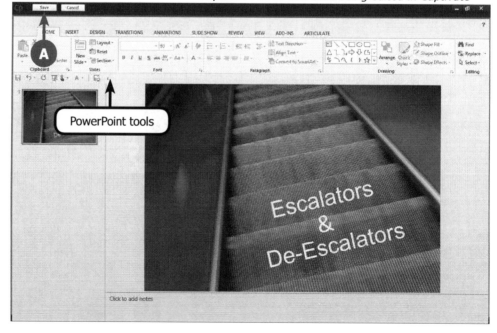

Update an Imported Slide

When you have a linked PowerPoint slide, changes made to the PowerPoint source file can be updated in the Captivate file, but it doesn't happen automatically. You need to initiate the update.

To update an imported PowerPoint slide:

1. Click the **Library** button to reveal the **Library** panel, if needed.
2. Right-click the presentation in the library.
3. Select **Update**.
4. Select which linked presentation you want to update.
5. Click the **Update** button.
6. Click the **OK** button.

If any new slides have been added to the PowerPoint file, you will be asked to select which ones you want to add.

Linking PowerPoint slides, p. 19
Library, p. 229

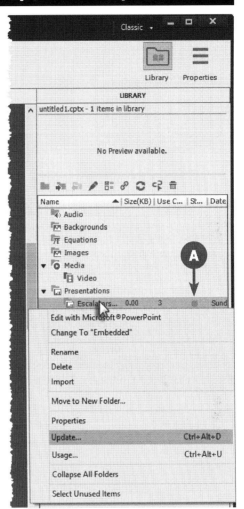

BRIGHT IDEAS

- Notice that there are other options on the library's right-click menu. For example, you can switch between linking and embedding the file.

- An embedded file also has a **Compact** option. This permanently deletes any slides from the original PowerPoint file that are not currently being used in the Captivate file.

- A green dot next to a linked presentation in the library **(A)** tells you that the file is current. The dot becomes orange if it is not current. It becomes a question mark if the link is broken because the file is renamed, moved, or unavailable from a network. Click the question mark to re-establish the link.

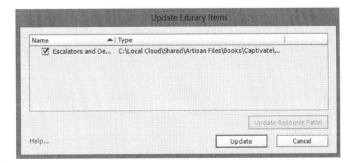

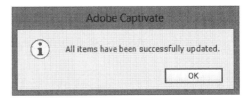

Add an Image Slide

When you add an image slide, the image is merged to the background of the slide.

Captivate accepts the following image types: **.jpg**, **.gif**, **.png**, **.bmp**, **.ico**, **.emf**, **.wmf**, **.pot**, **.potx**, and **.pict**.

To add an image slide:

1. Go to the **Insert** menu.
2. Select **Image Slide**.
3. Find and select the image you want to use.
4. Click the **Open** button.

The image is now the background of a slide. As such, it can not be repositioned, resized, or edited on the slide.

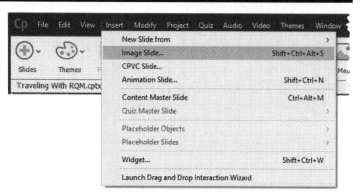

BRIGHT IDEA

If you want an image to "float" on the slide so that you can time, move, or resize it, add it as an image instead of as an image slide.

If you want to have the image as part of the background but want to make some changes first (move, resize, rotate, crop, etc.), add it as an image instead of an image slide. Then, once you have it how you want it, simply right-click it and merge it to the background. The option to merge to the background is not available if the slide has a master slide background.

Merge With Background, p. 157
Add an Image to a Slide, p. 61

You can swap out the image in a background in the **Background** section of the slide properties.

Slide Properties, p. 39

Slide Properties

Every slide and every object on every slide have properties. Click the **Properties** button **(A)** if the **Properties** panel is not visible. To see the properties for a slide, select the slide by clicking it in the filmstrip.

Slide Properties Panel

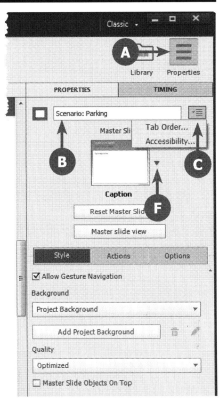

Name: You can give a unique name to each slide. **(B)** It shows up in the filmstrip and in any drop-down menus where you need to select a slide. Naming the slides makes it easier to identify the right slide quickly. In addition, the slide label is read to students using a screen reader if the accessibility features are turned on for a project.

Tab Order: When you select this option from the accessibility menu **(C)**, a dialog box appears **(D)** that lets you set the tab order of any interactive objects on the page. For students using a keyboard instead of the mouse for navigation (including those using a screen reader), it is important to put your objects in a logical order.

Accessibility: Click **Accessibility** on the menu **(C)** to get a dialog box **(E)** where you can enter a text description for the slide. This text will be read to students using screen readers who cannot see the content of the slide. Either type your text in the space provided, or click the **Import Slide Notes** button to use your slide notes for the accessibility text.

 Accessibility/Section 508, p. 289

Master Slide: Master slides in Captivate are very much like master slides in PowerPoint. You are able to create slide backgrounds that you can use over and over again. Select the master you want from the drop-down menu **(F)**.

Reset Master Slide: If you have modified any elements that are part of the master slide, such as moving or formatting the slide heading, you can click this button to reset all the objects back to their original size and format.

Master slide view: Click this button if you want to view the master slides to be able to edit them.

 Master Slides, p. 44

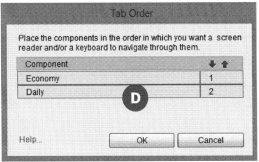

Slide Properties Panel (cont'd)

Style Tab

Allow Gesture Navigation: Checked by default, this option lets users navigate by touch when viewing on a mobile device. Uncheck the box if you only want students to use on-screen navigation.

 Mobile Gestures, p. 270

Background: This menu gives you three options for the slide background.

- **Master Slide Background**: This option uses the background image that comes with the master slide.

- **Project Background**: Use this option to select your own image to be merged to the background. Click the **Add Project Background** button that appears **(A)** to select an image from the library or your computer. Click the trash can icon to delete the current image. Click the pencil icon to edit the image, such as to crop it.

- **Custom**: This option lets you pick an image and/or a color for the background. From the **Solid** menu **(B)**, select whether you want a solid, gradient, or image fill. Then use the menu next to it to set the specific color, gradient, or image. Use the **Add Project Background** button and corresponding icons the same as for **Project Background**.

Quality: This drop-down menu lets you select the image quality of the slide.

Master Slide Objects On Top: By default, the master slide objects appear behind anything you add to an individual slide. Check this box if you want the master slide elements to appear on top of the individual slide elements. You cannot reorder the individual master objects, but they can be moved all to the front or all to the back.

 Master Slides, p. 44
Colors and Color Gradients, p. 98
Library, p. 229

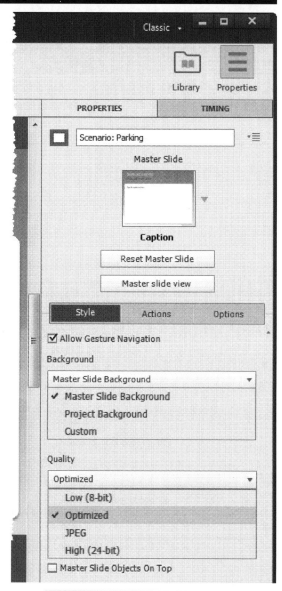

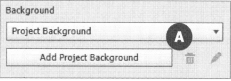

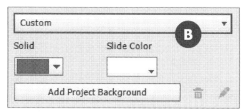

Slide Properties (cont'd)

Actions Tab

The **Actions** tab lets you designate certain actions when the slide first begins (**On Enter**) or when the course reaches the very last frame of the slide (**On Exit**). For example, you might want to disable a button when the student first views a slide.

 Actions, ch. 7 & 9

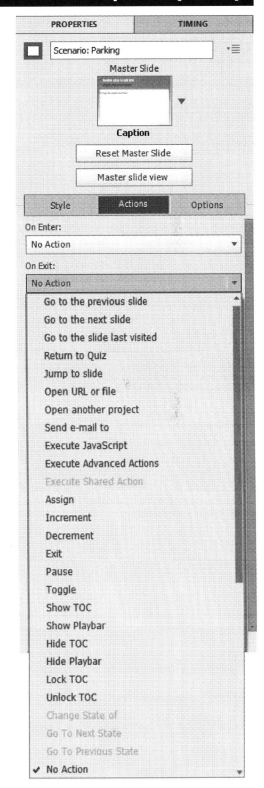

Slide Properties (cont'd)

Options Tab

The **Audio** section lets you add and manage audio attached to the slide. The options vary slightly based on whether or not there is already audio on the slide.

 Audio, ch. 5

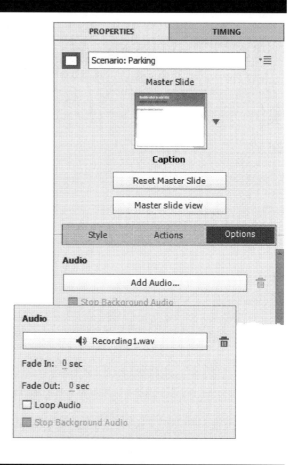

Timing Panel

Transitions: Transitions are effects that play when a project goes from one slide to the next. A slide transition plays at the beginning of a slide. For example, if a transition is applied to slide 3, it appears when the project goes from slide 2 to slide 3.

 BRIGHT IDEA

You can also apply transitions and effects to individual objects. Apply simple fade in/out transitions in the **Transition** pane for that object or apply special effects, such as motion paths or flying in/out, from the **Timing** tab.

 Object Transitions, p. 103
Object Effects, p. 118

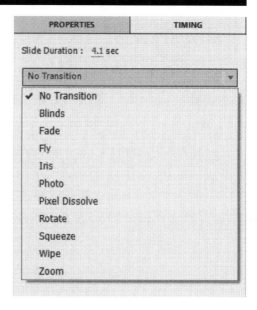

Slide Notes

Slide notes let you put text notes on individual slides. These might be development notes for your team or the transcript of your audio to show to your students. By default, slide notes are not included in your published project. Once you add your text to the **Slide Notes** panel, you can then:

- View the notes while recording audio.

- Convert the text to computerized audio using the text-to-speech converter.

- Create closed captions for accessibility purposes that *do* appear in the published course.

Text-to-Speech, p. 87
Closed Captioning, p. 88

TIME SAVER

When you import slides from PowerPoint, the slide notes from that file are automatically imported into your Captivate slide notes.

Add Slide Notes

To view the Slide Notes panel:

1. Go to the **Window** menu.

2. Select **Slide Notes**.

To add slide notes:

1. Select the slide you want.

2. Click the **Plus** button in the **Slide Notes** pane. **(A)**

3. Type or paste your text.

4. Repeat these steps to add more notes for that slide.

To remove slide notes:

1. Select the heading row **(B)** for the note you want to delete.

2. Click the **Minus** button. **(C)**

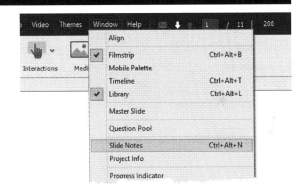

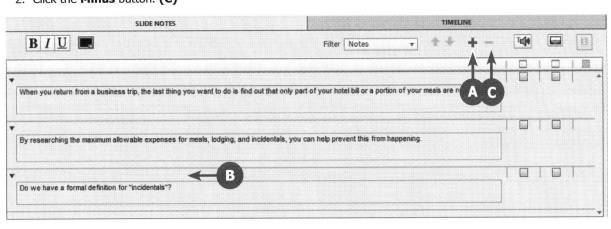

Master Slides

Master slides can help you create a consistent look quickly. Just as with Microsoft PowerPoint, you can add design elements to a master slide that can then be used as a template for one or more of your slides.

Master slides are managed in the **Master Slide** panel to the left of the interface where the filmstrip is normally found. (In previous versions, it was at the bottom of the interface.) Masters are applied to individual slides in the **Properties** panel.

There are three types of master slides: main, content, and question. The main master slide appears at the top of the **Master Slide** panel **(A)**. Content master slides are individual layouts based on the main master **(B)**. Changes made to the main master appear on all the content master slides, unless you choose to exclude those objects **(C)**. A question master is like a content master, but is for quiz questions.

Master slides (both main and content) can have regular objects and placeholder objects. Regular objects include text, images, and animations that can't be changed on each individual slide. Placeholder objects are formatted content frames, and the specific content is added in edit mode to each individual slide using that master. Some objects (mainly interactive objects) are grayed out in **Master Slide** view and cannot be added to a master slide.

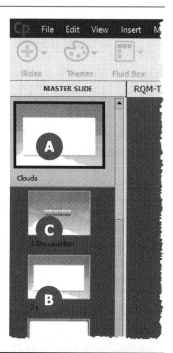

Show/Hide the Master Slide Panel

To show the Master Slide panel:

1. Go to the **Window** menu.
2. Select **Master Slide**.

To hide the Master Slide panel:

1. Click the **Exit Master** button.

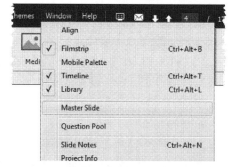

Modify a Main Master Slide

Changes you make to the main master slide appear on the content master slides, unless you exclude them.

To modify a main master slide:

1. Select the main master at the top of the **Master Slide** panel. **(A)**
2. Add standard content objects (such as text or images) from the **Insert** menu or the **Object** toolbar.
3. Configure the properties of the objects.

Create a Content Master Slide

To create a content master slide:

1. Go to the **Insert** menu.
2. Select **Content Master Slide**.
3. Configure properties in the **Properties** pane.
4. Add objects to the slide in the work area.

Content Master Slide Properties

Name: Names are very important for master slides, making it easier to later select the one you want.

Show Main Master Slide Objects: Leave this checked if you want your content master to inherit the objects on the main master. Uncheck it if you want to exclude these objects.

Background: Keep this drop-down menu set to **Master Slide Background** if you want to use the same slide background as the main master. If you want to have a different background, select **Project Background** or **Custom** from the menu.

 Backgrounds, p. 40

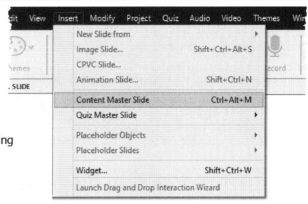

Add Placeholders to a Content Master

Content placeholders let you add consistent elements to your slides that can be customized each time you use them. For example, you can put an image placeholder and a text placeholder for a caption on the content master. Then, when you insert a slide using that master, you can use the image and the caption text you want.

To add a placeholder:

1. In the **Master Slide** panel, select the content master you want to work with.
2. Go to the **Insert** menu.
3. Select **Placeholder Objects**.
4. Select the object type you want.
5. Adjust the size, placement, and properties of the object.

Insert a New Slide Using a Content Master

To insert a new slide that uses a content master:

1. Go to the **Insert** menu.
2. Select **New Slide from**.
3. Select the content master you want.

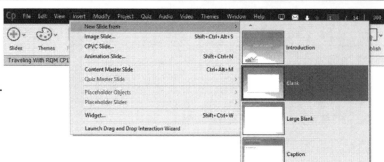

Apply a Content Master to an Existing Slide

To apply a content master to an existing slide:

1. In the filmstrip, select the slide(s) you want to apply the master to.
2. In the **Properties** panel, click the **Master Slide** drop-down arrow. **(A)**
3. Select the content master you want to apply to the slide(s).

 Slide Properties, p. 39

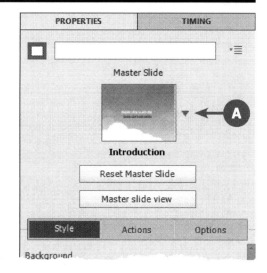

Themes

Slide themes in Captivate work very much like they do in PowerPoint. A theme is a family of pre-designed elements including master slides (main and content), object styles, skin settings, and recording defaults. They can help you design slides quickly and keep a consistent, professional look.

 CAUTION

When you apply a theme, your current formatting will be overwritten with the theme formatting.

Apply a Theme to a Project

To apply a theme to a project:

1. Click the **Themes** drop-down button.
2. Select the theme you want.

To set a theme as the default for all new projects:

1. Click the **Themes** drop-down button.
2. Right-click the theme you want.
3. Select **Set as Default Theme**.

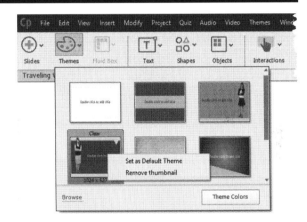

 DESIGN TIP

You can find additional design themes from third-party sources online.

Sample theme provided courtesy of eLearning Brothers eLearning Template Library.

 POWER TIP

You can make your own themes. Either start with an existing theme or a blank theme and customize the masters, objects, styles, etc. Then go to the **Themes** menu to save the new theme. Themes are saved as **.cptm** files. When you are ready to use a custom theme, click **Browse** from the **Themes** drop-down button.

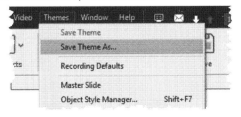

Managing Slides

Hide Slides

Just as in PowerPoint, hidden slides do not show up in preview mode or in your published course, but they remain in the filmstrip and work area.

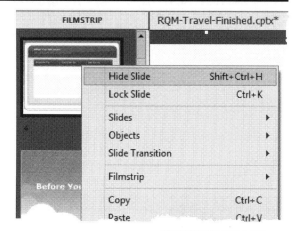

To hide a slide:

1. Right-click the slide thumbnail in the filmstrip.
2. Select **Hide Slide**.

To unhide a slide:

1. Right-click the slide thumbnail in the filmstrip.
2. Select **Show Slide**.

—— or ——

1. Click the "eyeball" icon under the thumbnail. **(A)**

BRIGHT IDEA

When capturing a software simulation, it is not uncommon to end up with extra captures. If you delete these slides and then later realize you need them, you may have a problem. Instead, you can hide the unwanted slides and delete them later once you are sure you don't need them.

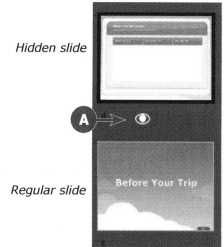

Hidden slide

Regular slide

Delete Slides

To delete a slide:

1. Right-click the slide thumbnail in the filmstrip.
2. Select **Delete**.

—— or ——

1. Select the slide in the filmstrip.
2. Press the **Delete** key on your keyboard.

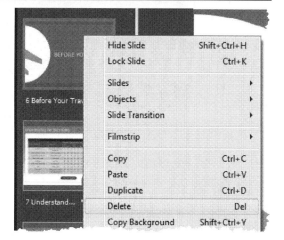

Move Slides

To move a slide to another position:

1. Click the slide thumbnail in the filmstrip, and drag it to the location you want.

Copy, Paste, and Duplicate Slides

Slides cannot be cut, but they can be copied and pasted. Once you select a slide in the filmstrip, you can copy, paste, and duplicate it in three different ways:

*   The **Edit** menu **(A)**
*   Keyboard shortcuts **(B)**
*   The filmstrip or work area right-click menu **(C)**

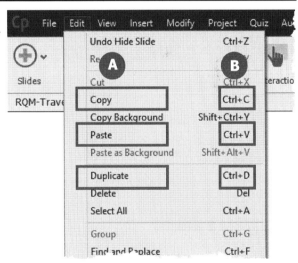

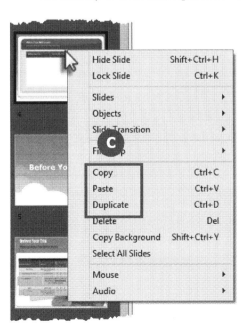

 TIME SAVERS

You can select more than one slide when you use these functions. For consecutive slides, press the **Shift** key while clicking the first and last slide in a range. If they aren't consecutive, press the **Ctrl** key while clicking each individual slide.

The **Duplicate** function combines the copy and paste actions into one step. The duplicated slide is pasted directly after the selected slide.

Lock Slides

If you want to ensure that certain slides don't get deleted, you can lock them. Locking a slide also prevents you from adding or editing objects on the slide.

To lock a slide:

1. Right-click the slide thumbnail in the filmstrip.
2. Select **Lock Slide**.

To unlock a slide:

1. Right-click the slide thumbnail in the filmstrip.
2. Select **Unlock Slide**.

———— or ————

1. Click the **Lock** icon in the top corner of the thumbnail. **(A)**

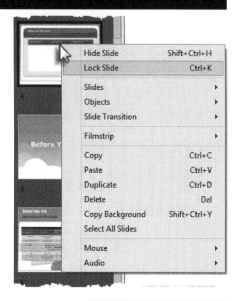

Locked Slide

BRIGHT IDEA

You can make the thumbnails in the filmstrip larger or smaller from the thumbnail right-click menu.

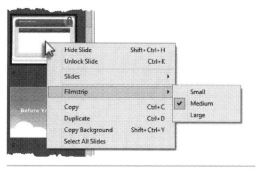

Group Slides

Grouping slides can help you manage a large project. When slides are grouped, you can identify them quickly and move, hide, or delete them as a group. Only consecutive slides can be grouped.

To group slides:

1. Select all the slides you want to group together.
2. Right-click any one of the selected slides.
3. Select **Group**.
4. Select **Create**.

Once you create a group, the slides are collapsed in the filmstrip with a placeholder slide. **(A)** When the placeholder is selected, the **Slide Group Properties** panel appears. **(B)**

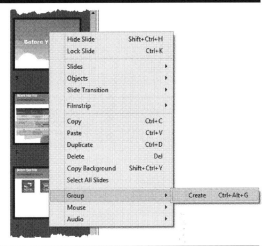

Slide Group Properties

Title: When you enter a title in the **Slide Group Properties** panel, it appears on the placeholder slide and under the thumbnail.

Master Slide: You can change the standard options for master slides for every slide in the group.

 Master Slides, p. 44

Color: Use the color swatch to set the outline color used in the filmstrip. Using different colors can make it easy to find the slides you are looking for. These colors only appear in the developing environment, not in the published course.

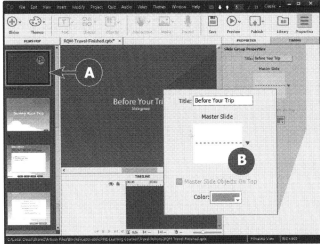

Managing Groups

To expand a group:

1. Click the down arrow icon on the group placeholder thumbnail. **(C)**

To collapse a group:

1. Click the up arrow icon on the thumbnail of the first slide in the group. **(D)**

To ungroup slides:

1. Right-click any one of the slides in the group.
2. Select **Group**.
3. Select **Ungroup**.

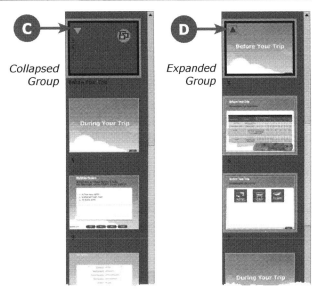

Collapsed Group

Expanded Group

Notes

Adding Content Objects

Introduction

The next several chapters cover how to add content to your slides.

- In this chapter, you'll learn about adding content objects, including captions, images, shapes, highlight boxes, and animations.
- Chapter 5 covers how to add audio and video to your projects.
- Chapter 6 covers object properties that relate to most object types, such as how to select colors, how to apply styles, and how to adjust timing.
- In chapter 7, you'll learn how to add interactive objects, such as rollover objects, text entry boxes, and buttons.
- In chapter 10, you'll learn how to add questions and quizzes.

In This Chapter

- Captions
- Images
- Characters
- Shapes and Highlight Boxes
- Animations
- Text Animations
- Zoom Areas
- Web Objects

Notes

Working With Captions

Captions are one way to add text to your slides, whether you want to point out a step in a computer procedure, provide feedback on a practice activity, provide instructions on what to do, or add text in a branching scenario.

Reinforce teaching points

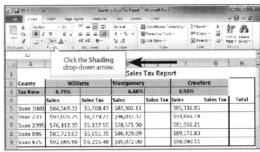

Provide feedback

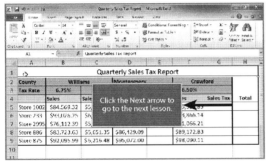

Give instructions

Add "non-caption" text

 DESIGN TIP

You can also add text to shapes. Shapes don't have all of the logic that captions have (like importing or exporting), but you have more formatting options, such as custom colors and gradients.

 Smart Shapes, p. 66

Add a New Caption

To add a new caption:

1. Click the **Text** drop-down button.
2. Select **Text Caption**.
3. Type your caption text.
4. Configure any settings in the caption **Properties** panel. (See following pages.)
5. Click off the caption.

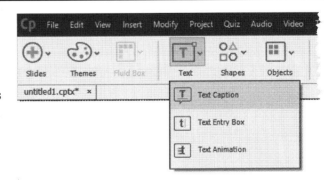

Edit Caption Text

To make text edits to your captions:

1. Double-click the caption to get a cursor.

2. Make your edits.

3. Click off the caption.

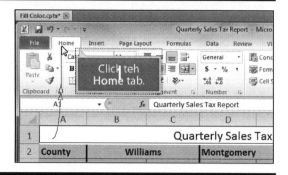

Change Caption and Callout Type

The *caption* type determines the color, shape, and outline of the captions. The *callout* type determines if and where the caption is pointing.

To change the caption type:

1. Select the caption you want to change.

2. On the **Style** tab, click the **Caption Type** drop-down menu.

3. Select the caption type you want.

To change the callout type:

1. Select the caption you want to change.

2. In the **Callout** field, click the type you want.

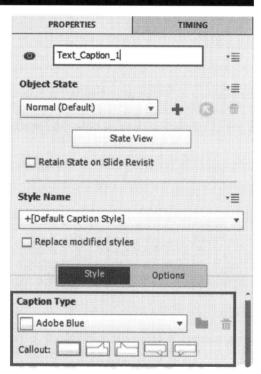

 BRIGHT IDEA

You can also insert caption widgets, giving you more choices for your caption type. From the **Insert** menu, select **Widgets**, and go to the **Captions** folder.

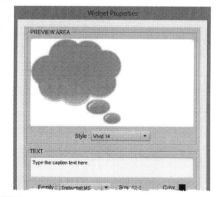

 Widgets, p. 231

DESIGN TIPS

- Use different caption types for different purposes. For example, use **Adobe Blue** when the student should read and **Glass Blue** when the student should act.

- Use a transparent caption to put plain text on a slide.

- You can use styles to save and apply formatting attributes.

 Styles, p. 110

Formatting Caption Text

Formatting is done in the **Properties** panel. Select the caption to format all text in the caption, or highlight just the part of the text you want to format.

Character Pane

Family (A): Select the font family you want, such as **Arial**.

Style (B): Select the font style you want, such as **Narrow**.

Size (C): Type or use the drop-down menu for the point size you want.

Format (D): Click the buttons for bold, italics, underlining, superscript, or subscript, as needed.

Bullets (E): Select a bullet/numbering option from the drop-down menu, as needed.

Align (F): Select the buttons you want for horizontal and vertical alignment of text within the caption.

Indentation (G): Click the **Decrease Indent** or **Increase Indent** buttons to change the left margin on the caption.

Insert (H): This toolbar is only active when your cursor is in the caption (instead of having the whole caption selected).

- Click the **Insert Symbol** button to insert symbols, such as a copyright symbol or a foreign currency symbol.

- Click the **Insert Variable** button to display the value of a stored variable.

 Variables, p. 169

- Click the **Insert Hyperlink** button to turn text into an active link that opens a website or runs an action.

 Add a Hyperlink to Text, p. 139

Spacing: Type or drag your mouse to change the vertical spacing between lines.

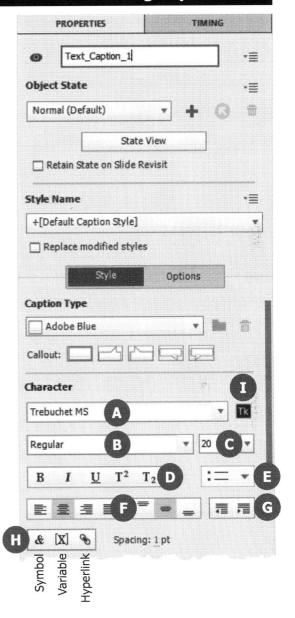

POWER TIP

If you have an Adobe Typekit account, you can now use those fonts in Captivate 2017. If you use a non-standard font in an HTML 5-published course, the text won't play properly for students who don't have that font installed. If you use Typekit, however, then the fonts will display properly for your students, even if they don't have a Typekit subscription.

To use a font from Typekit, click the **Go to Typekit. com** button, **(I)** which takes you to the Typekit website. Sync the font you want to use. Then, come back to Captivate, and the font will appear on the font family menu. **(A)**

Formatting Caption Text (cont'd)

Color: Click the drop-down menu to select the font color.

Highlight: Click the drop-down menu to select the color for highlighting the text.

 Colors, p. 98

Text Effects

When you select a caption or shape instead of the text within the object, there is an extra option in the **Character** pane: **Effects. (A)** Text effects are special font formatting options that can be applied to the entire object.

To apply a text effect:

1. Select a caption or a shape with text.
2. In the **Character** pane, click the **Effects** drop-down menu.
3. Select the effect you want.

To create your own effect:

1. Select a caption or a shape with text.
2. In the **Character** pane, click the **Effects** drop-down menu.
3. Click a button with a plus sign. **(A)**
4. In the dialog box, check the box for the attribute you want to modify. **(B)**
5. On the right, make the changes to the properties for that attribute. **(C)**
6. Repeat steps 4 and 5 to modify additional attributes.
7. Click **OK** to apply the effects to the selected object only, or click **Save** to add the effects to the options on the **Text Effects** drop-down menu.

Margins

Enter a number to put a margin on the inside of the caption, leaving more room between your text and the edge of the caption.

Remaining Properties

The rest of the caption properties are the same as for most objects. You can learn more about these properties in chapter 6.

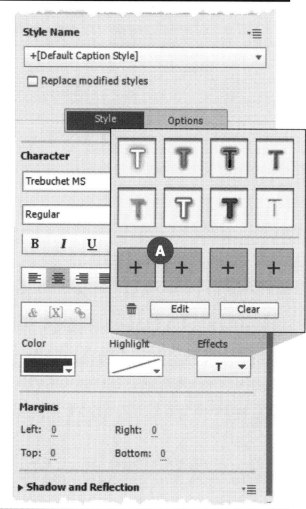

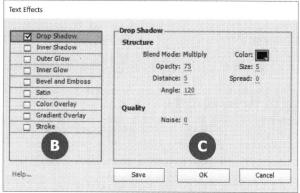

Exporting and Importing Captions

Exporting caption text into a Microsoft Word document can be useful for creating print materials, such as a job aid. You can also export captions, make changes to them, and import them back into your project—a huge time saver when you have lots of edits or if you need to translate/localize the captions.

When you use this option, caption text, smart shape text, and placeholder text boxes are all exported.

Slide Id	Item Id	Original Text Caption Data	Updated Text Caption Data	Slide
1012	2776	Go to **www.gsa.gov**.	Go to **www.gsa.gov**.	2
1542	2654	Click the link.	Click the **Per Diem Rates** link.	4
2038	2053	Select **California**.	Select the state you want.	6
2257	2272	Type **Los Angeles**.	Type the city you want to look	9

Caption as exported　　　*Edited caption to import*

Export Captions

To export captions:

1. Go to the **File** menu.
2. Select **Export**.
3. Select **Project Captions and Closed Captions**.
4. Find and select the folder where you want to save the Word document.
5. Click the **Save** button.

TIME SAVER

If you plan to use the exported captions in other documents, such as a help manual, set up a macro in Word to delete the unneeded columns and rows and take the text out of the table. Then, with one stroke, you have a ready-to-use list of steps.

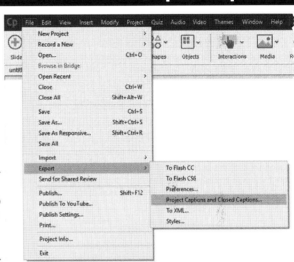

Import Captions

To import captions:

1. Go to the **File** menu.
2. Select **Import**.
3. Select **Project Captions and Closed Captions**.
4. Find and select the document previously exported.
5. Click the **Open** button.

CAUTION

- Make sure you import back into the *same* Captivate file and only change the **Updated Text Caption Data** column. Changing other text or adding/deleting rows can cause problems.

- White text in your course appears as white text in the table. You may want to apply a background color in Word to see it.

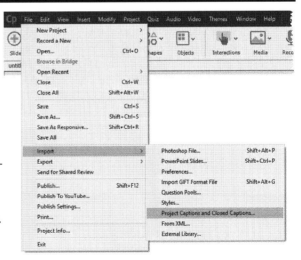

DESIGN TIPS

- For systems training, create a style guide for terminology so that your language is consistent. For example:

  - Do you refer to a "drop-down" or a "drop-down arrow"?

  - Do you bold the name of the feature or put it in quotations?

  - Do you always capitalize the name of a feature, never capitalize it, or match the capitalization that is in the system?

- You may end up resizing your finished course down to a smaller size to fit on a web page or in a course interface. If you are likely to do this, make your captions a larger font size than you think you need. That way they are still legible when you shrink the course.

- Never sacrifice legibility for creativity! Consider the color scheme of the software being captured, the color and size of the caption, and the color and size of the text to make sure the captions stand out and are easy to read.

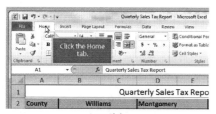

Legible

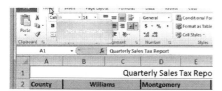

Not legible

 POWER TIP

You may use different terminology and punctuation than the automatically generated captions use. Rather than edit each caption, you can change the template used for the captions.

Original format   *Your preference*

First, you need to find the text template document for the language you want, which is in your program files. Make a backup copy in case you want to return to the original template. Then open the file in Notepad or Wordpad to edit it.

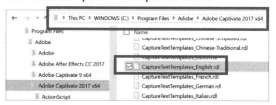

As you scroll through the document, it may seem overwhelming, but it is really quite simple. If you look at the end of every line, you'll see there is one group for each type of software feature (button, tab, etc.). Within each group, you can see the language to be used in the caption, shown in quotation marks. **%s** indicates the name of the software feature, such as **Home**, as in the example above.

Make whatever changes you want to the text INSIDE the quotation marks at the end of each line, being very careful not to change anything else or delete the **%s**.

Next, save the file. You can then share this file with anyone on your development team. They simply need to copy the file over the one currently in their program files.

Working With Images

Add an Image to a Slide

To add an image to a slide:

1. Click the **Media** drop-down button.
2. Select **Image**.
3. Find and select the image you want to use.
4. Click the **Open** button.

The image is now an object on the slide, which can be moved, resized, deleted, timed to audio, etc.

 TIME SAVER

You can also add an image by:

- Pasting it. For example, you can copy an image from a PowerPoint document or a Photoshop file and paste it onto a slide.
- Dragging and dropping it. Open the folder with the image, and drag the image onto the slide.

Image Properties

Many properties and options for an image, such as moving, resizing, and timing, are the same for most object types. Learn more about these settings in chapter 6. In this section, you will learn about properties unique to an image.

Image button (A): Click this button to select a different picture from the library or from your computer.

Transparency (B): You can select a single color and make it transparent in your image. This is useful for removing the white background in a photo or clipart. Click the drop-down menu, and select the eyedropper icon. Then click the color in the image you want to make transparent.

Reset to Original Size: If you have resized the image, click this button to return it to its original size. This option does not undo cropping.

Edit Image: See next page.

Fit to Stage: This option enlarges or shrinks the image to the largest size that will fit completely on the slide. Since the image and the slide may have different aspect ratios (height/width proportions), you may end up with empty space either above and below or to the left and right of the image.

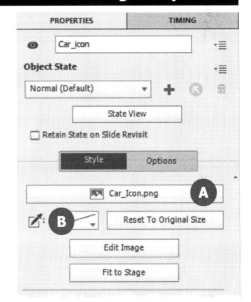

Original image   Image with white set as transparent

Editing Images

Resize/Crop Image Dialog Box

When you click the **Edit Image** button in the **Properties** pane for an image (see previous page), the **Resize/Crop Image** dialog box appears.

Brightness: Move the slider right or enter a positive number to brighten the image. Move the slider to the left or enter a negative number to darken the image.

Sharpness: Move the slider right or enter a positive number to better define edges in an image. Move the slider left or enter a negative number to soften them.

Contrast: Move the slider right or enter a positive number to increase the contrast (make darks darker, lights lighter, and colors brighter). Move the slider left or enter a negative number to decrease the contrast.

Alpha: Alpha refers to the opacity of an image. 100% means fully opaque. Use a lower number if you want to make the image partially or fully transparent.

Hue: Move the slider left or right to change the colors of the image, such as sliding it one way to make it more blue and the other way might make it more red.

Saturation: Move the slider right or enter a positive number to increase the saturation (richness) of the colors. Move the slider left or enter a negative number to make them less saturated.

Gray Scale: Check this box to remove all color in the image and convert it to gray scale.

Invert Color: Check this box to change darks to lights, lights to darks, and all colors to their opposite on the color wheel—as in a film negative.

Rotation Icons: Click any of the four rotation options to flip or rotate the image.

Fit to Stage: This option enlarges or shrinks the image to the largest size that will fit completely on the slide. You may end up with empty space either above and below or to the left and right of the image.

Crop: Select this radio button to show crop handles. Drag the handles and move the crop frame to indicate the part of the image you want to keep. That portion of the image will then be enlarged to fit the slide.

Constrain Proportions: If you are cropping the image, check this box to make the crop frame the same aspect ratio as the slide. Uncheck it if you want to be able to change the aspect ratio.

Retain Size: This is the default option whereby the image stays at whatever size you made it on the slide.

Reset All: Click this button to return the image to its original settings.

CAUTION

If you crop out areas of your image, you cannot come back later and bring those areas back (even if you click the **Reset All** button). If you want those parts of the image back, you either need to re-insert the image or find the uncropped version in the **Library** and add it back.

Library, p. 229

Using Photoshop Files

In addition to using image types such as **.gif** and **.png**, you can import Photoshop **.psd** files. When you do, you can bring in each layer individually for more control, edit the file in Photoshop without leaving Captivate, and update the image when the source file changes.

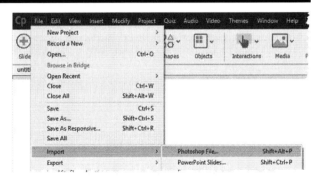

To import a Photoshop file:

1. Go to the **File** menu.
2. Select **Import**.
3. Select **Photoshop File**.
4. Find and select the file you want.
5. Click the **Open** button.
6. Select the options you want.
7. Click the **OK** button.

Photoshop Import Options

Photoshop Layer comps: In Photoshop, you can create several versions of a design in the same file. These versions are called layer comps. If you have more than one comp in your file, select **Multiple**, and then select the comp you want from the drop-down menu.

Scale according to stage size: If you check this box, Captivate will resize the image to be as large as possible and still fit on the slide.

Select Photoshop Layers to Import: If your Photoshop file has layers, check or uncheck the box for each layer to indicate which ones you want to import. Each layer will appear as its own image in Captivate.

Import As: If your file has layers, but you want to import them all as a single image, select **Flattened Image**. This brings it in as a single image without changing the layers of the underlying Photoshop file.

Merge Layers: If you don't want the image flattened but do want some of the layers combined, select the layers you want to merge (shift-click the layer names), and then click the **Merge Layers** button.

To edit a Photoshop file from Captivate:

1. Right-click the folder for the image in the **Library**.
2. Select **Edit PSD Source File**.
3. Make your changes in Photoshop.
4. Save your changes.

The first time you do this, you may only see **Edit with...** on the menu. If so, select that option, and then find and select the Photoshop program in your program files.

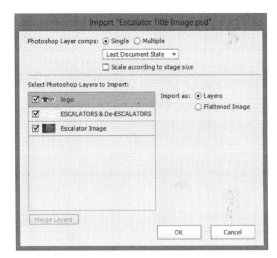

POWER TIP

If you have Adobe Photoshop installed on your computer, your imported **.psd** file is linked to the underlying source file. A green dot next to the file in the **Library** means you are working with the most updated version. A red dot means there has been a change to the source file. A question mark means the link has been broken. Click the red dot or question mark to update or relink the file.

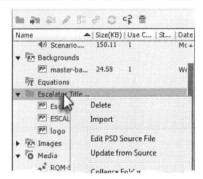

Using Scalable Vector Graphics

Starting in Captivate 9, you can use Scalable Vector Graphic (SVG) files to maintain image resolution and quality. A SVG file is an image created in a vector graphics editor, such as Adobe Illustrator. Unlike .png, .gif, .jpeg, or other image file types, SVG images can be scaled to whatever size you want without losing quality.

Scaled non-SVG imge.   Scaled SVG imge.

To add an SVG image:

1. Click the **Media** down-down menu.
2. Select **SVG**.
3. Find and select the SVG image you want to use.
4. Click the **Open** button.

To edit an SVG image:

1. Select the image.
2. In the **Properties** panel, click **Edit SVG. (A)**
3. Find and select a vector-based image editing application installed on your computer.
4. Click the **Open** button.
5. Make your changes in the editing program.
6. Save your changes.

POWER TIP

Because SVG images can be scaled to any size without losing image quality, they are ideal for responsive projects.

Creating Responsive Projects, p. 271

Characters

Captivate offers photographic and illustrated characters, each in a variety of poses, that you can add to your projects. Characters are available in the following categories: business, casual, illustrated, and medicine.

Insert a Character

To insert a character:

1. Click the **Media** drop-down button.
2. Select **Characters**.
3. Select the type of character you want from the **Category** drop-down menu.
4. Select the character you want from the thumbnails in the panel on the left.
5. Select the pose you want from the panel in the middle.
6. Select the cropping you want from the panel on the right.
7. Click **OK**.

 DESIGN TIPS

- The first time you use the characters, you need to download files using the link in a pop-up window.

- If you want to enlarge a character on the screen, it will look best if you check the **Use High Resolution Images** box when initially inserting the image.

- This dialog box includes even more design assets, such as access to templates and more images.

 Assets, p. 239

Drawing Shapes

The drawing tools in Captivate let you create basic shapes (such as rectangles, ovals, and lines), as well as special shapes (such as thought bubbles and flowchart elements). Refer to chapter 6 for information on shape properties, such as fill and stroke colors.

Draw a Shape

To draw a shape:

1. Click the **Shapes** drop-down button.
2. Select the shape type you want.
3. Drag your mouse to create the shape you want.

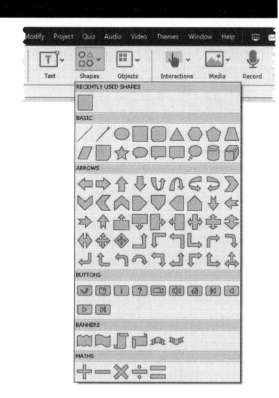

DESIGN TIPS

- When drawing a polygon, do not click and drag as with the other shapes. Instead, click where you want to add each point.

- To use the same shape several times, hold the **Ctrl** key when you click the shape, which lets you use that shape until you press **Esc** or select another tool.

- For a perfect square or circle, press and hold the **Shift** key while drawing a rectangle or oval.

- When drawing a line or polygon, press and hold the **Shift** key while drawing to keep the lines at 45º increments.

- To change the points on a polygon, right-click the shape, and select **Edit Points**.

- To edit the points of a different shape type, first right-click and select **Convert to freeform**. Then you can right-click and edit the points.

- To add text to a shape, double-click the shape, or right-click the shape to select **Add Text**.

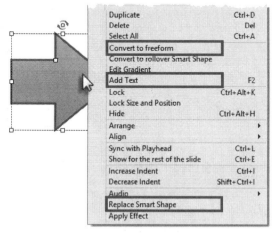

TIME SAVERS

- If you need to make changes to your shape, you don't need to start from scratch. Right-click the shape, and select **Replace Smart Shape** to draw a different shape. For polygons, right-click the shape and select **Redraw Smart Shape** to draw it over. With both of these options, the timing, formatting, and other properties remain, which wouldn't be true if you deleted the shape and started over.

- If you create your own custom polygon shape, you can save it for future use. Click the menu icon in the **Properties** pane and select **Save Shape** to save it. Then it will appear on the **Shapes** drop-down button.

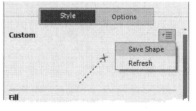

Add a Highlight Box

A highlight box is a different way to add a rectangle. It is commonly used to add visual emphasis to parts of the screen being discussed.

To add a highlight box:

1. Click the **Objects** drop-down button.
2. Select **Highlight Box**.
3. Move and resize the highlight box over the area you want to highlight.
4. Format the highlight box in the **Properties** panel.

Options: Fill Outer Area

By default, the inside of a highlight box is filled with your fill color. If you check this option, the *inside* of the box remains clear, and the *outside* of the box is filled, creating a spotlight effect.

Additional Properties

The rest of the properties for highlight boxes are the same as for most objects. You can learn about those properties in chapter 6.

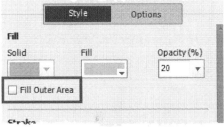

DESIGN TIP

How do you decide if you want a rectangle or a highlight box?

Rectangles:

- Have more formatting options, such as gradients.
- Can contain text.
- Can have alt text.
- Can have the points edited.

Highlight boxes:

- Can have an inner fill or an outer fill.
- Can be added automatically to highlight the object you are clicking during a screen capture session.
- Can be used to create a quick job aid using the **Print** option on the **File** menu, where just the part under the highlight box is exported to the print document.

Recording Settings, p. 27
Print, p. 262

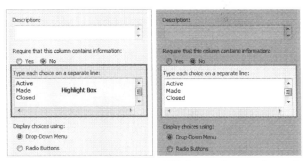

Default inner fill   *Fill Outer Area selected*

CAUTION

Don't worry if your fill area is not showing. Highlight boxes with an outer area fill do not show the fill color in edit mode. You can only see the fill when previewing or viewing the published course.

Adding Animations

Animations might come from: Adobe Flash or other software that outputs to Flash, an animated **.gif** that you create in Photoshop or purchase from stock clipart sources, or a published Captivate project. Animations are a great way to add specialized interactions, functionality, or visual effects.

When you add an animation *slide*, the animation becomes part of the background of the slide. This means that the animation cannot be resized, repositioned, or adjusted in the timeline. However, when you add an animation to an existing slide, it becomes an object on that slide, which can be edited, moved, etc.

 DESIGN TIP

Captivate comes with a gallery of Flash animations you can use in your projects. Look for the **Gallery** folder in your Adobe Captivate system files.

Add an Animation Slide

To add an animation slide:

1. Go to the **Insert** menu.
2. Select **Animation Slide**.
3. Find and select the animation you want.
4. Click the **Open** button.

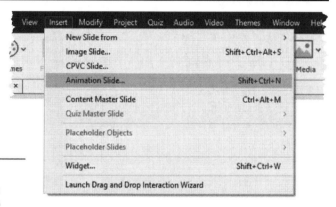

CAUTION

- Flash files added to your project will not convert to HTML5 when you publish. Adobe is discontinuing the Flash player in 2020, so coures that contain Flash content after that point won't play properly.

- Make sure the frame rate of any inserted animations is the same frame rate as your project. Otherwise, you may get some unpredictable results. The default setting for Captivate projects is 30 frames per second, which can be changed in **Preferences** on the **Edit** menu.

- If you are creating a Flash file for use in Captivate, use embedded fonts instead of system fonts. Otherwise, your text may not appear properly.

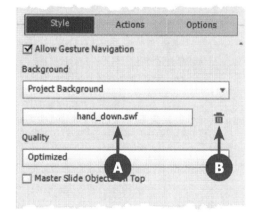

 BRIGHT IDEA

Even though the animation on an animation slide does not appear as its own object, you can still change or delete it. In the **Properties** panel for the slide, click the button with the file name **(A)** to select a different animation or the **Delete** button **(B)** to delete the animation from the slide.

Add an Animation

Captivate lets you add two types of animations to a slide. The **Animation** option lets you add a **.gif** or **.swf** file. The **HTML5 Animation** option lets you add animations created in Adobe Edge Animate (**.oam**).

To add an animation to a slide:

1. Click the **Media** drop-down button.
2. Select **Animation** or **HTML5 Animation**.
3. Find and select the animation you want.
4. Click the **Open** button.

Animation Properties

Animations have a few extra properties in the **Properties** panel versus other objects. (You can learn more about the standard properties in chapter 6.)

File switch: Click this button **(A)** with the file name to replace the animation with another animation, either from the library or from your computer.

Information: Click the information icon **(B)** to see the Flash version, size, duration, and other information about the animation. (Information provided varies based on the type of animation being used.)

If you have Adobe Flash installed on your computer, you have the following options available:

Linkage: This shows the link to the file.

Update: Click this button to update the animation if the linked file has changed.

Source: If your animation was created in Flash, you can link to the corresponding **.fla** file, making it quicker to edit the animation in Flash.

Edit: If the **.fla** file is shown in the **Source** field, you can click the **Edit** button to edit the **.fla** file.

Alpha: Reduce the percentage if you want the animation to become partially or fully transparent.

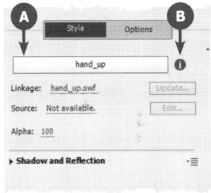

Timing Panel

In addition to the standard timing options, there are two additional options available for animations.

Synchronize with Project: Check this box to help synchronize your animation with the timeline speed. Try checking this box if your animation is not playing smoothly.

Loop: Check this box if you want the animation to continue from the beginning when it is finished, continuing to do so until the slide itself is finished.

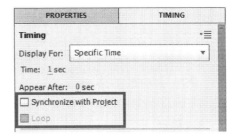

Timing Slide Objects, p. 122

 **POWER TIP**

To add an Adobe Edge Animate file, you will need to first save it in Adobe Edge Animate as an Animate Deployment Package (**.oam**).

Add a Text Animation

Captivate comes with a wizard that lets you quickly create your own text-based animations.

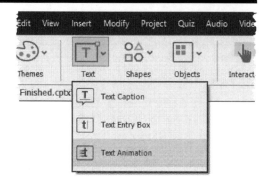

To create a text animation:

1. Click the **Text** drop-down button.
2. Select **Text Animation**.
3. In the **Text Animation Properties** dialog box, type your text in the **Text** field.
4. Format your text.
5. Click the **OK** button.
6. In the **Properties** panel, select the animation effect you want from the **Effect** drop-down list. **(A)**

To make text and font formatting changes later:

1. Click the **Animation Properties** button in the **Properties** panel. **(B)**
2. Make your changes in the dialog box.
3. Click the **OK** button.

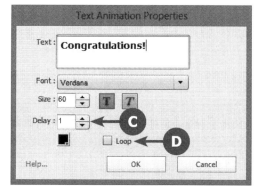

 DESIGN TIPS

- Make each individual letter appear faster or slower by changing the value in the **Delay** field **(C)**. This is the number of seconds between each letter.

- Check the **Loop** box **(D)** if you want the animation to play over and over until the end of the object's time in the timeline.

 CAUTION

Text Animations are Flash-based animations and are not supported on most mobile devices when published to HTML5. Consider using a HTML5-friendly effect instead.

 Object Effects, p. 118

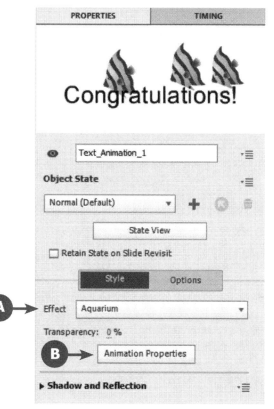

Zoom Areas

Zoom areas take a portion of your slide and magnify it for the student. For example, if you are doing a screen recording and want to emphasize a certain set of tools on screen, you can use a zoom area to magnify that section of the screen.

Insert a Zoom Area

To add a zoom area:

1. Click the **Objects** drop-down menu.

2. Select **Zoom Area.**

3. Move and resize the **Zoom Source** box over the area you want to magnify.

4. Move and resize the **Zoom Destination** box to the position and magnification you want.

5. Adjust the object in the timeline to control the speed and duration of the zoom. **(A)**

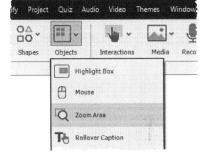

BRIGHT IDEA

You can swap out the zoom destination with your own image. For example, maybe you want to include a high-resolution version of a close up of a piece of equipment. In the **Properties** panel for the zoom destination, click the **Add new image** button to insert your own image.

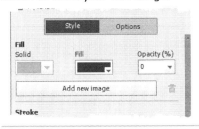

Objects as they first appear on the slide

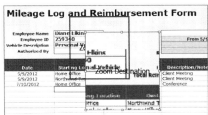

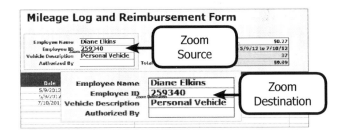

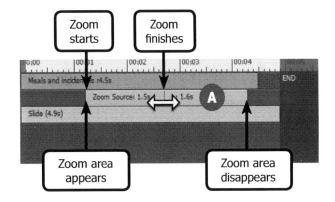

Timing Slide Objects, p. 122

Web Objects

You can use Web objects to insert anything that exists on a Web page into your course. While a hyperlink takes the student to a Website outside of the course, a Web object can embed the page into the course itself.

The student can interact with all buttons, links, etc., on the Website but does not have access to the **Address** bar. Using a Web object instead of a hyperlink helps keep the student focused on your course, prevents them from having to manage multiple windows, and avoids issues with pop-up blockers.

Insert a Web Object

To insert a web object:

1. Click the **Objects** drop-down button.

2. Select **Web**.

3. In the **Address** field, enter the Web address you want to use.

4. Adjust the frame so the Web content fits the way you want it.

5. Configure the rest of the properties. (See below.)

Web Object Properties

Embed Code

If you want to embed a video from a streaming service such as YouTube or Vimeo, select this option, and then paste the embed code for that video in the text field.

Auto Load

Keep this checked if you want the Web content to be immediately visible to your student. Uncheck the box if you would rather have a play button for the student to click.

Display In

By default, the Web page will display on the slide. Use this menu if you would rather have the Web content appear in a pop-up window.

Border

A small black border appears around the Web object. Uncheck this box if you don't want the border.

Scrolling

By default, the Web window has scrollbars if the window is smaller than the Web page. Uncheck this box if you do not want to allow scrolling.

Loading Animation

Check this box if you want the student to see a loading animation while waiting for the Web content to load.

 CAUTION

When previewing Web objects, you need to preview in a browser. Based on your computer's security settings, however, the content may not play properly until it is published and posted to a server.

 POWER TIP

If you click the folder icon next to the **Address** field, you can add your own **.oam**, **.pdf**, or **.zip** files.

Audio and Video

Introduction

Audio can be used to add voice-over narration, add fun or dramatic effects with sounds, or set a certain tone or mood with music. In Captivate, you can add audio files to individual objects, individual slides, or the project as a whole.

Audio can be either imported or recorded directly in Captivate. If you are recording screen captures, you can either record in Captivate while you capture or add it after the capture is finished. You can import **.mp3** and **.wav** files into Captivate.

Captivate also provides useful audio tools, such as text-to-speech, which adds automated narration based on the text you enter, as well as closed captions for those who are unable to hear your audio (for technical, environmental, or physical reasons).

In chapter 6, you'll learn how to time individual elements to audio, so that the right text, image, or other object appears exactly when it should.

In addition to audio, you can add video files to your projects. For example, you might want to introduce a course on a new policy with a video introduction from the CEO.

In This Chapter

- Working With Audio
- Closed Captioning
- Adding Video

Notes

Working With Audio

Import Audio to the Background

Background audio plays across slides—in the background. Even if you have background audio, you can still have slide-level audio, such as narration. For example, this is how you would add background music to your project.

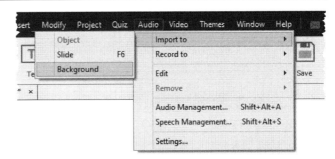

To import audio to the background:

1. Go to the **Audio** menu.
2. Select **Import to**.
3. Select **Background**.
4. Navigate to and select the file you want.
5. Click the **Open** button.
6. Set the background audio options you want. **(A)**
7. Click the **Save** button.
8. Click the **Close** button.

Background Audio Options

Fade In/Fade Out: If you want the background audio to fade in or out, enter the duration of each fade here, in seconds.

Loop Audio: By default, this box is checked, meaning the audio will play over and over until the course ends. Uncheck it if you want the audio to play only once.

Stop audio at end of project: By default, this box is checked, meaning that when the course is over, the audio will stop. Uncheck it if you want the audio to continue playing until the window is closed.

Adjust background audio volume on slides with audio: By default, background audio will lower to 50% volume on any slide with its own audio (such as voice-over narration). Uncheck this box if you don't want the audio automatically reduced, or use the slider to change how much to reduce the volume.

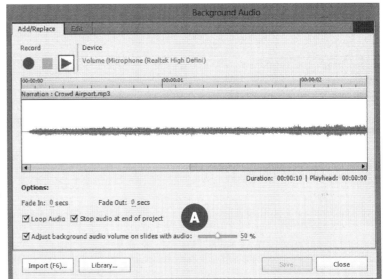

DESIGN TIP

Just because you can doesn't mean you should! Use background audio with care as it can easily overpower or distract from your instructional goals.

TIME SAVER

Captivate comes with music and sound effects in the Gallery!

> This PC > WINDOWS (C:) > Program Files > Adobe > Adobe Captivate 2017 x64 > Gallery > Sound >

Import Audio to an Object

You can add audio to individual objects such as a specific caption. For example, you can add a cheering sound effect to the correct feedback caption in a practice activity.

To import audio to an object:

1. Select the object you want to import the audio to.
2. Go to the **Audio** menu.
3. Select **Import to**.
4. Select **Object**.
5. Find and select the file you want.
6. Click the **Open** button.
7. Click **Yes** to extend the object length, if needed. **(A)**
8. Click the **Close** button. **(B)**

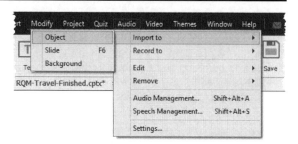

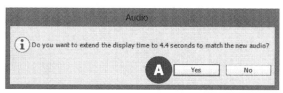

 CAUTION

You can still adjust the length of the object in the timeline. However, if you make the object shorter than the audio, the audio will get cut off.

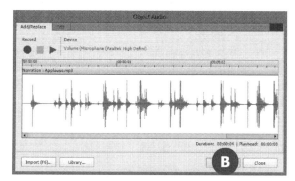

 BRIGHT IDEA

You can also add audio to an object from that object's **Properties** panel. Simply click the **Options** tab, and then click the **Add Audio** button. From there you can find and select the audio file you want. You can also delete or change the audio file from the same panel.

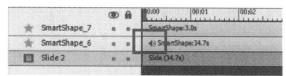

An audio indicator appears on the object in the timeline.

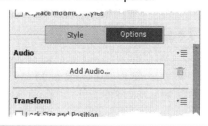

Import Audio to One or More Slides

To import audio to one or more slides:

1. Select the slide you want to import audio to, or select the first slide if the audio is for the whole course.
2. Click the **Media** drop-down button.
3. Select **Audio**.
4. Navigate to and select the file you want.
5. Click the **Open** button.
6. Choose how to import the audio. **(A)**
7. Click the **OK** button.

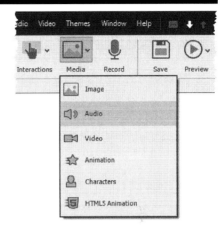

Audio Import Options

The dialog box in step 6 only appears if the imported audio is longer than the slide you are importing it into. These three options determine how that audio is distributed.

Show the slide for the same amount of time as the length of the audio file

Use this option if you are importing audio for a single slide and you want to make the slide as long as the audio.

Distribute the audio file over several slides

Use this option if you are importing audio for more than one slide, such as the whole course. This opens a dialog box that lets you split up the audio across the slides.

Retain current slide duration and distribute the audio files over several slides

Use this option if you are importing audio for more than one slide, but you want Captivate to split up the audio based on the current slide lengths.

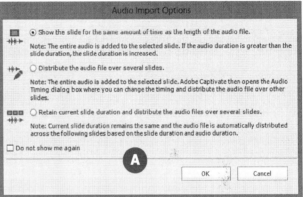

 DESIGN TIP

Which option is best? Generally, when you record voice-over for computer simulations, it is best to record the entire script in one file. This tends to take less time and create a more natural tone and flow than trying to record each slide's audio as a separate file. Then, all you need to do is add the one audio file to the first slide and select the second import option, which lets you chop up the audio across the slides.

The waveform for the audio appears in the timeline.

Distribute Audio Across Slides

If you import audio for several slides as a single file, you then need to distribute it across the slides. If you select the **Distribute the audio...** option when importing, the distribution dialog box appears automatically. Otherwise, you can go to the **Audio** menu to bring up the dialog box.

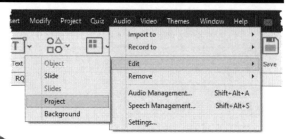

To distribute audio across multiple slides:

1. Go to the **Audio** menu.
2. Select **Edit**.
3. Select **Project**.
4. Click **Yes** in the warning dialog box (if appropriate).
5. Position the playhead in the waveform where you want the next slide to start (play the audio or click in the waveform).
6. Click the **Start Next Slide** button.
7. Click and drag slide dividers to adjust the position.
8. Click the **Save** button.
9. Click the **Close** button.

 CAUTION

Pay attention to the warning in step 4. If you have closed captions timed to audio, continuing with this process will remove the timing. It is best to time your closed captions at the end of production. After that, use only the slide-level audio editing.

> If you edit the project audio, all closed captions in the project will be disabled and the timing information of the captions will be lost. However, after editing the audio, you can:
>
> * Enable the closed captions by selecting the Audio CC check boxes in the Slide Notes panel.
>
> * Adjust the timing of the captions by clicking the Closed Captioning tab in the Slide Audio dialog box (Audio > Edit > Slide).
>
> Do you want to continue?

Closed Captions, p. 88

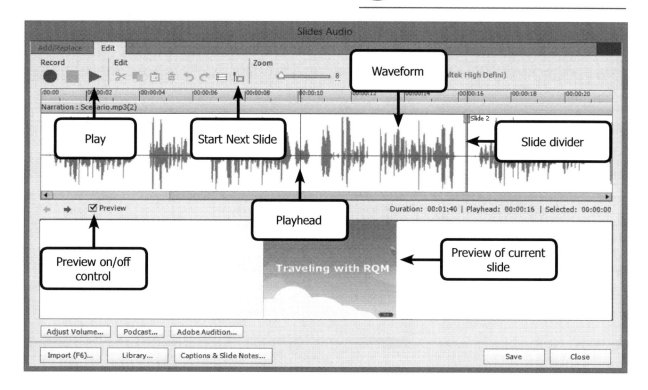

Configure Audio Compression

The audio settings apply to the entire published file, whether you import the audio or record it in Captivate.

To configure audio compression:

1. Go to the **Audio** menu.
2. Select **Settings**.
3. Select the compression level you want in the **Bitrate** section.
4. Click the **OK** button.

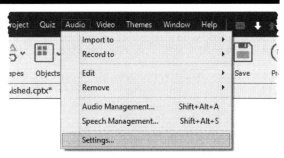

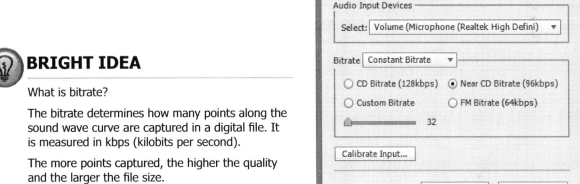

 BRIGHT IDEA

What is bitrate?

The bitrate determines how many points along the sound wave curve are captured in a digital file. It is measured in kbps (kilobits per second).

The more points captured, the higher the quality and the larger the file size.

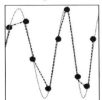   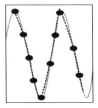

| Lower bitrate | Higher bitrate |

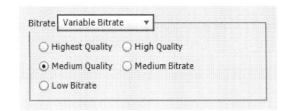

Constant Bitrate captures the same number of points for the entire project. **Variable Bitrate** adjusts the number of points based on what is happening in the audio. For example, variable bitrate uses fewer points during pauses than during spoken words. For voice-over, variable bitrate is likely to give you the same quality as constant bitrate, but at a lower file size.

For constant bitrate, the 48 to 96 range offers a good balance between compression and quality.

When you record audio in Captivate, it records at a high quality. The settings you choose here determine how it is compressed when you publish. The original high-quality recording is not affected, meaning you can come back and change your mind about these settings later.

 CAUTION

Make sure you test the audio settings by publishing your file and testing it on a target computer. A small change in bitrate can significantly affect quality and file size, so make sure you have the right balance.

Calibrate Audio Input

Before recording audio in Captivate, you will want to calibrate your microphone for the best volume levels. You will be prompted to do this the first time you record audio per session (once for every time you launch Captivate), or you can calibrate it yourself at any time.

To calibrate audio input:

1. Go to the **Audio** menu.
2. Select **Settings**.
3. Select the microphone you want to use (if you have more than one available). **(A)**
4. Click the **Calibrate Input** button. **(B)**
5. Click the **Auto calibrate** button. **(C)**
6. Speak into the microphone until you see the **Input Level OK** message. **(D)**
7. Click the **OK** button.

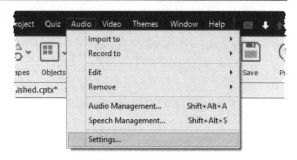

 POWER TIP

You can manually control the calibration. Instead of clicking **Auto calibrate**, click the **Record** button, and record some audio. Click the **Stop** button, and then the **Play** button to listen to it.

From there, you can adjust the **Pre-amplifier value** to get the volume you want during recording.

- **1** means no change in audio.
- Less than **1** means the recording volume will be reduced.
- Higher than **1** (up to **10**) means the recording volume will be increased.

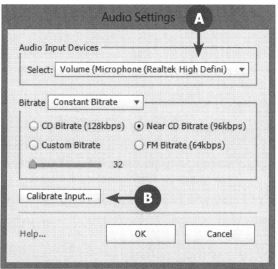

 BRIGHT IDEA

You will want to calibrate your audio every time you sit down to record audio. However, if you are recording more than one project in a sitting, you don't need to calibrate for each file you work on.

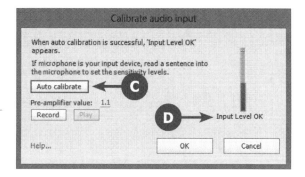

Record Audio to a Slide or Object

To record audio to a slide or object:
1. Select the slide or object you want to record audio to.
2. Click the **Record** button on the main toolbar.
3. Click the **Record** button in the dialog box.
4. Speak into your microphone.
5. Click the **Stop** button.
6. Click the **Save** button.
7. Click the **Close** button.

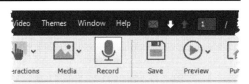

 BRIGHT IDEAS

- If you added your script in the **Slide Notes** panel, click the **Captions & Slide Notes** button **(A)** to see them while you record.
- If you'd like to record system audio instead of narration, click the **System Audio** button before recording.

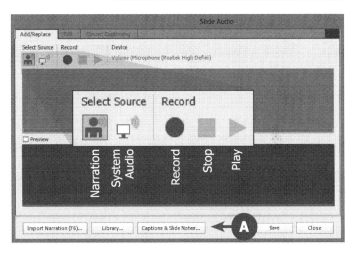

Record Audio Across Slides or to Background

To record audio across several slides:
1. Go to the **Audio** menu.
2. Select **Record to**.
3. Select **Slides**.
4. Indicate the range of slides you want to record.
5. Click the **OK** button.
6. Click the **Record** button. **(B)**
7. Speak into your microphone for the first slide.
8. Click the **Stop** button. **(C)**
9. Click the **Next Slide** button. **(D)**
10. Repeat steps 6-9 until all the slides are done.
11. Click the **Save** button.
12. Click the **Close** button.

To record audio to the background:
1. Go to the **Audio** menu.
2. Select **Record to**.
3. Select **Background.**
4. Click the **Record** button. **(E)**
5. Speak into your microphone.
6. Click the **Stop** button.
7. Click the **Save** button.
8. Click the **Close** button.

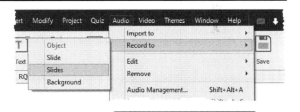

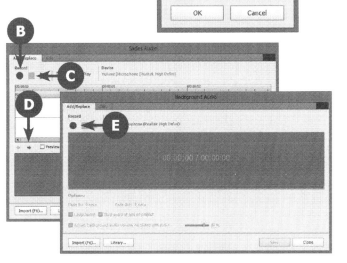

Record Audio While Capturing

If you want to record your narration while capturing a software simulation, you can set that up in your initial recording settings. Simply select the microphone you want to use from the **Audio** drop-down menu. Then, speak into your microphone while you are capturing.

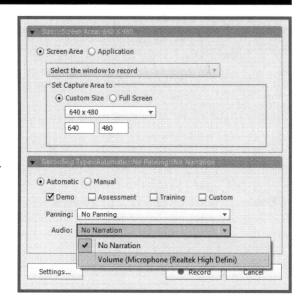

 Recording Settings: p. 25

 # CAUTION

Recording audio while you capture may seem like a time-saver, but in the long run, it may not be. It can be difficult to perform the steps and record the narration properly at the same time, meaning you may need several "takes" before getting it right. In addition, the editing process may take longer if you have to add or delete slides, change the script, etc. This option is best when you want a quick, casual sound. Add a scripted voice-over later if you want a more polished sound.

 # BRIGHT IDEAS

Setting up the Recording Environment

Microphone: Get the best results from a USB, unidirectional, headset microphone with a foam windscreen.

- The headset helps to keep the microphone a uniform distance from the speaker's mouth for a more consistent sound.
- The unidirectional feature helps eliminate background noise.
- The windscreen controls the popping and hissing sounds that come from letters such as "p" and "s."

Environment:

- Record in a room without a lot of hard, reflective surfaces such as large windows, tile floors, and metal or glass furniture. Instead, pick smaller rooms with carpet, curtains, and upholstered furniture.
- Record away from florescent lighting, electronic equipment, and air vents, which can cause background noise.
- To create a makeshift sound studio, glue "egg crate" foam sheets to a three-sided presentation board and prop it up in front of you.

Tips for Audio Quality

- Before you spend a lot of time recording, timing, importing, etc., do a quick test of all the settings. Create a single-slide course, record the audio, publish it, and play it. Adjust your tone, compression settings, and other elements until you are happy with the results. Then, proceed to record the rest of the audio.
- Listen to your audio using both your computer speakers and headphones. You may notice different quality issues using each method. Consider what your students will use when listening to your course to help you decide if you are happy with the audio quality.
- If audio quality is extremely important to you, consider recording it outside of Captivate and then importing it. Software made specifically for audio recording (such as Audacity or Wavepad) often provide useful noise filters and more precise editing control.

Edit Audio

To edit audio:

1. Go to the **Audio** menu.
2. Select **Edit**.
3. Select the scope of the audio you want to edit. **(A)**
4. Make your changes in the audio editor. (See below.)
5. Click the **Save** button.
6. Click the **Close** button.

To change the break between slides:

1. Click and drag the **Slide Divider** to the point where you want the break. **(B)**

To delete a section of audio:

1. Click and drag your mouse in the waveform to select the audio you want to remove.
2. Click the **Delete** button.

To cut or copy and paste audio:

1. Select the audio you want.
2. Click the **Cut** or **Copy** button.
3. Click in the waveform where you want the new audio to go, or select the audio you want to replace.
4. Click the **Paste** button.

 CAUTION

If you have closed captions, editing the *project* audio will delete the timing of your closed captions.

 BRIGHT IDEAS

- Select **Slides** or **Project** if you want to adjust the breaks between slides. Use **Project** for *all* slides, and **Slides** for whatever slides you have selected.
- To edit the audio for one slide, just double-click the audio item in the slide's timeline.
- You can edit audio in Adobe Audition right from the **Slides Audio** window **(C),** with Soundbooth, or with the software of your choice via the library.

 Library, p. 229

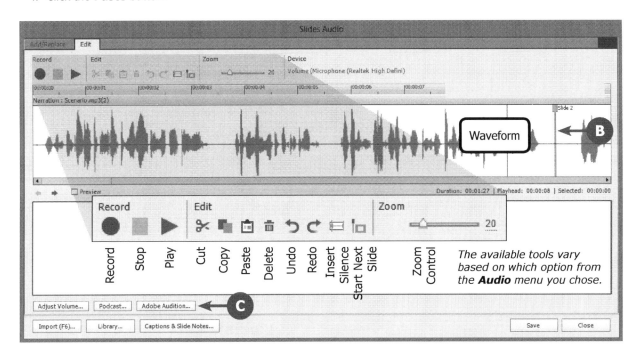

The available tools vary based on which option from the **Audio** menu you chose.

Edit Audio (cont'd)

To adjust volume:

1. In the waveform, select the audio you want to adjust.
2. Click the **Adjust Volume** button. (See previous page.)
3. Click and drag the **Volume** slider up to increase volume or down to decrease volume.
4. Click the **OK** button.

Audio Processing Options

Normalize: Use this option to have Captivate automatically adjust the audio to maintain a consistent volume between slides.

Dynamics: Use this option to have Captivate manage volume variations based on your settings. **Ratio** determines how loud to make the most quiet sections (**2** means the volume would double). **Threshold** determines the level of sound that shouldn't be amplified, such as background noise.

To insert silence:

1. Click in the waveform where you want the silence.
2. Click the **Insert Silence** button. (See previous page.)
3. Enter the amount of silence you want.
4. Select the location for the silence if you want it at the start or end of the audio instead of at the **Playhead Position**.
5. Click the **OK** button.

To record additional audio:

1. Click in the waveform where you want the new audio.
2. Click the **Record** button. (See previous page.)
3. Speak into the microphone.
4. Click the **Stop** button.

To import a new audio file into the waveform:

1. Click in the waveform where you want the new audio.
2. Click the **Import** button. (See previous page.)
3. Find and select the audio you want.
4. Click the **Open** button.

To import an audio file from the library:

1. Click the **Library** button. (See previous page.)
2. Select the file you want.
3. Click the **OK** button.

 The Library, p. 229

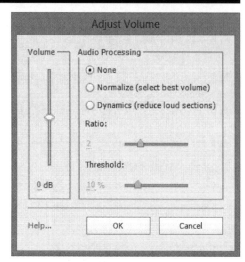

BRIGHT IDEA

One common reason to insert silence is because the length of the slide is longer than the length of the audio. For example, you might try to place a slide break where the playhead is, but the break actually shows up a little bit later.

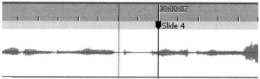

Or, you try to drag a slider to the left, and it won't go any farther.

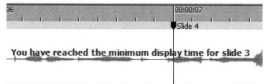

In both cases, you can insert silence to make the audio for the slide (slide 3 in these examples) longer to fit the timing better.

Export Audio

Exporting audio can be useful if you want to keep a backup of your audio or want to use it somewhere else.

To export audio:

1. Go to the **Audio** menu.
2. Select **Audio Management**.
3. Select the slides with the audio you want to export.
4. Check the boxes for the file types you want (MP3 and/or WAVE).
5. Click the **Export** button.
6. Find and select the location where you want to save the audio.
7. Click the **OK** button.
8. Click the **OK** button again.

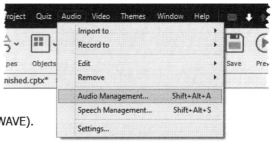

 BRIGHT IDEA

You can also export the audio for the entire project as a single **.wav** or **.mp3** file. Edit the audio for the whole project, and click the **Podcast** button.

Other Audio Management Options

You are able to perform several other tasks from the **Advanced Audio Management** dialog box.

- **Play**: Select an audio file in the list at the top, and click the **Play** button.
- **Remove**: Select an audio file in the list at the top, and click the **Remove** button.
- **Update**: Click the **Update** button to update the audio file from the library.
- **Add Closed Captioning**: Click the **Closed Caption** button to open the **Audio Editor** to the **Closed Caption** tab.
- **Edit**: Click the **Edit** button to open the **Audio Editor** to the **Edit** tab.

 Closed Captions, p. 88

Remove Audio

There are many ways to remove audio from a slide:

- Right-click the slide thumbnail, select **Audio**, and then **Remove**.

- Click the audio icon under the slide thumbnail, and click **Remove**. **(A)**

- Right-click the audio in the timeline, and select **Remove**. **(B)**

- Click the **Remove Audio** button in the **Audio Properties** pane. **(C)**

- Go to the **Audio** menu, select **Remove**, and then **Slide**.

- Go to the **Advanced Audio Management** dialog box, select the audio, and click the **Remove** icon. (See previous page.)

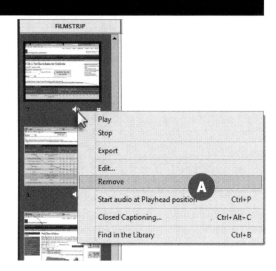

TIME SAVER

You can also *edit* audio from all of these locations.

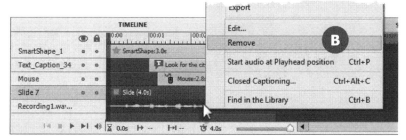

Audio-Related Properties

The **Options** tab in a slide's **Properties** panel has a few important audio settings.

- **Edit Audio**: Click this button **(D)** to go to the **Audio Editor**.

- **Fade In/Fade Out**: Adjust the number if you want your audio to fade in or out—used more often with music than with narration.

- **Loop Audio**: Check this box if you want the audio to continue playing until the slide is done playing, even if it means playing the audio more than once. Otherwise, the audio will play only once. This is used more often with music than with narration.

- **Stop Background Audio**: If you are using background audio, check this box if you do not want it to play on this particular slide.

POWER TIP

Interactive elements such as buttons have an extra option on the **Options** tab. Check the **Stop Slide Audio** box if you want the slide's audio to stop when the student clicks the button. For example, the button might reveal text that the student needs to read, and the slide audio would make that difficult.

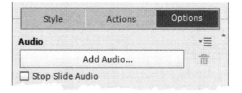

Create Audio With Text-to-Speech

The first time you use the text-to-speech (TTS) converter, you may be prompted to install it. If the **Slide Notes** panel isn't showing, select it from the **Window** menu.

To convert your text to speech:

1. Add your text in the **Slide Notes** panel for each slide.

2. Check the **Text-to-Speech** box next to each slide note you want to convert. **(A)**

3. Click the **Text-to-Speech** button. **(B)**

4. Select the voice option you want from the **Speech Agent** drop-down menu.

5. Click the **Generate Audio** button.

6. Click the **Close** button.

 Slide Notes, p. 43

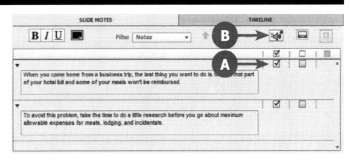

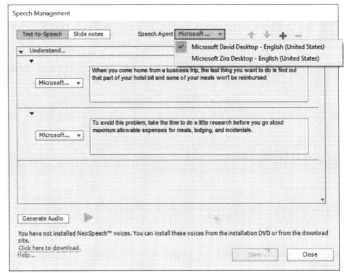

CAUTION

If you change the text in your slide notes, the changes are NOT automatically updated in your audio. You need to regenerate the audio anytime you make changes to your slide notes.

TIME SAVERS

- To generate audio for the whole project, go to the **Audio** menu, and select **Speech Management**. You'll see the same dialog box, but with the slide notes from all of your slides.

- Even if you plan to use "live" narrators, consider using TTS for early drafts. This lets you make quick edits during review cycles, recording the final narration at the end.

- To help you find the note you are looking for, use the **Filter** drop-down menu. This lets you look at all notes, just those selected for text-to-speech, or just those selected for closed captioning.

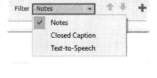

Closed Captioning

To help make your projects accessible to people who cannot hear your audio, you can convert your slide notes into closed captions that are timed to the audio.

To set up closed captions, you must first have slide notes and audio for your slides. (Closed captioning options are disabled on slides without audio.)

CAUTION

If you are using closed captions, be sure to enable the **Closed Caption** button on the playbar, which is DISABLED by default. If this button is not on the playbar, your students will not be able to see the closed captions.

Playback Controls, p. 244

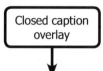

Closed caption overlay

When you come home from a business trip, the last thing you want to do is find out that part of your hotel bill and

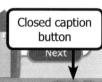

Closed caption button

Create Closed Captions

To convert your slide notes to closed captions:

1. Add your text in the **Slide Notes** panel for each slide.

2. Check the **Closed Captioning** box next to each slide note you want to convert. **(A)**

3. Click the **Closed Captioning** button. **(B)**

4. If you have more than one caption per slide, drag the caption markers in the waveform to where you want each caption to begin.

5. Click the **Save** button.

6. Click the **Close** button.

Slide Notes, p. 43

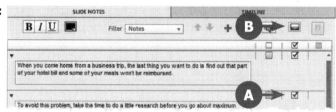

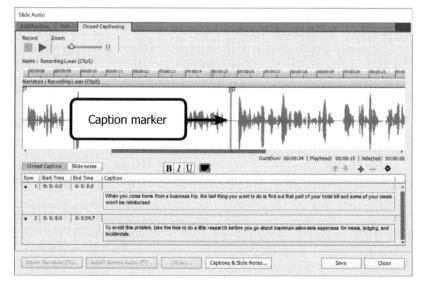

Caption marker

Change Closed Caption Settings

To change the closed captioning settings:

1. Click the **Closed Captioning** button in the **Slide Notes** panel. (**B** on previous page)
2. Click the **CC Project Settings** button. **(A)**
3. Change the settings you want.
4. Click the **Apply** button.
5. Click the **Close** button.

Settings

Show Closed Captions: By default, closed captions are hidden when the course is viewed. To view them, students must click the **CC** button in the playbar (assuming it is enabled). If you check this box, the closed captions will show when the course initially plays. Students can turn them off by clicking the **CC** button in the playbar (if it is enabled).

Font attributes: Use the size, color, and alignment tools to format the text of the captions. Center alignment is the preferred choice.

Slide menu: If you select **Project** from this menu, then the settings apply to the whole project. Or you can select a specific slide and modify the settings for just that slide. For example, if you have a slide with a dark background, it might need different formatting.

Align: This field lets you designate where you want the closed caption panel to appear. For example, if you have important content at the bottom of the slide, such as in an Excel demo, then you might want to move the captions to the top. Bottom center alignment is the preferred choice.

X/Y/W/H: Use these fields to use precise size and placement of the caption panel. **X** is distance from the left edge. **Y** is distance from the top edge. **W** and **H** are width and height. These attributes are measured as a percentage to allow for multiple device sizes.

Reset to Project: If you changed settings on a specific slide, click this button if you want to change them back to the settings for the whole project.

Background: Click the color swatch to pick the color of the caption panel.

Opacity: Use the slider to determine how opaque or transparent you want the caption panel to be.

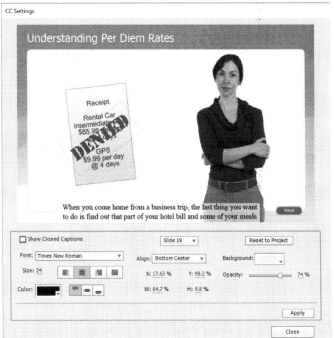

 DESIGN TIP

Consider the space used by the overlay when taking your initial captures. Avoid showing anything important in the space that will be covered by the captions.

Adding Video

Video is a great way to provide demonstrations of procedures, interviews with experts, scenarios, or visual effects.

Captivate accepts **.flv**, **.f4v**, **.avi**, **.mp4**, **.mov**, and **.3gp** movie types.

You can also use video deployed to a Web server, Flash Video Streaming Service, or Flash Media Server.

There are two ways to add video to your projects: multi-slide synchronized video or event video. Both options have their advantages, as listed in the table.

Use the multi-slide method when you want:	Use the event video method when you want:
• The video to be distributed over several slides. • The video in the library. • The video on the slide or in the table of contents. • Closed captioning. • The video to play in sync with the timeline.	• More than one video on the slide. • Playback controls on the video. • The video to play separately from the timeline.

Insert a Multi-Slide Synchronized Video

To insert a multi-slide synchronized video:

1. Click the **Media** drop-down button.
2. Select **Video**.
3. Select **Multi-Slide Synchronized Video**.
4. Click the **Browse** button.
5. Find and select the file you want.
6. Click the **Open** button.
7. Select the **Video Type** you want. (See below.)
8. From the **Show Video On** menu, select **Stage** to put the video on the slide or **TOC** to put it in the project's table of contents.
9. Select the timing option you want. (See below.)
10. Click the **OK** button.

Video Type:

By default, video is played via progressive download. If you would instead prefer to host the video on a streaming server, select either **Streaming** or **Flash Video Streaming Service** from the drop-down menu, and then enter the URL for the host location.

Timing Options:

- Select **Modify slide duration...** if you want to extend the slide to be as long as the video.
- Select **Distribute video...** if you want to split the video among several slides, based on the current slide durations. For example, a 30-second video might be split across a 10-second slide and a 15-second slide, with the rest going on the following 20-second slide.
- You can go back later and adjust how the video is distributed. (See next page.)

Change Slide Distribution

Whether you choose to extend the slide duration to match the video length or choose to distribute the video across several slides, you can adjust how the slide video is distributed. (This option is only available when you add a multi-slide synchronized video.)

To change how the video is distributed:

1. Go to the **Video** menu.

2. Select **Edit Video Timing**.

3. Drag the orange slide markers to where you want the slide breaks to happen. **(A)**

4. Click the **OK** button.

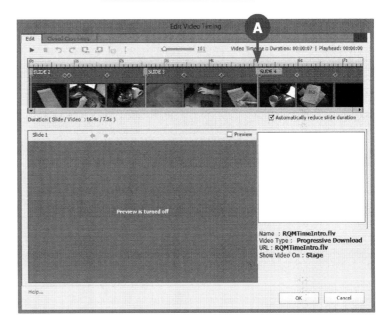

 BRIGHT IDEAS

- Don't worry about adding Flash video to a project that will be viewed on an iPad. If you publish to HTML5, the video is converted to **.mp4** format.

- Video closed captions work very much like audio closed captions. Click the **Closed Captioning** tab to enter and time the captions.

 Closed Captioning, p. 88

Insert an Event Video

To insert an event video from a file:

1. Click the **Media** drop-down button.
2. Select **Video**.
3. Select **Event Video**.
4. Click the **Browse** button.
5. Find and select the file you want.
6. Click the **Open** button.
7. Click the **OK** button.

To insert an event video from a server:

1. Click the **Media** drop-down button.
2. Select **Video**.
3. Select **Event Video**.
4. Click the **Already deployed...** radio button.
5. In the **URL** field, enter the Web address of the video file.
6. Click the **OK** button.

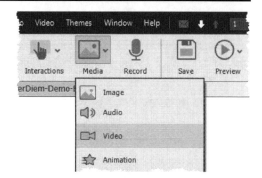

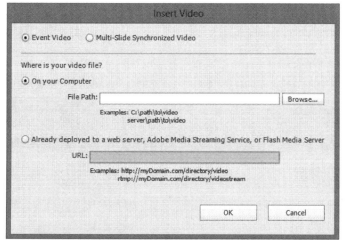

BRIGHT IDEA

If you want to include a YouTube video into your course, use the YouTube widget found in Learning Interactions or insert a Web Object with an embed code.

Learning Interactions, p. 125
Web Objects, p. 72

DESIGN TIP

Once the video is on the slide, you can move, resize, and adjust timing just as with any object.

Event Video Properties

Event video comes with special properties unique to this type of video. Standard object properties are covered in chapter 6.

Properties Panel

Video Type

Use this menu if you want to change how the video is hosted. For example, you may want to use progressive download during the development cycles, but then move the video to a streaming server once the course is ready to go live. Select the video type you want from the drop-down menu. Additional fields will appear based on the type you choose.

Detect Size

Click this button to adjust the size of the video to be at 100% of its original size.

Auto Play

By default, the video does not start until the student clicks the **Play** button on the video controls. Check this box if you want the video to play automatically.

Auto Rewind

Check this box if you want the video to go back to its starting point when it is finished.

Skin

The skin is the video control toolbar that appears underneath the video. You can select a different look for the controls (or choose not to have one) from this drop-down menu.

Timing Panel

Pause Slide Till End of Video

Because the video is not synchronized to the slide, your slide might finish before the video does. Keep this box checked if you want the slide to pause until the video is done. Uncheck it if you want the slide to finish even if the video is not done.

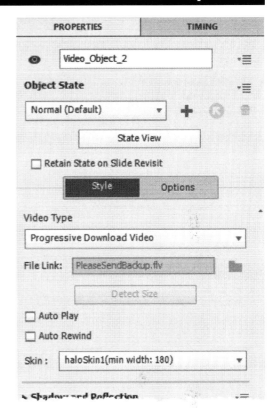

Video Management

Video Management (available from the **Video** menu), lets you perform a number of functions for multi-slide video:

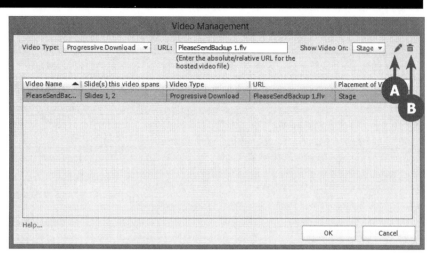

- **Edit the video timing**: Select the video, and click the **Edit Session** icon. **(A)**

- **Delete a video**: Select the video, and click the **Delete Session** icon. **(B)**

- **Move the video to the Table of Contents**: Select the video, and then select **TOC** from the **Show Video On** menu.

DESIGN TIP

Put the video in the table of contents (TOC) when you want the video to be the secondary visual. For example, you may have an expert explaining a process in the TOC while the main slide area shows a diagram of that process.

CAUTION

If you put a video in the table of contents, make sure you enable the TOC for your project.

Table of Contents, p. 246

Update Project Video

If you make changes to the video, you can update your project to include the most recent version of the video.

To update project video:

1. Right-click the video in the library.
2. Select **Update**.
3. Select the video you want to update.
4. Click the **Update** button.

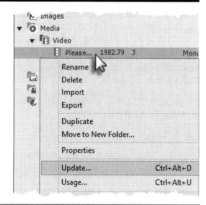

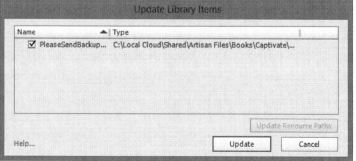

Managing Objects

Introduction

Every object has properties—every caption, every graphic, every highlight box. This chapter focuses on the properties that are common to most object types, whether sizing and rotating, changing colors, or applying styles.

In addition to these common properties, many object types have additional properties unique to that type of object. For example, captions let you choose fonts and character formatting. You can learn more about these unique properties in the chapter for that object type, such as:

- Captions and other content objects, ch. 4
- Audio and video, ch. 5
- Interactive objects, ch. 7
- Questions & quizzes, ch. 10

In this chapter, you'll also learn about ways to work more efficiently with objects, such as with layering, alignment, and grouping tools.

In This Chapter

- Object Properties Panel
- Colors and Formatting
- Managing Objects
- Styles
- States
- Effects
- Timing

Notes

Object Properties

You can find an object's properties by selecting the object in the work area or in the timeline. The **Properties** panel appears on the right side of the interface by default. If you do not see the **Properties** panel, go to the **Window** menu, and select it.

Visible in Output

By default, all objects are visible in the finished output. Click the eyeball icon **(A)** if you want the object to be initially invisible. Then you can add an action that causes the object to appear, such as when the student clicks a button.

 Show/Hide Actions, p. 136

Name

Here you can enter a name for each object. **(B)** This makes it easier to identify an object in the timeline or when selecting the object from a drop-down menu. It also serves as the alt text for an object if the **Auto Label** box is checked (see below).

Accessibility

To help make your course accessible to visually-impaired students using screen readers, you can add a text description to objects, known as alt text. Alt text is read by a screen reader to students who cannot see your content. Click the menu button **(C)** and select **Accessibility (D)** to get the **Item Accessibility** dialog box.

When the **Auto Label** box is checked in the pop-up window **(E)**, the name of the object is read to the screen reader. Uncheck this box if you want to use your own text.

 Accessibility, p. 289

Object State

The options in this section let you create multiple variations of the same object.

 Object States, p. 114

Style

Styles let you group formatting elements and apply them all at once.

 Object Styles, p. 110

Use as Button

You can turn a shape into an interactive object with actions by checking this box.

 Actions and Interactions, ch. 7

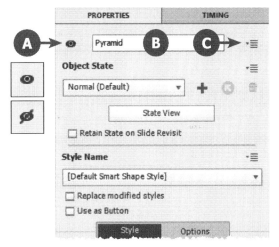

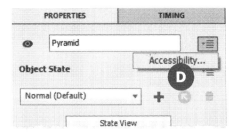

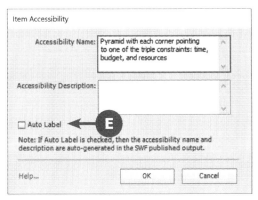

CAUTION

Accessibility text will only appear in your published course if you enable accessibility for the project.

Fill Pane and Stroke Pane

The **Fill** and **Stroke** panes are available on shapes, highlight boxes, rollover objects, and hot spot areas.

Gradient: The first menu lets you choose between a gradient fill, a solid fill, or an image fill. The name above the menu changes based on what is chosen.

Fill: Click the swatch to select the color to fill the object.

Opacity: Enter a percentage for the transparency for the fill color. 0% = transparent / 100% = opaque

Style: Some objects let you select the style of the outline, including **Solid**, **Dash**, **Dot**, **DashDot**, and **DashDotDot**.

Stroke: Click the swatch to select the color you want to outline the shape.

Width: Enter the point size for the width of the outline.

Start and End: With lines, you can choose what the ends look like. Options include **None**, **Square**, **Round**, **Diamond**, and **Arrow**.

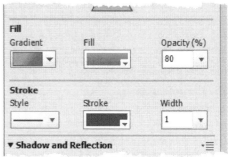

Rectangle options

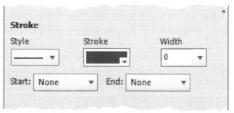

Line options

Solid Fill Colors

Whether you are selecting a fill color, text color, or any other color, the **Fill** palette appears when you click a color swatch. This palette gives you many ways to select color.

Theme Colors (A): This opens a palette of colors you chose for the project. (See the next page for more.)

Standard Palette (B): Click this icon to return to the palette shown here.

Color Picker (C): If you click the **Color Picker** button, a new window appears with additional color choices.

- Use the slider and the color area to mix a color.
- Enter RGB (red, green, blue) values.
- Enter the six-digit (hexadecimal) value. **(D)**

Pick Color/Eyedropper (E): To match a color somewhere on the screen, click the **Pick Color** icon, and click on the color you want to match.

Recent Colors (F): Click any of the recently used colors to select that color.

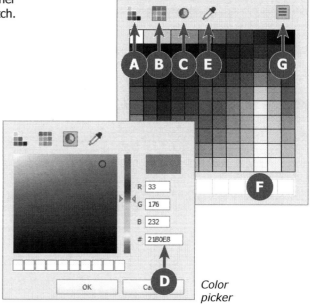

Color picker

 POWER TIP

If you click the menu button **(G)**, you get the **Swatch Manager** (also available on the **Window** menu). Here you can save even more colors for future use. You can create your own, more extensive palette, save and share palettes, and even import palettes from other sources such as Photoshop.

Theme Colors

Just as in Microsoft PowerPoint, you can set up theme colors, which give you a customized palette unique to your project. Setting up themes saves you development time and helps give your projects a more consistent, professional look.

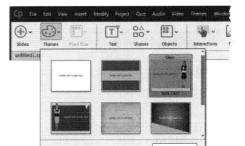

To apply a pre-made color theme to a project:

1. Click the **Themes** drop-down button.
2. Click the **Theme Colors** button.
3. In the dialog box, click the **Select Theme Color** drop-down menu.
4. Select the color scheme you want.

To create a custom color theme:

1. Click the **Themes** drop-down button.
2. Click the **Theme Colors** button.
3. Click the **Customize** button. **(A)**
4. Click the name of the theme to enter a new name. **(B)**
5. Use the swatches to set up the colors you want.
6. Click the **Save** button.
7. Click the **Close** button.

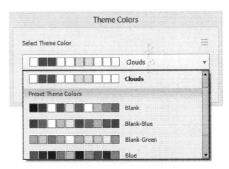

To access the theme palette when selecting colors:

1. Click the color swatch for the object you want to modify.
2. Click the **Shades** icon on the color menu. **(C)**
3. Click the square with the color you want.

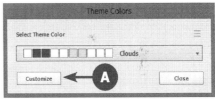

 BRIGHT IDEAS

- Save time by starting with a pre-made theme that is close to the color palette you want. You may be able to keep some of the existing colors.

- Click the icon in the top-right corner of the **Theme Colors** dialog box to delete a custom theme.

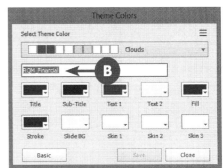

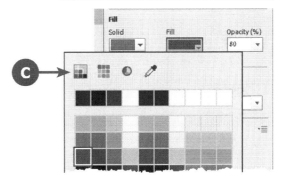

Color Gradients

With some fill color palettes (such as for slide backgrounds and shapes), you have the option of using a gradient. When you select **Gradient** from the first menu in the **Fill** pane, the **Fill** menu shows your gradient options.

Pre-Made Gradients (A): Click an icon in the top row of swatches to use one of the pre-made gradients.

Direction (B): Click any of the swatches to change the direction of the gradient (horizontal, vertical, diagonal, etc.).

Custom Gradients (C): If you have saved any custom gradients, click the swatch to apply that gradient.

Gradient Bar (D): Use the gradient bar to customize an existing gradient or create your own.

- Click an existing color stop **(I)** to change the color for that stop.

- Click and drag a color stop to change where that color starts/stops.

- Drag a color stop away from the gradient bar to delete it.

- Click below the gradient bar to add a new color stop.

Linear Gradient and Radial Gradient (E): Click either of these icons to indicate the type of gradient you want.

Reverse Colors (F): Click this icon if you want the colors on the left to move to the right and vice-versa.

Add to Custom Gradients (G): If you create a gradient you want to use again, click this icon to add it to the **Custom Gradients** area. Custom gradients will be available for your other projects.

Remove Custom Gradients (H): If you want to remove one or more of your custom gradients, click this icon. This puts a small red **X** on each of your custom gradients. Click the red **X** on a gradient to delete it from your custom gradient palette.

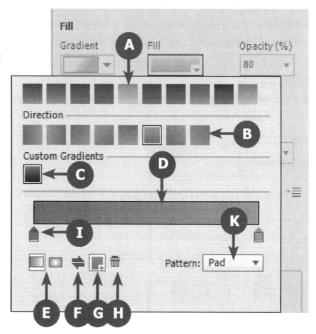

Linear Gradient

Radial Gradient

 POWER TIP

You can edit the direction of a gradient. Right-click a gradient-filled shape, and select **Edit Gradient**. This gives you a controller **(J)** you can click and drag to change the direction and the start/end points.

If the gradient is shorter than the shape, use the **Pattern** drop-down menu **(K)** to determine how to fill the remaining space.

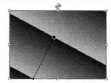

Pad *continues the end colors*

Reflect *continues the gradient in reverse*

Repeat *starts the gradient over at the beginning*

Fill Texture

With some fill color palettes (such as for slide backgrounds and smart shapes), you have the option of using a texture fill. To access these options, you must first select **Image** from the first drop-down menu. Then the **Fill** menu populates with the texture options.

Pre-Made Textures: Click an icon in the top rows of swatches to use one of the pre-made textures.

Custom Image: You can fill your shape with the image of your choice. Click the **Browse** icon (folder) to find and select the image you want to use. Click the **Edit** (pencil) or **Delete** (trash can) icons to change or delete the chosen image.

Tile: If the image used for the texture is smaller than the shape being filled, the image will be repeated within the shape, creating a tiled effect. Uncheck this box if you don't want the tiling. This option is used in conjunction with the next two options below.

Tile Type: If you are using the **Tile** option, you can use this drop-down menu to indicate the part of the object where the first tile should be placed.

Stretch: If you are not using the **Tile** option and the texture image is smaller than your shape, you can either have the image stretch to fill your shape or have the image stay at its normal size. Check or uncheck this box based on the option you want.

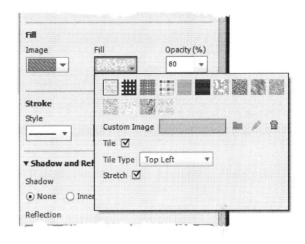

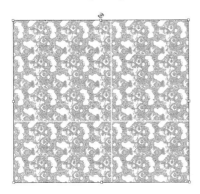

Tile = yes

Tile = no; Stretch = no

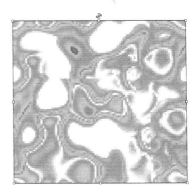

Tile = no; Stretch = yes

Shadow & Reflection Pane

Shadow

You can add drop shadows to objects such as shapes, captions, and images.

Shadow: Select **Inner** or **Outer** to turn on the shadow, based on the type of shadow you want. Then select the icon **(A)** for the angle of lighting you want, which determines on which side of the object the shadow falls.

What would you do?	What would you do?
Outer shadow	*Inner shadow*

Color: Click the swatch to select the color for the shadow.

Angle: If you do not want to use a pre-set direction, you can indicate your own angle for the shadow.

Blur: Enter a number to indicate how sharp or how blurry the edges of the shadow are. A higher number makes the shadow appear bigger.

What would you do?	What would you do?
Blur of 3 pixels	*Blur of 15 pixels*

Opacity: Select the opacity of the shadow. A lower number gives you a lighter shadow, and a higher number gives you a darker shadow.

Distance: Enter a number to determine how far away from the object you want the shadow. A larger number means it is farther away, making the object look more like it is coming off the surface of the screen.

What would you do?	What would you do?
Distance of 4 pixels	*Distance of 15 pixels*

Reflection

To add a reflection to an object, go to the **Reflection** pane, and select the reflection option with the size and distance you want.

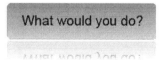

What would you do?

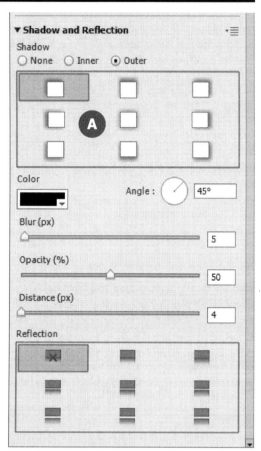

TIME SAVER

Many of the object properties have an **Apply to All** icon in the top-right corner of the pane. Click the icon, and then select the option you want. You can either apply the new settings to all of that type of item (all captions, all highlight boxes, etc.) or just the items that have the same style (all captions using the "success" style).

Transform Pane

The **Transform** pane on the **Options** tab lets you move, resize, and rotate objects numerically. You can do these same things in the work area with your mouse.

Lock Size and Position: Check this box to lock an object in place. When you do, you cannot move or resize it. You can still change other properties, such as color or text.

X: Enter, in pixels, how far from the left edge you want the object to be.

Y: Enter, in pixels, how far from the top edge you want the object to be.

W: Enter, in pixels, how wide you want the object to be.

H: Enter, in pixels, how high you want the object to be.

Constrain proportions: If you check this box, when you change the value in width or height, Captivate will automatically adjust the other dimension so that the object keeps its current proportion.

Angle: Enter, in degrees, any rotation for the object.

Rotate buttons: Rotate an object in 90 degree increments by clicking either the **Rotate Left** or **Rotate Right** button. **(A)** Use the other two buttons to flip an object vertically or horizontally. **(B)**

Using Your Mouse Instead:

- **Position**: Drag the object where you want it.
- **Size**: Click and drag a side or corner handle on the object to resize it. Hold the **Shift** key while doing so to constrain the proportions.
- **Rotation**: Click and drag the rotation handle on top of the object. Hold the **Shift** key while dragging to rotate the object in 15-degree increments.

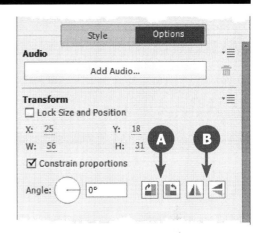

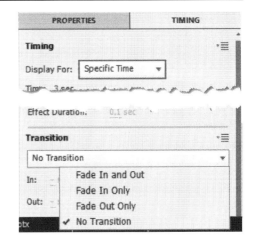

TIME SAVER

To make two or more objects the same size, use the resize tools on the **Align** toolbar.

  Aligning Objects, p. 107

Transition Pane

The settings in the **Transition** pane on the **Timing** panel determine whether an object fades in and fades out or just appears and disappears. First, select the transition you want from the drop-down menu, and then use the **In** and **Out** fields to make any fade longer or shorter.

DESIGN TIP

For a more dramatic entrance or exit (such as flying in and out), use effects instead of transitions.

  Effects, p. 118

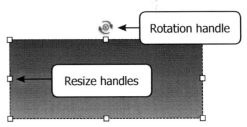

Managing Objects

In this section, you will learn how to:

- Cut, copy, and paste objects.
- Delete objects.
- Group/ungroup objects.
- Show/hide objects.
- Lock/unlock objects.
- Align objects.
- Adjust layering of objects.

Cut/Copy/Paste/Duplicate Objects

You can cut, copy, and paste objects using the following methods:

- Right-click the object in the work area or the timeline and select **Cut**, **Copy**, or **Paste**.
- Select the object(s), and press the keyboard shortcut shown to the right of the menu item.

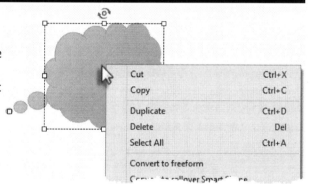

 TIME SAVER

Use the **Duplicate** function to copy and paste all in one step.

Delete Objects

There are two options for deleting an object.

- Right-click the object in the work area or the timeline, and select **Delete**.
- Select the object(s), and press the **Delete** key on your keyboard.

Group/Ungroup Objects

Grouping objects can make them easier to manage. When you group objects, you can:

- Move, resize, and time them all at once.
- Apply certain properties to all objects in the group.
- Expand and collapse the group in the timeline, making it more organized.
- Use the whole group as the target of an action, such as a **Show** or **Hide** action.

To group objects:

1. Select them in the timeline or the work area.
2. Right-click any of the selected objects.
3. Select **Group**.

To ungroup objects:

1. Right-click any item in the group.
2. Select **Ungroup**.

To remove a single object from a group:

1. Click the group.
2. Click the individual object you want to remove.
3. Right-click that same object.
4. Select **Remove From Group**.

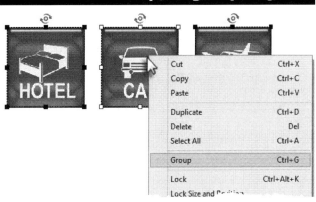

BRIGHT IDEAS

- You can still work with the individual objects in a group. Click the object once to select the whole group, and then click the object again to select just that object. From there, you can move it, resize it, change its properties, etc.
- Click the triangle next to the name of the group in the timeline to expand or collapse the group.
- When the group is selected, any active property in the **Properties** panel can be changed, affecting all the objects in the group.

Show/Hide Objects in Edit Mode

While you are working on a slide, you can hide certain objects in the work area. This is useful when you have overlapping objects (such as a correct and incorrect caption on a quiz), and you want to more easily work with the one on the bottom.

- To hide an object in the work area, click the dot under the "eyeball" icon for that object in the timeline.

- To bring an object back, click the red X that appears in the dot's place.

- Click the eyeball icon itself to show or hide all objects on the slide.

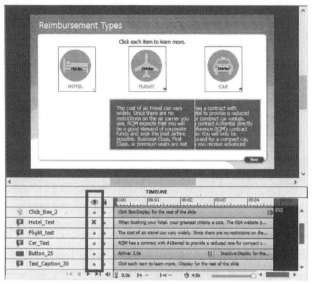

 CAUTION

Hiding an object in the timeline does not change how it appears in the published project. If you want to hide an object in a published project, either click the "eyeball" icon in the Properties panel or use a **Hide** action on it.

Rollover caption on the left is hidden, making it easier to work with another caption it was covering.

 Visibility, p. 97
Hide Actions, p. 136

Lock Objects in Edit Mode

If you lock an object, you cannot do ANYTHING to that object. You cannot move, edit, or delete it. You can't even see its properties. You can also just lock size and position, in which you can't move or resize the object, but you can change other properties, such as color or text.

The **Lock** column in the timeline has three settings. Click in that column for an object until you see the icon for the setting you want. The icon can also be seen next to the object on the slide.

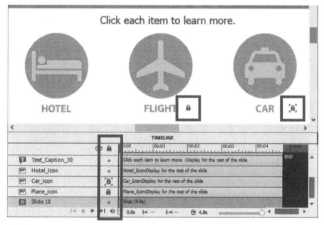

- ◎ Unlocked
- 🔒 Size and position locked
- 🔒 Fully locked

 DESIGN TIP

Locking objects can be useful if you want someone else to work on certain elements of your project but not others, or you simply want to keep from accidentally changing an object yourself.

 BRIGHT IDEA

Remember that you can also lock the entire slide. Not only does it lock all the objects on the slide, but it keeps you from deleting the slide or changing the slide properties.

 Lock Slides, p. 50

Aligning Objects

You have several options for aligning objects on the slide to help make your project look more professional.

Transform Pane

On the **Options** tab of the **Properties** panel, you can view and change the numerical coordinates for the location of objects. If more than one object is selected, you can adjust the location for all of them at one time. **X** is how far from the left edge you want an item to be. **Y** is how far from the top you want the item to be.

Alignment Toolbar

Select the objects you want, and then use the buttons on the **Align** toolbar to align them. If the **Align** toolbar isn't showing, go to the **Window** menu, and select it.

These same alignment options are available on the object's right-click menu.

Show Grid/Snap to Grid/Snap to Object

These three features can be found on the **View** menu.

Show Grid: You can show a grid on the work area to help you visually align objects. To change the size of the grid, go to the **Edit** menu, and select **Preferences**.

Snap to Grid: In addition, you can turn on the snap feature, which snaps the object into place along one of the gridlines as soon as you get close to it. This prevents your objects from being a pixel or two off.

Snap to Object: If you want to draw a line that goes right up to the edge of another drawn object (rectangle, etc.), turn on **Snap to Object**. When you draw a line up to a shape, a small circle appears when you are right at the edge of the object. If you stop the line there, it will be perfectly lined up without a gap or overlap.

Example of a grid

Smart Guides

When you use your mouse to position objects, a blue dotted line appears when the center of that object is aligned with the center of the nearest object. (You can turn this feature off from the **View** menu if you don't want it.)

Smart guide showing center alignment of objects

Aligning Objects (cont'd)

Ruler

On the **View** menu, you can toggle a ruler on and off. You can use this as a visual guide to help you place items on the slide or as a way to decide what numerical value you want to use when setting X and Y coordinates for something. When you move your cursor, you can see a small black line **(A)** move along the ruler to let you know its coordinates.

Guides

Where as the grid is a set of lines with pre-defined patterns and spacing, guides are lines that you can move yourself for more precise control and placement. **(B)**

To add a guide:

1. With the ruler showing, click and drag from the ruler onto the work area.

To move a guide:

1. Position your mouse over the guide until you see a double-sided arrow. **(D)**
2. Click and drag the guide to the new position.

To delete a guide:

1. Right-click the guide.
2. Select **Delete Guide**. **(E)**

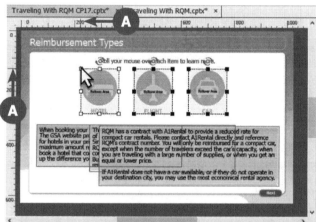

Once you have the guides in place, you can use the **View** menu to:

- **Hide Guides**: This hides them from view but still keeps them there. Select **Hide Guides** again to bring them back.

- **Clear Guides**: This gets rid of all guides completely.

- **Lock Guides**: This keeps you from accidentally moving the guides.

- **Snap to Guide**: When you drag an object on the slide, it snaps into place along the guide as soon as you get close to it. This prevents your objects from being a pixel or two off.

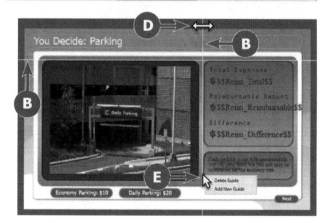

 DESIGN TIPS

- If you are using a column structure to design your slide, select **Create Multiple Guides** from the **View** menu. This lets you set up guides in equally spaced columns or rows.

- You can change the color of the guides in the **Preferences** dialog box on the **Edit** menu.

Layering

When you have overlapping objects on a slide, you want to make sure they are layered in the right order. For example, you may want the mouse movement to go in front of a caption instead of behind it, or have a logo appear on top of a colored box.

Drag-and-Drop Method

In the timeline, the objects at the top appear in front of other objects on the slide. The objects on the bottom appear behind other objects on the slide. To change the layering order, drag and drop the objects up and down in the timeline. Note that changing the top-to-bottom order in the timeline does not affect *when* the objects appear, but rather what appears in front of or behind what.

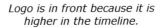

Logo is in front because it is higher in the timeline.

Logo is in back because it is lower in the timeline.

Right-Click Method

You can access layering tools from an object's right-click menu, under the **Arrange** sub-menu.

- **Bring Forward**: Bring the selected object one layer forward (up one layer on the timeline).

- **Send Backward**: Send the selected object back one layer (down one layer on the timeline).

- **Bring to Front**: Bring the selected object to the very front layer (very top of the timeline).

- **Send to Back**: Send the selected object to the very back layer (very bottom of the timeline).

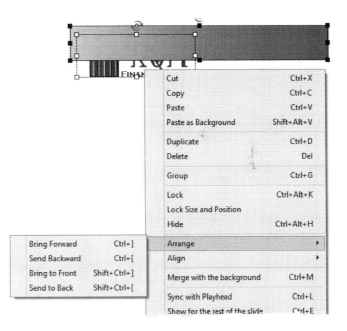

Styles

Styles are groups of format settings that can be applied all at once to an object. For example, for a caption, you can create a style that includes the type, font style, size, color, etc. Styles can help you save time and create a consistent look.

You create and modify styles from the **Object Style Manager** (found on the **Edit** menu). Once the style has been created, you then apply it to the object. For most object types, you can apply the style from the **Properties** pane for that object. With some object types, you can also apply a style from the settings for that object. For example, you can select the style of caption during a capture session from the **Recording Settings** dialog box.

BRIGHT IDEA

Runtime dialog refers to system messages in the published project.

Styles can be created for:

Standard Objects	Quizzing Objects
• Captions (text, rollover, success, failure, and hint) • Buttons • Text entry boxes • Text entry box buttons • Highlight boxes • Rollover areas • Rollover slidelets • Slidelets • Zoom area (zoom source and zoom destination) • Smart shapes • Runtime dialog	• Captions (correct, incorrect, retry, timeout, incomplete, partial correct, advance feedback, title, question text, answer/FIB text, header (matching/Likert), matching entries, Likert question, scoring result, and scoring result label) • Buttons (skip, back, continue, submit, clear, review, retake, and submit all) • Answer area • Progress indicator • Review area • Hot spot • Short answer

---

Modify an Existing Style

All object types come with at least one style—the default style. You can modify that default style and any custom styles from the **Object Style Manager**.

1. Click the **Edit** menu.
2. Select **Object Style Manager**. (See next page.)
3. Select the type of object you want to modify. **(A)**
4. Select the specific style you want to modify. **(B)**
5. Make the formatting changes you want. **(C)**
6. Click the **OK** button.

The options on the right vary based on the object type you select and contain many of the same options you'll find on that object's **Properties** panel.

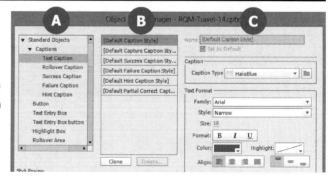

BRIGHT IDEA

If you make any changes to styles while you are in a project, the style changes affect only that project. But if you modify styles with no project open, the style changes will be available in all future projects.

Create a New Style

To create a new style:

1. Click the **Edit** menu.

2. Select **Object Style Manager**.

3. In the pane on the left, select the type of object you want to modify.

4. In the pane in the middle, select a style that is most similar to the style you want to create.

5. Click the **Clone** button.

6. In the **Name** field, type the name for the new style.

7. In the panes on the right, make the formatting changes you want.

8. Click the **OK** button.

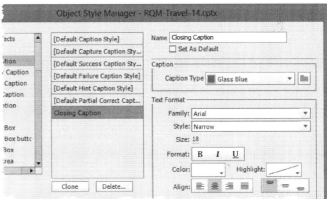

Set the Default Style

The default style is the style used when an object is first created. For example, when you create a new highlight box or button, it appears on your slide in the default style.

To change the default style, you can go to the **Object Style Manager**, select the default style, and modify it. Or, you can create a new style, and then designate it as the default.

To designate the default style:

1. Click the **Edit** menu.

2. Select **Object Style Manager**. (See above.)

3. In the pane on the left, select the type of object you want to work with.

4. In the pane in the middle, select the style you want to use for the default.

5. Check the **Set As Default** box.

6. Click the **OK** button.

Now when you create a new object of that type, it will automatically use that new style.

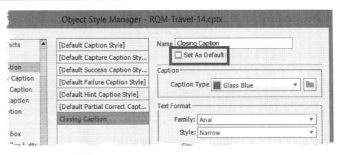

 BRIGHT IDEA

You can also change the default styles from **Preferences** (on the **Edit** menu).

Apply Styles to an Object

To apply a style to an object:

1. Select an object on the slide.
2. Click the **Properties** tab.
3. In the **Style Name** drop-down menu, select the style you want.

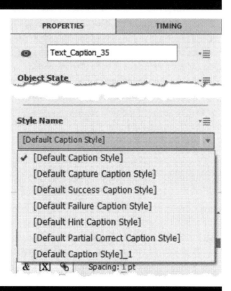

Additional Style Options

If you make any changes to properties that are governed by a style (caption type, fill color, font, etc.), you are given additional style options from a drop-down menu at the top of the **Properties** pane.

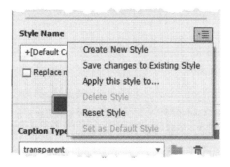

Create New Style: Rather than going to the **Object Style Manager**, you can create a new style right here. Format your object on the slide, and then select this option to create a new style based on that object. For example, if you have a highlight box with a red border, you can give one a blue border and save that as a new style.

Save changes to Existing Style: Instead of making a new style from your revised object, you can override the existing style with the new changes. For example, if your font isn't big enough, you can change the size and resave the style.

Apply this style to: If you change the style of an object, you can apply it to all other objects in the project with any given style. For example, you can apply a new green caption style to all of the objects that currently use the blue caption style.

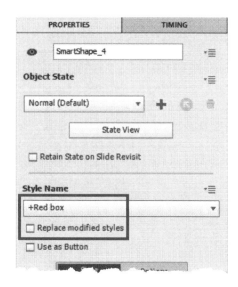

Delete Style: Select this option to delete the style from the project.

Reset Style: If you have made changes to the object, click this button if you want to revert back to the original style.

Set as Default Style: Select this option if you want all future objects of this type to use the current style.

Replace modified styles: If you change the style-related properties of an object, it is considered modified. Modified objects have a plus sign next to the name of the style. If you make changes to a style, it does not apply to any objects that are overridden, unless you check this box.

Import and Export Styles

If you are working on a team, you can share styles with teammates so you maintain a consistent look, and you don't all have to set up the styles individually. You can also import and export project-specific styles from one project to another.

To export styles:

1. Go to the **Edit** menu.
2. Select **Object Style Manager**.
3. Click the arrow to the left of the **Export** button.
4. Select the option for the styles you want to export.
5. Click the **Export** button.
6. Navigate to where you want to save the style.
7. Click the **Save** button.
8. Click the **OK** button.

To import styles:

1. Click the **Edit** menu.
2. Select **Object Style Manager**.
3. Click the **Import** button.
4. Find and select the style (**.cps**) you want to import.
5. Click **Open**.
6. Click **OK**.

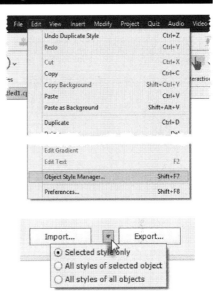

BRIGHT IDEA

If you manage styles with a project open, the changes affect that project only. If you manage styles with no projects open, then it affects all future projects.

Delete Styles

To delete a style:

1. Go to the **Edit** menu.
2. Select **Object Style Manager**.
3. Select the type of object whose style you want to delete. **(A)**
4. Select the specific style you want to delete. **(B)**
5. Click the **Delete** button.

If there are no objects in the project using that style, then you are done. If, however, there are any objects in the project that use the deleted style, you need to choose what style you want to give them instead.

6. In the dialog box that appears, select the style you want from the drop-down menu.
7. Click **OK**.

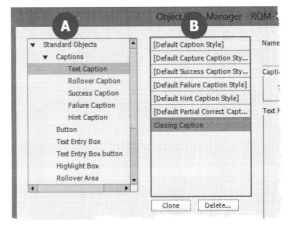

Object States

Just about any object can have multiple states. States are variations of an object that can be used for different purposes. For example:

- A button can have one look if it has been visited and another look if it has not.

- A character can have one expression if the student gets a question right and another expression if the student gets it wrong.

- A text box can say one thing when the slide loads and then say something else when a student clicks a button.

Each state can have different formatting, different sizes, different placement, and even additional objects. You can create as many states as you want. In chapter 7, you'll learn how to add actions that change the state of an object.

You create and modify states for an object from the **Object State** section of the **Properties** panel.

 CAUTION

Not all objects support multiple states, and some objects only support certain types of states.

- All smart shapes, text captions, objects, buttons, and media can have multiple states.

- The following object types have built-in states but do not support adding custom states: question slide buttons, feedback captions, rollover objects, and text entry buttons.

Image with "Normal" state

Image in new "Approved" state with text added

Image in new "Denied" state with text added

Add a New State

To add a new state:

1. Select the object you want to add states to.

2. Click the plus button **(A)** in the **Object State** section of the **Properties** panel.

3. Enter the name of the new state. **(B)**

4. Click **OK**.

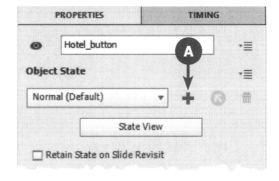

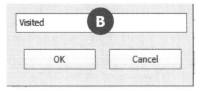

Edit States

Once you create one or more states for an object, you'll want to edit those states to customize the way they look.

To edit a state:

1. Select the object you want to edit the state(s) of.
2. Click the **State View** button **(A)** in the **Properties** panel.
3. Locate and select the state you want to edit. **(B)**
4. Make your changes to the object.
5. Click the **Exit State** button. **(C)**

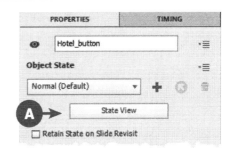

BRIGHT IDEA

- Quickly add additional states to an object while in **State View** by clicking the **New State** button.
- To switch to a different object while still in **State View**, select the objects from the **States of** drop-down menu.

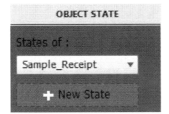

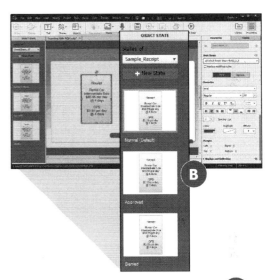

CAUTION

Remember to click the **Exit State** button when you are finished. Many of the software features are not available while you are in the **State View** mode.

Managing States

Once you create one or more states for an object, you may want to rename, delete, or duplicate the states.

The following procedures are all performed once you are in the **Object State** mode.

To rename a state:

1. Right-click on the state you want to rename.
2. Select **Rename State**.
3. Enter the new name.
4. Click **OK**.

To delete a state:

1. Right-click on the state you want to delete.
2. Select **Delete State**.
3. Click **OK**.

After making changes to a state, you can reset the state back to how it looked before you made any changes to it.

To reset a state:

1. Right-click on the state you want to reset.
2. Select **Reset State**.

After creating your own states, you can set one of them as the default state. The default state is the initial state that the student sees when the slide initially loads.

To set state as default:

1. Right-click on the state you want to set as the default.
2. Select **Set As Default**.

To duplicate a state:

1. Right-click on the state you want to duplicate.
2. Select **Duplicate State**.

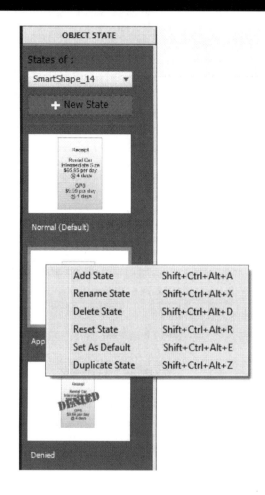

Built-In State Types

Interactive objects, such as buttons, smart shapes used as buttons, and objects used in drag-and-drop interactions have built-in states that can be customized. These states are automatically programmed to work—you don't need to set up actions for them to function.

Button or smart shape used as button:

- Normal: The default state of an object.
- Rollover: The state when a student hovers the mouse cursor over the button.
- Down: The state while a student clicks the button.
- Visited: The state after the student clicks the button. This is a built-in state, but it does have to be manully added by clicking the **New State** button.

Drop Sources:

- DragOver: The state of an object when a student drags it over a drop target.
- DropAccept: The state of an object when a student drags it to a correct drop target.
- DropReject: The state of an object when a student drags it to an incorrect drop target.
- DragStart: The state of an object when a student starts dragging it.

Drop Targets:

- DragOver: The state of a drop target when a student drags an object over it.
- DropAccept: The state of a drop target when a student drops a correct object on it.
- DropReject: The state of a drop target when a student drops an incorrect object on it.
- DropCorrect: The state of a drop target when a student drops a correct object on it and submits the answer.
- DropIncorrect: The state of a drop target when a student drops an incorrect object on it and submits the answer.

 Drag-and-Drop Interaction Wizard, p. 200

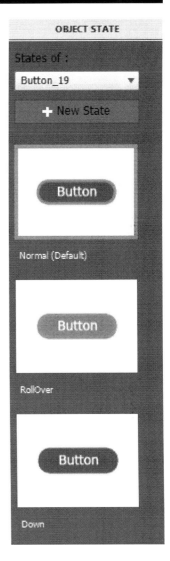

BRIGHT IDEAS

- What's the difference between the **Down** state and the **Visited** state? The **Down** state is a temporary state that appears as the click happens—and then goes away. It happens every time the object is clicked. The **Visited** state is a permanent state that indicates the button has been clicked once. Once the button has been clicked, the **Visited** state remains in place.

- When a student leaves a slide and comes back, states are reset back to their defaults. If you'd like to keep the state of an object when the student comes back to a slide, check **Retain State on Slide Revisit** in the **Properties** tab. This is especially useful for the **Visited** state so that you and the student can keep track of what has been clicked.

Object Effects

Object effects let you create visual interest as objects appear, disappear, or move across the slide, similar to animations in PowerPoint. Effects in Captivate can either be triggered based on the timeline (ease in at 3.5 seconds) or based on an action (the page loading or the student clicking a button).

Effects are managed in the **Effects** section of the **Timing** tab.

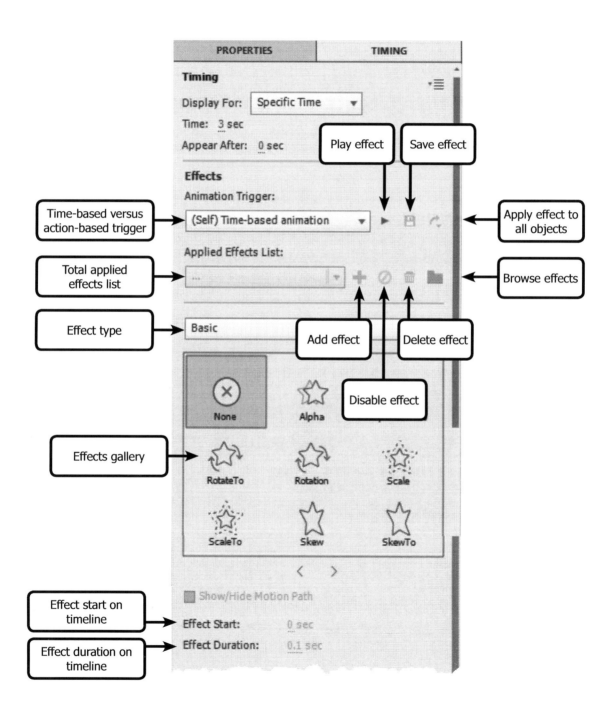

Add a Time-Based Effect

Time-based effects start and end based on the timeline. When a time-based effect is added to an object, an event for that effect is added to the timeline. In the example here, the rectangle is visible on the slide for four seconds, and the fly-in effect is two seconds.

To add a time-based effect:

1. Select the object you want to add the effect to.

2. In the **Effects** panel, click the drop-down menu to choose a type of effect. **(A)**

3. Select the effect you want from the gallery. **(B)**

4. Adjust the **Effect Start** and **Effect Duration** fields **(C)** to change when the effect happens and how long it will last on the object.

——— or ———

4. Move and resize the effect item on the timeline to change the starting time, end time, and duration. **(D)**

5. Repeat steps 2-4 to create additional effects for that object.

 BRIGHT IDEAS

- To see the option for adjusting the timing of the effect in the timeline **(D)**, click the expand icon for the object with the effect. **(E)**

- Some effects have options just below the effects gallery. For example, the **Alpha** effect lets you indicate how much transparency you want.

- You can add entrance and/or exit transitions (fading in and out) at the bottom of the **Effects** panel. **(F)**

- If you choose an effect that involves motion (such as a motion path or a fly-in effect), a red line appears on the screen for you to view and change the path. Check the **Show/Hide Motion Path** box if you don't want to see it.

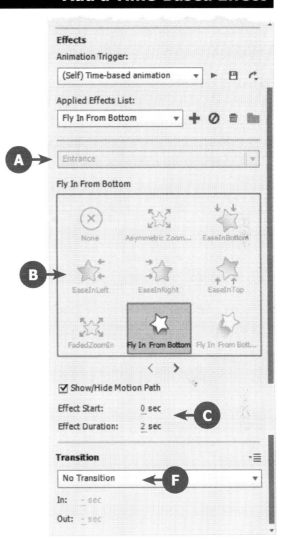

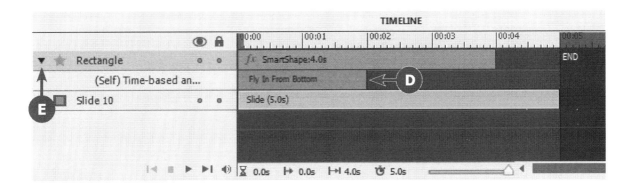

Add an Action-Based Effect

Setting up an action-based effect starts with the trigger, meaning the item that will trigger the event. For example, if you want the animation to start when the student clicks a button, then you would start by adding a trigger to the button.

To add an action-based effect:

1. Select the object that will trigger the effect.

2. On the **Actions** tab of the **Properties** panel, click the drop-down menu for the action (such as **On Success**).

3. Select **Apply Effect**.

4. Click the **Object Name** drop-down menu that appears.

5. From the menu, select the object with the effect you want to trigger.

6. On the slide, select the object that will have the effect.

7. In the **Effects** section of the **Timing** panel, click the **Animation Trigger** drop-down menu.

8. Select the name of the action that will initiate the trigger.

9. Add your effect. (See steps 2-4 on previous page.)

 Actions, ch. 7

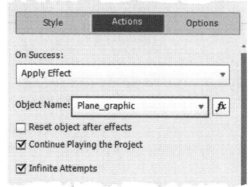

Properties panel for the button

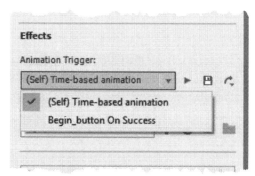

Timing panel for the object with the effect

 **BRIGHT IDEA**

If you want the object to reset after the effect is done, check the **Reset object after effects** box.

Managing Effects

Preview Effects

To preview effects, select an object with an effect and click the **Play Effect** button in the **Effects** section. **(A)**

You can also select an object and hover over an effect in the **Effects** section, or preview a slide to see all object effects.

Disable an Effect

To temporarily disable an effect, select the effect in the **Applied Effects List**, and click the **Disable** button. **(B)**

Remove an Effect

To remove an effect, select the effect in the **Applied Effects List**, and click the **Delete** button. **(C)**

Save and Reuse Effects

You can reuse effects for a given object so that you don't have to set them up over and over again. Effects are saved as XML files. All time-based effects for that object are included in the file.

To save an object's effects:

1. Select the object with the effects.
2. In the **Effects** section, click the **Save** button. **(D)**
3. Designate a name and location for the file.
4. Click the **Save** button.

To reuse a saved effect:

1. Select the object you want to give the effects to.
2. Click the **Add Effect** button. **(E)**
3. Select **Browse**.
4. Find and select the saved effects file.
5. Click the **Open** button.

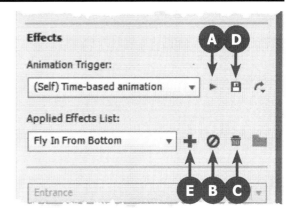

POWER TIPS

- Click the plus button if you want to add more than one effect to an object.
- Reused effects are also available for use with advanced actions.

  Advanced Actions, ch. 9

TIME SAVER

If you use the same type of effect with different objects, even with different timing, use the **Apply to all** button. You can choose either of the following:

- **Apply to all items of this type**: This applies the effect to all objects of the same type (e.g., shape).
- **Apply to all items of same style**: This applies to all objects with the same applied style.

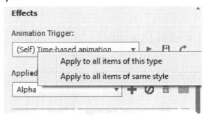

Timing Slide Objects

A Captivate project plays like a movie along the timeline. Once your objects are on the slide, you may want to time them to appear in the appropriate sequence and to stay on screen for the appropriate length of time. For example, a caption needs to stay up long enough to be read, and a highlight box or image might need to appear at a certain point in the audio.

On the timeline for each slide, you can quickly adjust the start, duration, and finish of each slide object, as well as the length of the slide as a whole. If your timeline isn't showing, go to the **Window** menu, and select **Timeline**.

CAUTION

When a slide is finished playing, the project automatically goes on to the next slide. If you want the student to choose when to advance to the next slide, you'll need to add a button or other object that pauses the slide until the student clicks it.

 Buttons, p. 142

Adjust Timing of Slide Elements

To adjust timing in the Timeline:

- Drag the left edge of an item to adjust the start time.
- Drag the right edge of an item to adjust the end time.
- Drag the entire object to move it to a different place on the timeline.

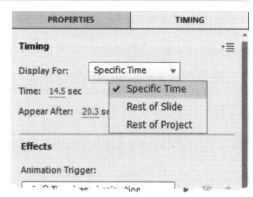

To adjust timing in the Properties panel:

1. Select the object in the timeline or the work area.
2. Click the **Timing** panel.
3. On the **Timing** panel, enter the duration for the object in the **Time** field.
4. Enter the start time for the object in the **Appear After** field.

Timing Options

The **Display For** drop-down menu has additional timing options.

- **Specific Time**: This is the default. This displays the object for the amount of time set in the timeline or in the **Timing** pane of the **Properties** panel.
- **Rest of Slide**: This extends the object to the end of the slide and "locks" it in place. If the slide is extended or shortened, the object is moved so that it stays at the end of the slide.
- **Rest of Project**: This extends the object to the end of the project. The object will only appear on this slide's timeline, but will show up on every other slide for the rest of the project.

BRIGHT IDEA

Use the zoom control to zoom the timeline in or out for more or less detail.

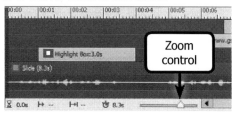

Actions & Interactions

Introduction

Actions are commands that can either be triggered by the student (such as clicking a button) or triggered automatically (such as reaching the end of a slide). Actions let you customize the functionality of the course and make it more interactive.

In this chapter, you will first learn about pre-made interactive objects and templates, such as rollover captions and interactive diagrams. From there, you'll learn how to build your own custom interactions. You'll learn the individual actions available in Captivate, as well as the interactive objects you can apply them to. These become building blocks that let you create any number of features from branching navigation to games.

The following table describes the action options for the various interactive objects.

Object	Action options
Rollover Caption	A text caption appears when the student rolls over the hot spot.
Rollover Image	An image appears when the student rolls over the hot spot.
Rollover Slidelet	A mini slide (with text, graphics, audio, etc.) appears when the student rolls over the hot spot. You can add an additional action for when the student clicks the hot spot.
Learning Interactions	You can create interactive diagrams, games, and other interactions from templates using your own text and media.
Slide	Although this technically isn't an interactive object, you can assign an action for when the slide starts and finishes.
Text	You can use text hyperlinks to perform most action types.
Click Box, Button, Text Entry Box, Quiz Question	You can select one action for when the student clicks/answers successfully and/or one action when failing to click/answer successfully after a specified number of attempts.

Many properties for interactive objects are the same as for other objects (such as size, layering, and shadows). This chapter explains the properties specific to the interactivity. Refer to the Object Properties chapter for information on the standard properties. Quiz questions are covered in the Questions & Quizzes chapter.

Object Properties, ch. 6
Questions & Quizzes, ch. 10

In This Chapter

- Learning Interactions
- Rollover Objects
- Action Types
- Adding Actions
- Click Boxes
- Buttons
- Text Entry Boxes

Notes

Learning Interactions

Learning interactions are pre-built interactive templates that come with Captivate. You can choose from over 30 different templates and then customize them to your content.

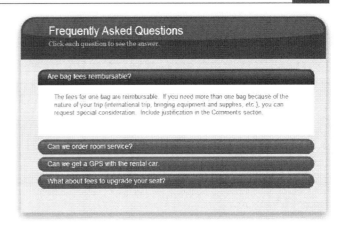

Add a Learning Interaction

To add a learning interaction:

1. Click the **Interactions** drop-down button.
2. Select **Learning Interactions**.
3. Select the interaction template you want.
4. Click the **Insert** button.
5. In the **Configure interaction** dialog box, select a design theme from the column on the left.
6. Enter your content. (See next page.)
7. Click the **OK** button.

 DESIGN TIPS

Click the **Custom** button **(A)** to configure the colors and fonts used in the interaction.

Configure Interaction Content

To configure an interaction:

- Double-click an element, such as a bar or tab, to add your content.

- Click the plus button **(A)** to add additional elements, if available.

- Double-click an element, and then click the minus button **(B)** to delete that element.

- Double-click a content area, and click the audio or image icons **(C)** to add media, if available.

To edit an interaction after it is on the slide:

- Click the edit button in the **Properties** panel. **(D)**

 BRIGHT IDEAS

- Each learning interaction has different options for configuration. Advanced interactions such as the games, walk you through a wizard to help you set it up.

- The properties for an interaction are the same for other animations.

 Animation Properties, p. 69

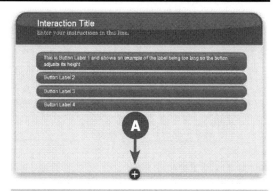

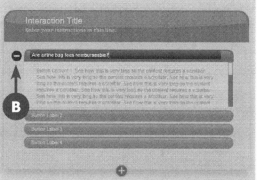

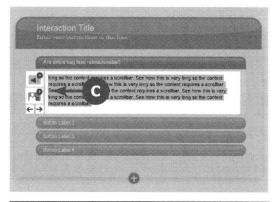

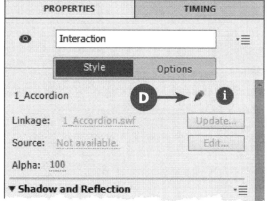

Interaction Gallery

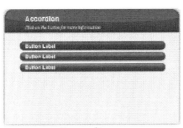

Accordion

Tabs

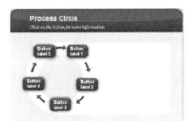

Process Circle

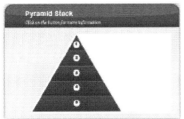

Pyramid Stack

Timeline

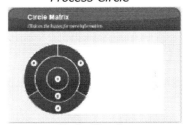

Circle Matrix

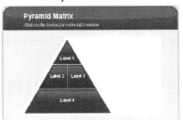

Pyramid Matrix

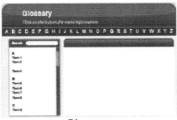

Glossary

Certificate

Word Search

Bookmark Widget

Bulletin Widget

Carousel Widget

Catch AlphaNums (Accelerometer)

Checkbox Widget

Checkbox Widget

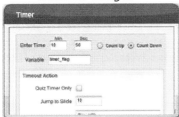

Timer

Drop Down

Hangman

Interaction Gallery (cont'd)

Hourglass

Image Zoom

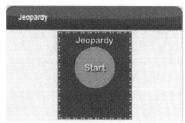

Jeopardy

Jigsaw Puzzle

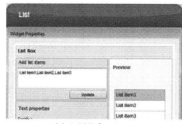

List Widget

Memory Game

Who Wants to Be a Millionaire

Notes Widget

Radio Button Widget

Table Widget

Scrolling Text

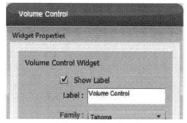

Volume Control

YouTube

Rollover Objects

The three types of rollover objects let you quickly create interactive objects where students roll their mouse over a hot spot **(A)** to reveal additional content **(B)**.

- **Rollover Captions**: Place hot spots on the slide that the student rolls over to view a text caption.
- **Rollover Image**: Place hot spots on the slide that the student rolls over to view an image.
- **Rollover Smart Shape**: Place hot spots on the slide that the student rolls over to view a smart shape.
- **Rollover Slidelets**: Place hot spots on the slide that the student rolls over to view a mini-slide that can contain text, images, audio, etc.

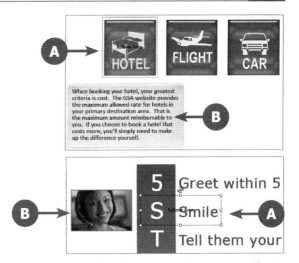

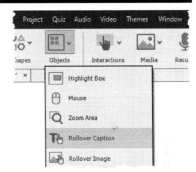

Insert a Rollover Caption

To add a rollover caption:

1. Click the **Objects** drop-down button.
2. Select **Rollover Caption**.
3. Move and resize the rollover area over the portion of the screen to serve as the hot spot for the caption.
4. Enter text, format, and position the caption.
5. Format the objects in the **Properties** panel.

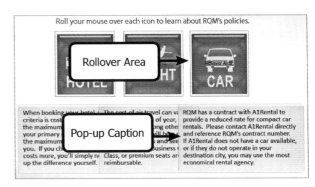

 TIME SAVER

If you are placing the rollover area over an object, such as an image, you can save yourself a little time. Right-click the rollover area and select **Auto-adjust Rollover Area**. This "snaps" the rollover area to the same size as the object below it.

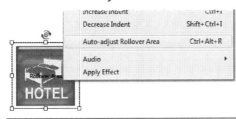

 CAUTION

Your project will not automatically stop and let students explore all of the hot spots. To give them enough time, either extend the length of the slide, or add a **Continue** button that pauses the slide until they want to continue.

 Buttons, p. 142

Insert a Rollover Image

To insert a rollover image:

1. Click the **Objects** drop-down button.
2. Select **Rollover Image**.
3. Find and select the image you want to use.
4. Click the **Open** button.
5. Format and position the rollover area and the image.

BRIGHT IDEA

Rollover objects don't actually require a mouse. When a student using keyboard navigation tabs to the rollover area, the caption, image, or slidelet appears.

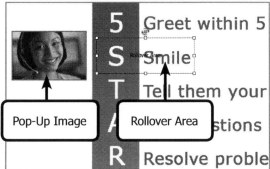

Insert a Rollover Smart Shape

To insert a rollover smart shape:

1. Create the shape you want to have appear.
2. Right-click the shape.
3. Select **Convert to rollover Smart Shape**.
4. Format and position the rollover area that appears.

Drawing shapes, p. 66

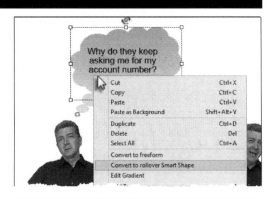

Insert a Rollover Slidelet

To insert a rollover slidelet:

1. Click the **Objects** drop-down menu.
2. Select **Rollover Slidelet**.
3. Move and resize the rollover area over the portion of the slide to serve as the hot spot.
4. Move and resize the slidelet frame to the size and location you want for the pop-up slidelet.
5. Select the slidelet frame in the work area.
6. Add objects to the slidelet as you would to a regular slide.

Objects as they first appear on the slide

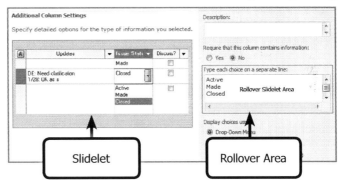

Slidelet   Rollover Area

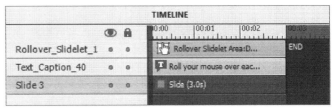

Slide timeline

CAUTION

When you are adding objects to the slidelet, make sure you have the slidelet selected. Look at the bottom layer on the timeline and make sure it says slidelet.

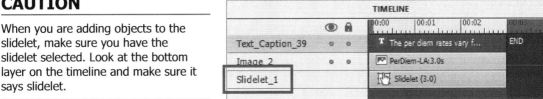

Slidelet timeline

Rollover Slidelet Properties

Properties

Both the rollover area and the slidelet have their own properties, which are similar to other object types. Both have some additional properties unique to that object type.

Rollover Area: Style Tab

Show Border: If you select this option, a thin border appears around the rollover area when the student's mouse is *not* on the area.

Show Runtime Border: If you select this option, a thick border appears around the rollover area while the student's mouse is over it. This is useful when you have more than one rollover area on a slide as it lets the students know which object they are viewing.

Rollover Area: Actions Tab

On Click: You can designate an action to execute if the student clicks in the rollover area rather than rolling over it.

CAUTION

If you use an **On Click** action, be sure to test everything carefully to make sure the actions don't contradict with each other.

Shortcut: You can type a keyboard command to run the **On Click** action if the student types it. If there is no **On Click** action, the keystroke does nothing.

On Rollover: In addition to having the slidelet appear, you can set an action to execute upon rollover, such as showing an object elsewhere on the slide. Please note, however, that the action does not undo when the student rolls off the rollover area.

Stick Slidelet: By default, the slidelet disappears when the student moves off the rollover area. If you check this box, the slidelet stays up. A close button appears on the slidelet that the student would click to close it.

Slidelet: Style Tab

Show Runtime Shadow: If you check this box, the slidelet area will have a drop shadow when it appears.

Add New Image: If you'd like to have an image serve as the background for the slidelet, click this button and select an image from the library or from your computer.

Slidelet: Options Tab

Stop Slide Audio: If your slide and your slidelet both have audio, you probably want to check this box so that both audio files don't play at the same time when the student views the slide.

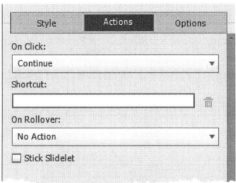

Rollover area properties

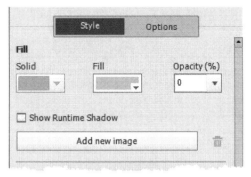

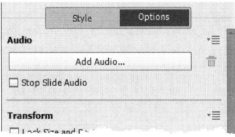

Slidelet properties

Actions

The following pages describe the types of individual actions you can use to create your own interactivity and custom functionality. Objects that can serve as triggers (such as buttons and hyperlinks) have an **Actions** tab in the **Properties** panel. The available actions vary somewhat based on the type of object.

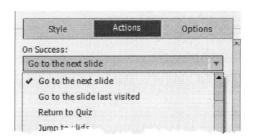

Action Overview

Action	Brief Description
Continue	Play the slide along the timeline.
Go to the previous slide	Go to the start of the previous slide (in order).
Go to the next slide	Go to the start of the next slide (in order).
Go to the slide last visited	Go to the start of the slide the student was just on.
Return to Quiz	Go back to the quiz (if that's where they came from).
Jump to slide	Go to the start of a slide you specify.
Open URL or file	Go to a Web page or launch a document.
Open another project	Open a Captivate file, template, or published course.
Send e-mail to	Open the student's email and create a new message.
Execute JavaScript	Run JavaScript to extend Captivate's capabilities.
Execute Advanced Actions	Run a series of actions that may have conditions.
Execute Shared Action	Run an action you saved for reuse.
Play Audio	Play an audio file other than that on the timeline.
Stop Triggered Audio	Stop the audio triggered with the **Play Audio** action.
Show	Make a hidden object visible.
Hide	Make a visible object invisible.
Enable	Make a disabled button functional.
Disable	Turn off the function of a button.
Assign	Set the value of a variable.
Increment	Increase the value of a numerical variable.
Decrement	Decrease the value of a numerical variable.
Pause	Pause the timeline.
Exit	Close the published project.
Apply Effect	Trigger an animation effect.
Toggle	Turn the TOC, playbar, or closed captions on and off.
Show TOC	Show the table of contents.
Show Playbar	Show the playbar.
Hide TOC	Hide the table of contents.
Hide Playbar	Hide the playbar.
Lock TOC	Disallow navigation from the table of contents.
Unlock TOC	Allow navigation from the table of contents.
Change State of	Change the state of an object.
Go To Next State	Change to the next state of an object.
Go To Previous State	Change to the previous state of an object.
No Action	Do nothing.

Action Types

Continue

The slide continues to play along the timeline. This action is useful if the timeline is paused, perhaps because of a click box or button.

Go To and Jump Actions

These actions allow for custom navigation and branching.

- **Go to the previous slide**: Go to the beginning of the previous slide.
- **Go to the next slide**: Go to the beginning of the next slide.
- **Go to the slide last visited**: Go to the beginning of the slide the student was on before the current slide.
- **Return to Quiz**: See page 189.
- **Jump to slide**: Go to the beginning of the slide specified on the **Actions** tab.

Open URL or File

You can go to a Web page (such as a page on your Website or a PDF document stored on your intranet). For this action, type the URL in the space provided.

You can link to a file (such as a file on your computer or a network drive). Click the **Browse** button **(A)** to find and select the file you want to link to. The file needs to be manually added to your published files, or the link will not work.

For both options, click the drop-down menu **(B)** to indicate how you want the Web page or file to open.

  Current: The Web page or document replaces the Captivate course in the current browser window.

  New: The Web page or document opens in a new window.

  Parent and Top: These only apply if your course will play on a Web page with frames. **Parent** replaces all the frames in the current frameset, while **Top** opens the Web page or document in the topmost frame.

    With all but the **Current** option, you can check the box to indicate whether you want the course to continue playing once the new Web page launches.

Open Another Project

Open a Captivate project file, template, or published course. Click the folder icon **(C)** to find and select the file, and then click the drop-down arrow **(D)** to indicate how you want to open it. This action works with the following file types: **.cp**, **.cptx**, **.cptl**, **.rd**, **.swf**, and **.cpvc**.

CAUTION

Don't confuse the following actions:

Go to the previous slide and **Go to the last slide visited**: Imagine the student is on slide 3 and then goes to slide 6. **Go to the previous slide** takes the student to slide 5. **Go to the last slide visited** takes the student back to slide 3.

Continue and **Go to the next slide**: With a **Continue** action, the project keeps playing from that point in the timeline. With a **Go to the next slide** action, it goes immediately to the next slide and does not finish playing the slide it is on.

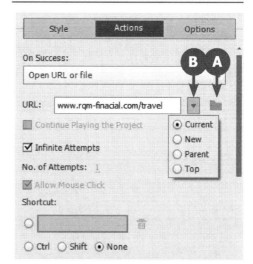

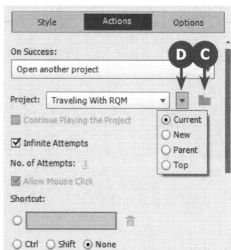

Action Types (cont'd)

Send E-Mail To

Open the student's default e-mail program with a message addressed to the e-mail address entered on the **Actions** tab. Click the **Continue Playing the Project** checkbox to indicate if you want to continue playing the project or you want to pause the project when the e-mail message opens.

CAUTION

The e-mail action does not trigger Web-based e-mail programs (such as Gmail), and some corporate server configurations may not allow this action. Be sure to test the e-mail function carefully.

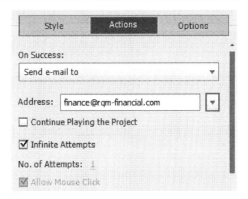

Execute JavaScript

Run JavaScript code entered on the **Actions** tab. This lets you extend the capabilities of Captivate. For example, you could:

- Manipulate something on the HTML page.
- Create a custom pop-up message window.
- Communicate with other Captivate courses.

To enter your code, click the **Script_Window** button, enter your code in the dialog box, and click the **OK** button.

BRIGHT IDEAS

If you don't know JavaScript, you can often find sample code in the Captivate forum or blogs.

JavaScript is interpreted by a browser, so use one of the browser-based preview modes to test your work.

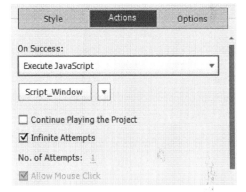

Execute Advanced Actions

Advanced actions let you perform more than one action at once, use conditional actions (only perform an action if something is true), or build customized actions. After you build the advanced action in the **Advanced Actions** dialog box, then you run it with this action.

Advanced Actions, ch. 9

Execute Shared Action

In the **Advanced Action** dialog box, you can create actions that you can save and use over and over again across projects. This action runs one of those saved actions.

Saving and Reusing Actions, p. 178

Action Types (cont'd)

Play Audio/Stop Triggered Audio

Play Audio plays an audio file separate from the timeline. For example, you can add a sound that plays when the student clicks a button or answers a question incorrectly. The **Stop Triggered Audio** action stops any audio that is playing from a **Play Audio** action.

Show/Hide

The **Show** action makes a hidden object visible. (Objects can be hidden by clicking the visibility icon in the **Properties** panel **(A)** or with a **Hide** action.) For example, you could have a hidden hint caption on a question with a **Help Me** button that shows the hint when clicked.

The **Hide** action makes an object invisible. For example, you might want the student to click a button to make an image disappear, revealing information beneath it.

 BRIGHT IDEA

If you need to show and hide objects based on time, simply adjust them on the timeline. Use **Show/Hide** actions if you want them to appear/disappear based on actions or conditions.

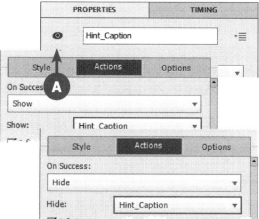
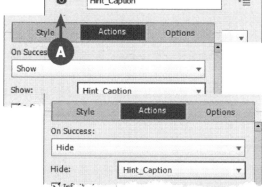

Enable/Disable

Enable lets you activate an interactive object (such as a button or click box) that has previously been disabled. For example, a **Next** button might be disabled until certain tasks are performed. Once they are performed, the button could be enabled.

Disable de-activates an interactive object (such as a button or click box). The object will still be visible on the screen, but associated actions will not work.

With **Enable** and **Disable**, select the object you want to enable/disable from the drop-down menu that appears. Only eligible objects appear on the drop-down menu.

Assign/Increment/Decrement

These actions let you adjust the value of a variable.

 Variables, p. 169

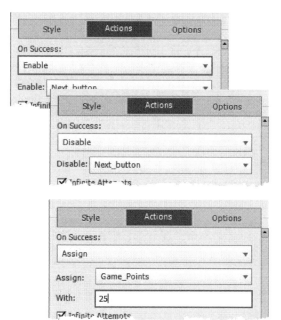

Pause

This action pauses the timeline for the slide. (You can use a **Continue** action or have the student click the **Play** button on the playbar to resume.)

Exit

This action closes the published project.

Apply Effect

You can use this action to trigger an effect, such as a fly-in or fly-out animation.

 Action-Based Effects, p. 120

Player-Based Actions

The following actions control the visibility and function of the table of contents (TOC), playbar, mute button, and closed captioning when you don't want to use the standard playbar and TOC controls. For example, you might set the TOC to be unlocked for the course as a whole. But on the quiz slides, you want to hide or lock the TOC so students can't go back into the content.

- **Toggle**: This action creates an on/off toggle for: playbar, mute, locking the TOC, closed captioning, TOC visibility, and custom variables. Each time this action is fired, the setting goes back and forth between yes/no, on/off, etc. When used on a custom variable, the value toggles between 0 and 1.
- **Show TOC/Hide TOC**: Use the show action to make the TOC visible. Use the hide action to make it disappear.
- **Show Playbar/Hide Playbar**: Use the show action to make the playbar visible. Use the hide action to make it disappear.
- **Lock TOC/Unlock TOC**: Use the lock action if you don't want the student to use the TOC for navigation. Use the unlock feature to allow navigation again.

State Actions

The following actions control the state of an object. For example, you can change the expression (state) of a character when the student clicks a button or answers a question right/wrong.

- **Change State of**: Use this action to change the state of an object.
- **Go To Next/Previous State**: Use these actions to change the state of an object to its next or previous state. For example, you can change the appearance of an object in succession each time a student clicks a button.

 Object States, p. 114

No Action

This does nothing—on purpose.

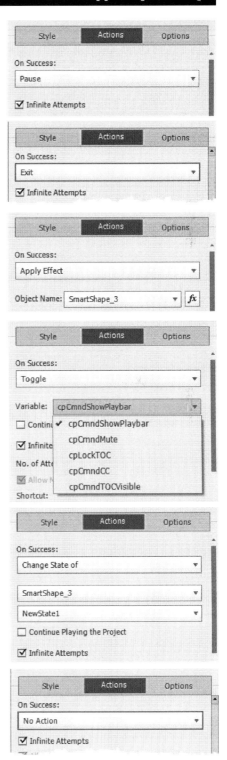

DESIGN TIPS

Creating Branching Scenarios

In a branching scenario, students make choices that determine where they go next. For example, in a customer service scenario, the student can choose between several things to say. Each option takes the student to a different slide for feedback and a continuation of the scenario.

To create a branching scenario, it is usually best to sketch it out first. This will help you make your basic design decisions before you build it.

- Do you want to give students the chance to go back and change their answers?
- After getting feedback, do all students go to the same question next, or do they get different questions based on their responses?
- How many content slides do you need for instructions and to set up the scenario?
- Can the new question be on the same slide as the feedback for the previous question, or do you need separate slides?

Once you have your structure determined, create the slides and give them logical names. Before adding your content, set up the logic: buttons with the branching actions, quiz questions, etc.

Once you have the logic working, then you can add your content.

Using Branching View

To help you manage the flow of slides in any project with branching, you can use the branching view. Branching view is a flowchart-style view that helps you quickly determine where the student can go from each of the slides.

To show branching view:

1. Go to the **Window** menu.
2. Select **Branching View**.

From branching view, you can:

- Create and manage slide groups. **(A)**
- Export the view as an image. **(B)**
- View or change the action of an interactive object. Click the navigation line **(C)** for the action box to appear. **(F)**
- View success, failure, and navigational paths. **(D)**
- Expand and collapse sections. **(E)**
- View or change the action of a slide. **(F)** Click a thumbnail or an action to make the action box appear.

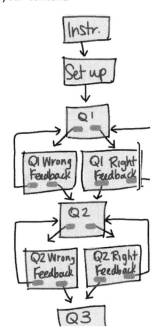

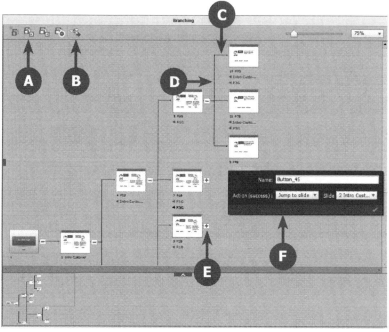

Adding Actions

Now that you know your options for actions, you can add them to your projects using the various interactive objects, covered on the next few pages.

Add Actions to a Slide

Actions can be triggered when the project goes to the first frame of a slide (**On Enter**) or the last frame of a slide (**On Exit**). For example, you might want to run an advanced action at the end of the slide that branches to different slides based on whether the student has indicated if he or she is a supervisor.

To add an action to a slide:

1. Select the slide(s) you want in the filmstrip.
2. Select the action from the **On Enter** and/or **On Exit** menus on the **Actions** tab.

 CAUTION

An **On Exit** action will only execute if the project reaches the last frame of the slide. It will not execute if the student leaves the slide in the middle, such as by clicking a button that takes them to the next slide.

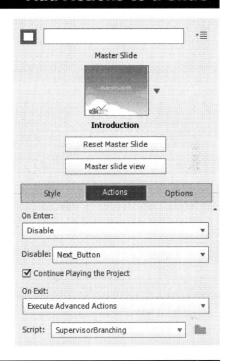

Add a Hyperlink to Text

You can add a hyperlink to text in a caption or a shape.

To add a hyperlink to text:

1. Select the text you want to use for the hyperlink.
2. On the **Style** tab, click the **Insert Hyperlink** button. **(A)**
3. Select an action from the **Link To** drop-down menu that appears.
4. Configure the rest of the action in the pop-up window.
5. Click the **OK** button.

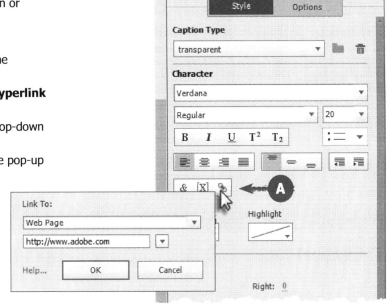

Add a Click Box

Click boxes are useful for turning images into hot spots. For example, you can show a diagram with a click box over three key parts of the diagram. Each of the click boxes could link to a slide with more information.

Click boxes can have success and failure captions as well as success and failure actions.

To add a click box:

1. Click the **Interactions** drop-down button.
2. Select **Click Box**.

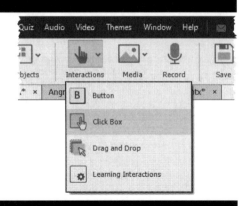

Click Box Properties

Actions Tab

On Success: Select an action that executes if the student clicks in the click box.

Continue Playing the Project: Click boxes pause the timeline so students interact with the content. By default, the timeline restarts when the click box is clicked. But what if you have three click boxes? You wouldn't want the timeline to start up again after the first box is clicked. In this case, uncheck this box so that pause still holds. Then you would add a separate action for when it is time to continue.

Infinite Attempts: If you leave this checked, students can keep clicking on the slide until they get it right. If you uncheck this box, you can enter the number of attempts they are allowed. **(A)** When you do this, you can also add an extra action in the **Last Attempt** field that triggers when they have reached the final number of attempts without successfully clicking in the click box.

Allow Mouse Click and **Shortcut**: Click boxes are designed to be...clicked! However, sometimes you might want to test the student on a keystroke command. There is not a designated Captivate object for this, but you can use a click box object to allow and grade a keystroke command.

- Type the keyboard shortcut in the **Shortcut** field.
- By default, students can still click the click box even if you set up a keyboard shortcut. Uncheck **Allow Mouse Click** to only accept the keyboard shortcut.
- To clear the **Shortcut** field, click the **Clear** button. **(B)**
- Your shortcut can include the **Shift** or **Ctrl** keys (such as **Ctrl + B**). If you want just the **Ctrl** or the **Shift** key, use the radio button for that key.

 CAUTION

Test your shortcuts to make sure they don't conflict with standard browser shortcuts like **Ctrl + P**.

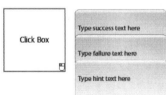

Click Box Properties (cont'd)

Display

Check the boxes to select which captions you want to include with the click box.

- **Success** shows when the student clicks in the click box (or presses the correct keyboard shortcut).

- **Failure** shows when the student clicks somewhere other than the clickbox (or presses the incorrect keyboard shortcut).

- **Hint** shows when the student's mouse hovers over the click box area.

Others

- **Pause for Success/Failure Captions**: Success and failure captions are not in the timeline. If you include these captions, you'll need to decide if you want the project to pause long enough to read them. The project pauses by default. Uncheck this box if you don't want the project to pause.

- **Hand Cursor**: Check this box if you want the student's cursor to change from an arrow to a hand when it is over the click box area. This is an indication to students that their cursor hovered over a hot spot area.

- **Double-click**: Check this box if you want the student to double-click the box instead of single-click the box.

- **Disable Click Sound**: When a student clicks the click box, Captivate plays a click sound. Check this box if you don't want the sound to play.

- **Pause project until user clicks**: A click box pauses the project until the student clicks successfully in the box or uses up all of the incorrect attempts. Uncheck this box if you don't want to pause the project.

- **Right-Click**: Check this box if you want the student to right-click the box instead of the traditional left-click.

Reporting

Include in Quiz: Check this box if you want to count the click box interaction as a question in a quiz.

- **Points**: Enter the number of points the student should receive for clicking the click box within the specified number of attempts. The value can be between 0 and 100.

- **Add to Total**: Check this box if you want to include the points in the quiz total.

- **Report Answers**: Check this box if you want to send the scores to a learning management system (LMS). Uncheck it if the score does not need to be reported.

Interaction ID: Enter an ID to be used when sending the data to the LMS. This can help you identify the data in the LMS.

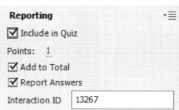

 LMS Reporting, p. 252

 # CAUTION

If you use multiple click boxes or keyboard shortcuts on a slide, be sure to test the slide carefully to make sure everything works, especially in a Web browser.

Add a Button

Buttons are a flexible way to add interactivity, because there are so many ways you can format them. Use buttons for course navigation, branching scenarios, questions built outside of the question wizard, pop-up interactions, etc.

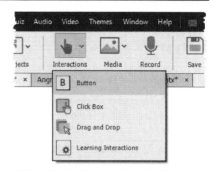

To add a button:

1. Click the **Interactions** drop-down button.
2. Select **Button**.

Button Types

This section covers the formatting options on the **Style** tab for the three types of buttons: text, transparent, and image. The properties on the **Actions** tab are the same as for a click box, except that some of the defaults are different.

 Click Box Properties, p. 140

Button Type: Select the type of button you want from the drop-down menu. **(A)**

- **Text Button**

  Type the text for the button in the **Caption** field. Format the text in the **Character** pane.

- **Transparent Button**

  Use the **Fill** and **Stroke** panes to change the button's fill color, transparency, and stroke color and weight. A transparent button works very similarly to a click box.

- **Image Button**

  Select a button from the options provided, or click the **Browse** button **(B)** to select your own.

Make Transparent: Check this box to make the background of a button transparent.

BRIGHT IDEAS

- When you select **Transparent Button**, it doesn't actually make the button transparent! Instead, it enables the **Fill** and **Stroke** panes that let you make the button transparent (set **Opacity** to 0%) or any other color.

- When you select **Image Button** and then click the **Browse** button, **(B)** you are taken (by default) to the Captivate Gallery. If you open the **More** folder, there are a number of other image buttons to choose from.

Button Widgets

Button widgets offer additional button formats and effects. The button widgets come in two forms:

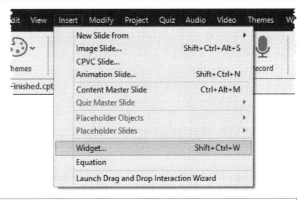

- **Interactive**: Interactive buttons have the same basic action properties as a regular button: action on success, action on failure, and success, failure, and hint captions.

- **Static**: Static buttons have a single action, no failure action, and no captions.

To add a button from the button widgets:

1. Go to the **Insert** menu.
2. Select **Widget**.
3. In the Adobe Captivate gallery, open the **Buttons** folder.
4. Select the interactive or static option.
5. Click the **Open** button.
6. In the **Widget Properties** dialog box, select the options, including the success action and button text.
7. Click the **OK** button.

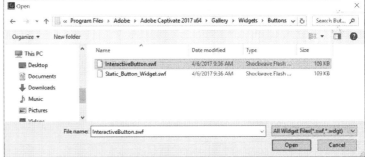

To make changes later, click the **Edit** button in the **Properties** panel. **(A)**

For interactive buttons, use the **Actions** and **Options** tabs to configure the attempts, captions, etc.

Add a Text Entry Box

Text entry boxes let the student enter text. This text can then be validated (graded), sent to the LMS, and stored to be used later for conditional logic or to display back to the student. (You can also use a fill-in-the-blank question for similar purposes.) Text entry boxes can have success and failure actions and captions.

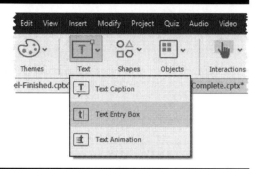

To add a text entry box:

1. Click the **Text** drop-down button.
2. Select **Text Entry Box**.

Text Entry Box Properties

Style Tab

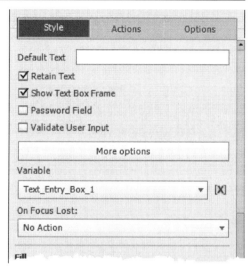

Default Text: If you don't want the text entry box to appear blank to the student, you can enter default text here. For example, you can add default text that says "Enter name here." This text can be edited by the student.

Retain Text: By default, the student's answer stays in the text box if the student navigates away from the page and returns during the same session. Uncheck this box if you want the answer cleared when the student leaves the page.

Show Text Box Frame: By default, there is an outline around the text entry box. Uncheck this box if you don't want the frame. For example, if you are laying the text box over a shape, you may not need the frame.

Password Field: If you are using the text entry box as a real or simulated password field, check this box. Then the student's typing is captured as typed but is shown as asterisks.

Validate User Input: By default, a text entry box is not graded. However, if you want to grade the answer, check this box. When you do, a small dialog box appears on the slide that lets you add one or more correct answers and indicate if you want the answer to be case-sensitive. **(A)**

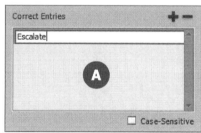

More options: Click this button for a menu of validation and display options. **(B)** You can specify a maximum number of characters. When you do, you can check the **Auto Submit** box to evaluate the student's answer when that number is reached. Select **Numbers** to only accept numbers. Select **Uppercase** or **Lowercase** to display all characters in the selected format. Select **Allow All** to reset the radio buttons and accept all text.

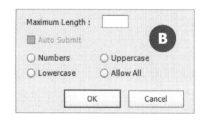

Variable: A variable is a stored piece of data you can use later. All text entry boxes are assigned a variable. You can use the name provided, select a variable that already exists from the menu, or click the **[X]** button to create a new variable.

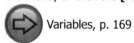

Variables, p. 169

Text Entry Box Properties (cont'd)

Actions Tab

The properties on the **Actions** tab are very similar as for a click box. This page explains any properties that are different.

 Click Box Properties, p. 140

Shortcut: By default, click boxes and buttons do not have keyboard shortcuts. By default, text entry boxes come with a shortcut of **Enter**.

With non-validated text entry boxes (and most other interactive objects), the keyboard shortcut activates the **On Success** action. But for text boxes that are validated, the shortcut triggers the validation. The **On Success** action is only activated if the answer is *correct*.

On Focus Lost: Select an action to execute when the student clicks off of the text entry box.

Display

Captions: The success and failure options are only available if you are validating the student's entry.

Others

Pause for Success/Failure Captions: If you have success or failure captions enabled, this box is checked by default. This means that the slide pauses so the student has time to read the feedback captions.

Show Button: By default, a **Submit** button is added with your text entry box to validate the student's input. Uncheck this box if you don't want this button. For example, you might want to use the keyboard shortcut for validation or don't have any validation. You can click the **Submit** button on the slide to view and manage its properties.

Show Scrollbar: Check this box if you want to add a scrollbar to the text box, letting the student enter more text in a smaller amount of space.

Reporting

Include in Quiz: This option is only available if you are validating the student's entry.

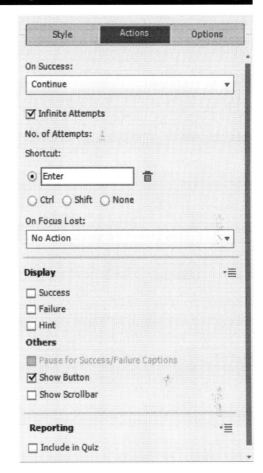

Notes

Editing Software Simulations

Introduction

In chapter 2, you learned how to capture software simulations. Your raw captures get you off to a great start when creating your simulations. However, there is usually a fair amount of clean-up to be done after your initial capture. You will often spend more time on editing than you do on the initial capture. That's why it is important to know what your options are and how to work quickly.

In previous chapters, you learned about many features to edit and customize your recordings:

- Add/modify slides, chapter 3
- Add/modify captions and highlight boxes, chapter 4
- Add audio, chapter 5
- Adjust timing of on-screen objects, chapter 6
- Add rollover objects, chapter 7

This chapter shows you features that are specifically designed to help you edit your captures:

- Add/modify mouse movements
- Add/modify typing
- Make changes to the underlying captures
- Edit a full-motion recording clip
- Recapture additional screen shots or video demo clips
- Manage click box slides and text entry slides for interactive practices
- Edit video demos

In This Chapter

- The Editing Process
- Editing Typing
- Mouse Movements
- Editing Full-Motion Recording
- Editing Slide Backgrounds
- Recording Additional Slides
- Managing Practice Slides
- Managing Video Demos

Notes

The Editing Process

Once you have your "raw" capture, it is time to edit it. You might need to:

- Correct errors, such as multiple or missing captures.
- Refine placement of automatically added elements, such as the exact position of a mouse click.
- Add instructional elements, such as an extra caption.
- Modify underlying images, such as hiding sensitive information or changing the name of a button.
- Recapture new screen shots.

CAUTION

Always save your raw capture before making edits. That way, you can revert back to your original if you make mistakes during the editing process.

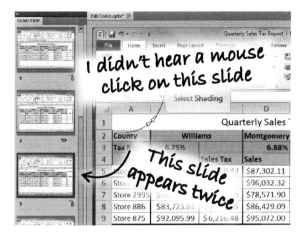

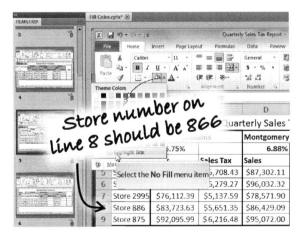

Editing Typing

By default, when you type during a capture, Captivate captures the keystrokes and plays them back one character at a time in the published course. If you make a mistake in the typing, it is often easier to re-do the slide while capturing. However, sometimes you don't realize you need to make a change until much later, and recapturing the typing again would be too time consuming. Fortunately, you are able to go in and edit the typing by converting the typing into a text animation.

Edit Typing

To edit typing:

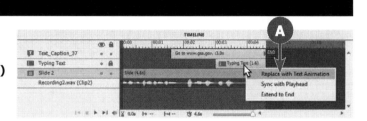

1. Right-click the typing item in the timeline.

2. Select **Replace with Text Animation**. **(A)**

3. In the **Properties** panel, click the **Animation Properties** button. **(B)**

4. In the dialog box that appears, make your text edits in the **Text** field. **(C)**

5. Click the **OK** button.

 Text Animations, p. 70

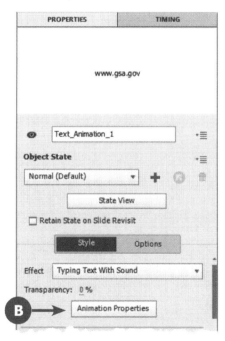

 ## CAUTION

- Converting the typing to a text animation may change how the characters look. You may need to adjust the formatting or placement of the typing on the screen to make it match.

- Changing the typing on one screen does not change it on later slides, so you may need to do photo editing on the background of later slides. For example, if you changed a Web address from **.com** to **.gov**, the later screens will need to be changed to show the **.gov** address.

Mouse Movements

When you capture a procedure, you have the option to include the mouse movements. Captivate keeps track of where you click the mouse on each screen and then creates an animated path from point to point on each slide.

Because the mouse movement is "layered" on top of the slides, it is easy to make changes to the movement. For example, you can adjust where the mouse click occurs and what the cursor looks like.

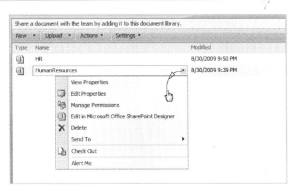

Move the Mouse Click Position

You may need to adjust where the mouse is positioned when it clicks. For example, you may have clicked a menu item in the empty space on the right of that item, which seemed natural during the capture. However, when you review the course, it seems odd to click off to the side.

To move the mouse click position:

1. Click and drag the mouse cursor to the location you want.

Mouse position from original capture

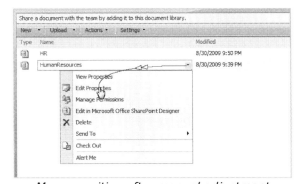

Mouse position after manual adjustment

Change Initial Mouse Position

On each slide, mouse movements start from where they left off on the previous slide. However, on the first slide, there is no such point of reference. Instead, the mouse starts in the upper-left corner. In many cases, this works just fine. However, if your first click is very close to the upper-left corner, your students might not see the mouse move. In cases like this, you might want to change the initial mouse position.

To change the initial mouse position:

1. Click and drag the four red dots to the location you want.

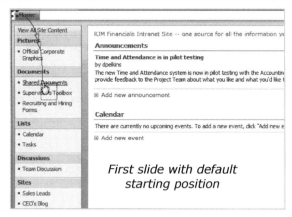

First slide with default starting position

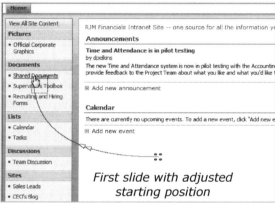

First slide with adjusted starting position

Align Mouse Paths

Because the mouse movement on a slide picks up where the previous slide left off, you should see smooth, fluid movement. However, if you have a slide where you don't want the mouse to move at all, there still might be a little jump in movement because the mouse is not in exactly the same place as it is in the previous slide. You can fix this by aligning the mouse to the previous slide or the next slide.

To align mouse paths with another slide:

1. Right-click the mouse cursor on the slide.
2. Select **Align to Previous Slide** or **Align to Next Slide**.

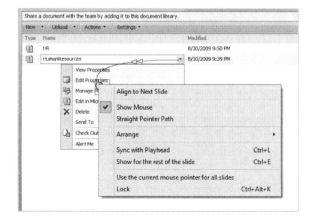

Hide/Show Mouse Movement

Based on how you configured your recording settings, Captivate automatically includes the mouse movements. However, you may want to hide the movement on certain screens.

If you didn't choose to include the mouse when you initially captured, Captivate still "knows" where you clicked on each slide. This means you can add the mouse movement back to any slide during editing.

To hide the mouse movement on a slide:

1. Right-click the mouse cursor on the slide **(A)** or click the mouse icon under the filmstrip thumbnail. **(B)**
2. Deselect **Show Mouse**.

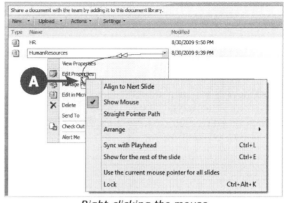

Right-clicking the mouse

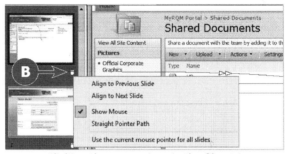

Clicking the mouse icon in the filmstrip

To show the mouse movement on a slide:

1. Right-click the slide or the thumbnail.
2. Select **Mouse**.
3. Select **Show Mouse**.

——— or ———

1. Click the **Objects** drop-down button.
2. Select **Mouse**.

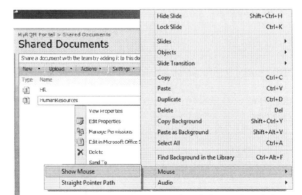

Right-clicking the slide

TIME SAVER

You can hide the mouse for the entire project in the **Publish Settings** section of **Preferences**.

 Publish Settings, p. 250

Objects menu

Change Mouse Properties

When you select the mouse cursor on a slide, the **Mouse Properties** panel appears, giving you additional options for how the mouse behaves.

Display

Captivate adjusts the look of the cursor based on what it looks like in the software. For example, you might see an arrow when clicking a button or an "i-beam" when editing text. You can change the look of the mouse if you need something different.

You can select one of the mouse options shown in the gallery or click the **Browse** button to select from any cursor type included with your operating system.

Double Mouse Size

If you'd like to give the mouse more emphasis, check this box so the mouse appears larger than normal.

Straight Pointer Path

By default, the path of the mouse curves slightly. If you would prefer that it be straight, check this box.

Reduce Speed Before Click

If you check this box, the mouse slows down before the click, which may make the movements appear less abrupt and easier for your students to absorb.

Mouse Click Sound

By default, a click sound is played for every click in the published course. If you want to change that setting for a given slide, check or uncheck this box.

In addition, you can select the sound used for the click. From the drop-down menu, you can select a single-click sound or a double-click sound. You can also click the **Browse** button **(A)** to select your own sound. The **Play** button **(B)** lets you hear the selection.

Show Mouse Click

By default, a small blue glow appears with every click in the published course. If you want to change this for a given slide, check or uncheck this box. In addition, you can click the color swatch to change the color, select **Custom** from the menu to pick from several other options, or browse for your own **.swf** file.

Timing Panel

The **Timing** panel lets you adjust when the mouse moves. This can also be done on the timeline.

 Timing Slide Objects, p. 122

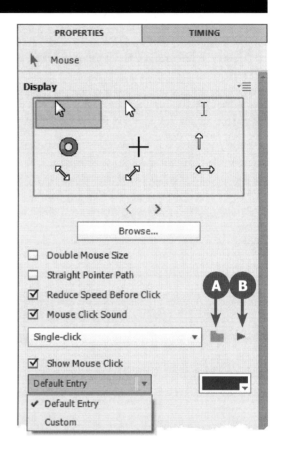

 CAUTION

Don't confuse **Show Mouse** with **Show Mouse Click**. **Show Mouse** determines whether the mouse cursor and movement appear. **Show Mouse Click** determines whether or not there is a glow or other effect associated with the click.

 POWER TIP

In addition to the cursor options shown and those available with your operating system, you can use any **.cur** file for Windows or **.pict** file for Mac.

Editing Full-Motion Recording

During a capture, certain actions (such as a dragging action) trigger a full-motion recording (FMR). You can also manually start FMR in a capture. On screens with FMR, the on-screen action is not presented as an image with the mouse layered on top, but as a video clip in **.swf** format. On FMR screens, the **Options** tab has an **FMR Edit Options** pane which lets you perform the steps below.

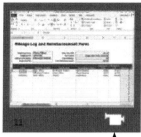

FMR indicator ↑

 Recording Settings, p. 25

Edit FMR

To insert another .swf file onto the slide (A):

1. Click the **FMR Edit Options** drop-down menu.
2. Select **Insert**.
3. Indicate the point when you want to add the clip:
   - Enter the time in the **Insert At** field.
   - Drag the black time marker to the time.
   - Click the **Snap to Playhead** button.
4. Click the **Insert** button.
5. Find and select the **.swf** file you want to insert.
6. Click the **OK** button.

To split the FMR file into two slides (B):

1. Click the **FMR Edit Options** drop-down menu.
2. Select **Split**.
3. Indicate the point when you want to split the clip:
   - Enter the time in the **Split At** field.
   - Drag the black time marker to the time.
   - Click the **Snap to Playhead** button.
4. Click the **Split** button.

To trim the front and/or end from a clip (C):

1. Click the **FMR Edit Options** drop-down menu.
2. Select **Trim**.
3. Enter the times you want to start and end the clip:
   - Enter the start and end points in the **Trim From** and **To** fields.
   - Drag each of the two black time markers to indicate the start and end points.
   - Click the **Snap to Playhead** button for the start or end point.
4. Click the **Trim** button.

To combine multiple FMR slides into one (D):

1. Select the slides you want to combine.
2. Go to the **Modify** menu.
3. Select **Merge FMR Slides**.

Time marker | Playhead

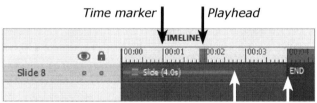

Video length   Slide length

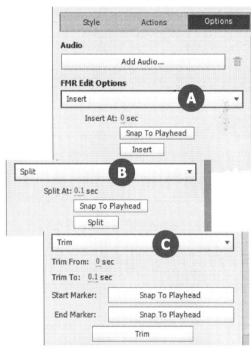

Editing Slide Backgrounds

Each step in your software simulation is saved as an image. This makes it fairly easy to make changes to those images either using photo editing software or the tools that come with Captivate. For example, you may be creating training for a new software rollout, and at the last minute, the developers change the name of one of the buttons. Instead of redoing the entire capture, you can make background edits to your slides.

Copy and Paste Backgrounds

You can copy the background image of any slide to either paste into another slide or to edit in photo editing software.

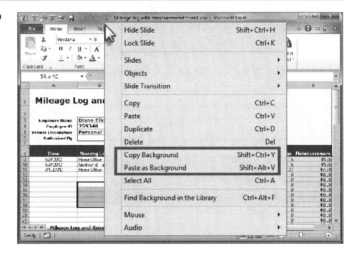

To copy a slide background:

1. Right-click the slide.
2. Select **Copy Background**.

To paste an image as a slide background:

1. Copy the image you want to use.
2. Right-click the slide.
3. Select **Paste as Background**.

 POWER TIPS

- If you ever need to go back to your original background, you can find it in the library.
- You can save time on editing by launching your photo editing software from the library. Right-click the background image you want and select **Edit with**. Then, navigate to your photo editing software. This lets you make edits without having to go through the copy and paste steps.

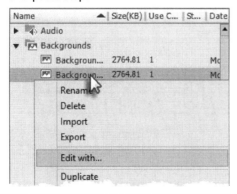

 CAUTION

Be careful about using **Paste** instead of **Paste as Background**. When you use **Paste as Background**, the existing background is replaced with the new image. If you use **Paste**, the new background appears as its own item in the timeline on top of the old background. This adds some risk, because that object could be deleted or moved in the timeline, causing the original background to show.

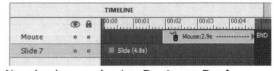

*New background using **Paste as Background***

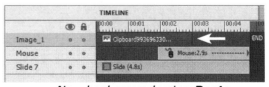

*New background using **Paste***

Merge With Background

In addition to using photo editing software to modify your backgrounds and then pasting them back into your capture, you can also use many of the object tools in Captivate to make simple changes, such as a rectangle, text box, or small image. When you do this, it's best to merge that item with the background.

Merging with the background combines the existing background and the new object being merged. This keeps the object from being deleted or moved.

The option to merge to the background is not available if the slide has a master slide background.

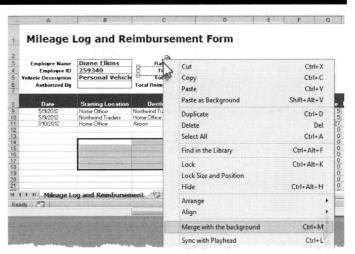

To merge an item into the background:

1. Paste or create the object on the slide.
2. Right-click the object.
3. Select **Merge with the background**.

CAUTION

- If your new objects are even a pixel off, your students may notice a "jump" when they are viewing your course. Before merging, check your edits carefully by going back and forth between the previous and next slides or by toggling the visibility icon for that object to make sure the edit isn't noticeable.

- Use **Merge with the background** when you have an object to add to the background. Use **Paste as Background** when you want to replace the background.

Text caption incorrectly pasted as background

Text caption pasted and then merged into background

DESIGN TIP

Here are some helpful hints about how to use objects to edit your backgrounds.

Shapes
Use the shape tools (rectangle, line, etc.) to cover over solid color areas. This is a great way to cover over a tooltip, a feature that shouldn't be showing, or text that you'll be replacing. Use the eye dropper tool to match the background perfectly.

Captions
Use a transparent caption to replace text. Change sensitive information, such as a customer name, update the name of a feature that has changed, or fix a typo on a non-typing slide.

Sections of Other Slides
Use a screen capture tool to capture a small part of another slide to reuse. For example, if an **Enter** button was renamed **OK**, and you have another slide with a similar **OK** button, capture just the area with the **OK** button, and paste it on the slide you need to fix.

Recording Additional Slides

After your initial capture, you may need to return to your software application and get additional captures. For example, you may find an error that can't be fixed by photo-editing the background, or you may have missed a few steps. You can record new slides inside an existing capture. You can also add a video demo into an existing project.

Record Additional Slides

To record additional slides:

1. Click the **Slides** drop-down button.
2. Select **Software Simulation**.
3. Select the slide after which the recorded slides should be inserted.
4. Click the **OK** button.
5. Configure your capture settings.
6. Click the **Record** button.
7. Capture your screens as you did before.
8. Press the **End** key on your keyboard.

 Record a Software Simulation, p. 22

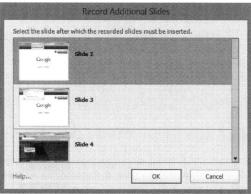

 TIME SAVERS

- Set up everything for the new slides before you click **Record**. You may need to undo some of the steps you performed in the original capture, especially if the new slides go in the middle of the project. For example, if you approved a vacation request at the end of a project, you may need to "unapprove" it before you can recapture an earlier step.

- Use the **Snap to window** feature during the initial recording and any additional recording to reduce the chance of your new captures being misaligned with your original captures.

 CAUTION

Not all of the recording options are available when you are adding additional captures. For example, the size of the recording window is locked to the size of the existing project.

Managing Practice Slides

When you create an interactive practice (such as training or assessment mode), Captivate adds either click boxes or text entry boxes to create the student interactivity. You can manage the properties of the click boxes and text entry boxes, and you can also add your own click boxes and text entry boxes if you want to.

Here are some special considerations when dealing with practice slides: click boxes and text entry boxes.

Elements of a Click Box Slide

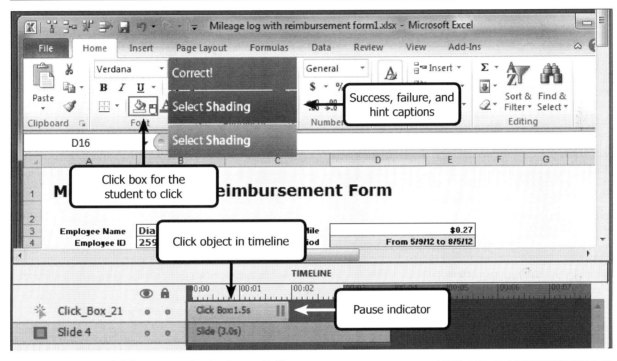

You learned about click box properties in chapter 7. Here are a few notes about how to use these properties in a practice slide.

Placement: Be sure that the click box fully covers the area that the student should click. In some cases, the default placement only covers half of the button, menu item, etc. Click and drag the click box to move or resize it.

Actions Tab

- Students go directly to the next slide when they click correctly, but the slide continues if they do not click correctly within the maximum attempts. Since the rest of the slide plays, you can put a caption with feedback after the pause indicator. Only the students who don't answer correctly will ever see that caption.

- In the **Shortcut** field, you can enter a keyboard shortcut that will be accepted in place of a click.

- In the **Others** section, you can change a left-click to a double-click or right-click.

Click Box Properties, p. 140

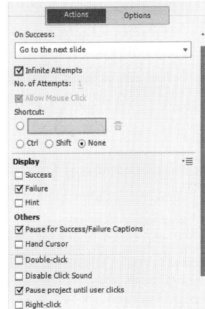

Elements of a Text Entry Box Slide

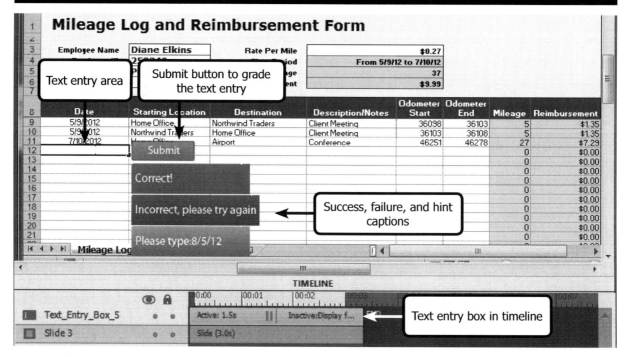

You learned about text entry box properties in chapter 7. Here are a few notes about how to use them in a practice slide.

Placement: You may need to adjust the formatting or size of the text entry box to match everything else on the screen.

Grading the Answer: When a student types in an answer, Captivate needs to know when to grade it.

- **Keyboard shortcut**: If you enter a shortcut **(A)**, the students' entries are graded when they type that shortcut.

- **Submit button**: If you check **Show Button (B)**, a **Submit** button appears next to the text box. The student's answer is graded when he or she clicks the **Submit** button.

- **Combine the Submit button with the next step**: If the next step in the procedure is a click, use **Show Button**, but make it transparent and place it over the step. When the student clicks the next step, the text entry will be graded.

- **Grade the answer after limit has been reached**: If you click **More options (C)**, you can set a character limit and have the answer evaluated when the limit is reached.

 ## CAUTION

With the first two options, the student performs a step that is not part of the procedure. The student might get used to pressing **Enter** or clicking **Submit**, and then try to do it in the real system.

 Text Entry Box Properties, p. 144

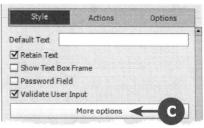

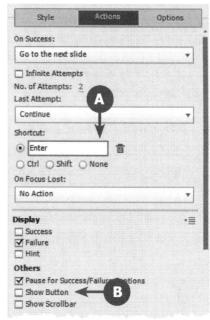

Managing Video Demo Projects

As you learned in chapter 2, you can create a screen recording in real-time that works more like a movie than a filmstrip. When you open one of these video composition files, you will not see the filmstrip or individual slides. Instead, your video appears on a single timeline.

As with any project, you can add audio, captions, shapes, and other static objects to your project and adjust the timing in the timeline. In addition, you can perform special functions available only in a video demo project:

- Trim and split the recording.
- Add pan and zoom effects.
- Add pop-up captions.
- Add transitions.
- Create a picture-in-picture effect.

Trim and Split the Recording

To trim the start or end points:

1. Click and drag the yellow marker. **(A)**

To trim a section out of the middle:

1. Click the **Trim** button. **(B)**
2. Drag the sliders to highlight the portion to be removed. **(C)**
3. Click **Trim**. **(D)**

To split the recording:

1. Click in the timeline where you want to split the video.
2. Click the **Split** button. **(E)**

If you have more than one section of video because of splitting and trimming, you can move the individual segments on the timeline.

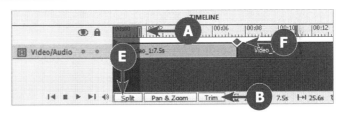

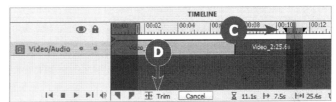

Add Transitions

At the beginning, the end, and any split or trim point in your video, you can add a transition. A gray diamond or triangle **(F)** indicates a point where you can add a transition.

To add a transition:

1. Click a transition marker. **(F)**
2. On the **Transitions** tab that appears, select the transition type you want.
3. From the drop-down menu at the top, select the speed for the transition.

Add Pan & Zoom Effects

To add a pan or zoom effect:

1. Click in the timeline where you want the effect to start.

2. Click the **Pan & Zoom** button. **(A)**

3. On the **Pan & Zoom** tab, position the blue frame to indicate the portion of the screen to zoom to.

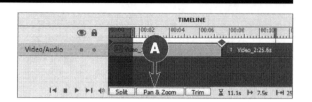

Options

Scale: Rather than manually resizing the blue frame, use the slider or numerical entry box to set the frame based on a scale of the original.

Speed: Use the slider or the text entry box to indicate how long it takes to zoom in/zoom out/pan.

Size & Position: Use the width and height fields as a different way to adjust the size of the blue frame. Use the X and Y coordinates as a different way to position the frame.

 DESIGN TIPS

- A magnifying glass icon appears in the timeline for each change in pan/zoom. **(B)** Click the icon to change its properties in the **Pan & Zoom** panel. Drag the icon to change when the change happens. Right-click it to delete it.

- To end a zoom effect, click in the timeline where you want to end the effect, and click the **Zoom Out** button on the **Pan & Zoom** tab. **(C)**

- To create a pan effect, put two zoom effects (each focusing on a different part of the slide) next to each other. Captivate will transition between the two with a pan effect.

- If you have splits or trims, the video will zoom out at the end of each segment.

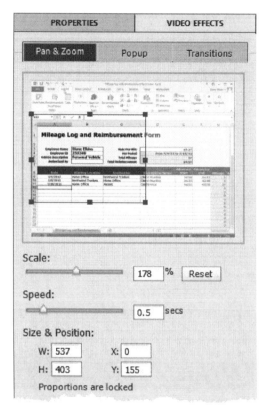

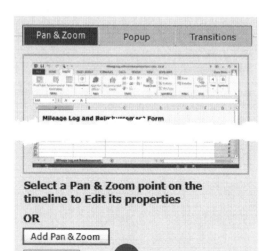

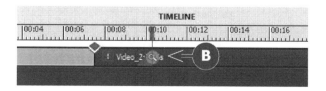

Create Picture-in-Picture (PIP) Effects

You can add a video that appears in a small window on top of your existing video demo. Acceptable file types include **.flv**, **.f4v**, **.avi**, **.mp4**, **.mov**, and **.3gp**. If you insert one of these file types other than **.mp4**, the file will be converted to **.mp4** for you.

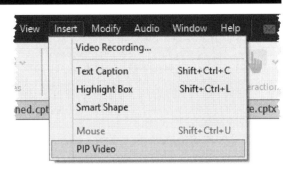

To add a picture-in-picture effect:

1. Click in the timeline where you want the PIP to start.
2. Go to the **Insert** menu.
3. Select **PIP Video**.
4. Find and select the video you want to add.
5. Click the **OK** button.
6. Position the video where you want it on the slide.
7. Position the video where you want it in the timeline.

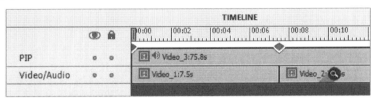

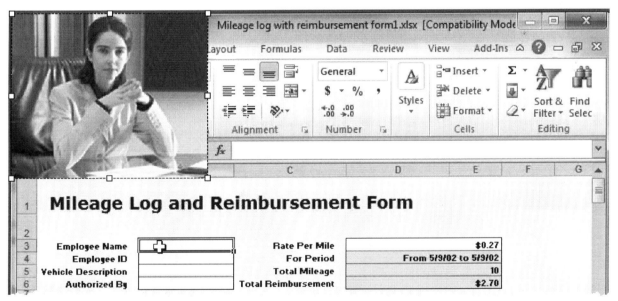

Clean Popup Windows

When you are recording a video demo, you might have a tooltip appear if your mouse stays in one place to long, or you might have an email or instant message notification window appear in the bottom corner of your screen. Captivate comes with an easy way to clean up these unwanted pop-up windows. You can either automatically or manually add a freeze frame of the background that appears on top of the video in the timeline, hiding the pop-up window you don't want.

To clean a pop-up window automatically:

1. Click in the timeline at a point when the pop-up is visible.

2. On the **Video Effects** panel, click the **Popup** tab.

3. Click the **Cleanup** button.

4. Click and drag your mouse around the area you want to clean up. **(A)**

5. Click the **Cleanup** caption that appears once you release the mouse. **(B)**

To clean up a pop-up window manually:

1. Click in the timeline at a point when the pop-up is visible.

2. On the **Video Effects** panel, click the **Popup** tab.

3. Click the **Replace** button.

4. Click and drag your mouse around the area you want to clean up.

5. Click and drag the plus icon **(C)** to the left until you find a frame where the pop-up does not appear.

6. In the timeline, click and drag the right edge of the freeze frame image **(D)** to extend the duration of the image until the pop-up is gone.

To remove a freeze frame image, simply delete it from the timeline.

 CAUTION

The **Cleanup Popup** function uses static image overlays. Therefore, it will not be effective if the area around the pop-up area is moving, panning, or changing.

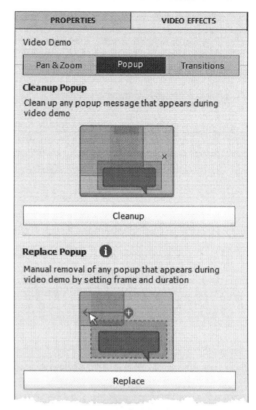

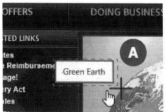

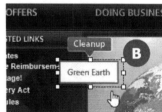

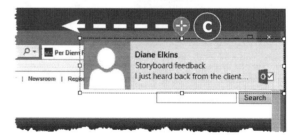

Add a Video Demo Slide to a Project

You can add an existing video demo capture (CPVC) to an existing project or record a new video demo within an existing project. The video demo is added as a full-motion recording.

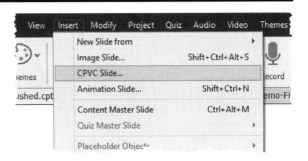

To add an existing video demo to a project:

1. Go to the **Insert** menu.
2. Select **CPVC Slide**.
3. Find and select the CPVC slide you want.
4. Click the **Open** button.

To edit a CPVC file that has been inserted into another project:

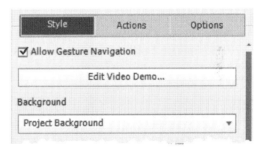

1. Select the CPVC slide.
2. In the **Properties** panel, click the **Edit Video Demo** button.
3. Make your changes as described on the previous pages.
4. Save your changes.
5. Click the **Exit** button.

Note that the changes you make are saved to the underlying CPVC file.

To create a new video demo to insert into an existing project:

1. Click the **Slides** drop-down button.
2. Select **Video Demo**.
3. Select the slide after which the recorded slides should be inserted.
4. Click the **OK** button.
5. Record your demo as you normally would.

Notes

Variables & Advanced Actions

Introduction

Variables and advanced actions let you expand and customize the functionality of Captivate. They are like building blocks that you can use however you want to create special features.

A variable is a stored piece of logic within the project that you can use to:

- Track information provided by the student, such as an option that the student selects or text that the student enters.
- Control course functionality, such as turning the audio or the control playbar on and off.
- Display something back to the student, such as the current time or points earned in a test or game.
- Set up conditional logic, such as whether a student is a supervisor or uses a screen reader.

Advanced actions give you more choices than you have on the **Actions** tab of an object's properties. Use the **Advanced Actions** dialog box when you want to:

- Apply more than one action to a single object. For example, in a game, you might want a single button click to show a message, add points to a score, and advance to the next slide.
- Create a conditional action. For example, you can ask students if they are a supervisor or not, and then have a button that branches to one slide if they click **Yes** and a different slide if they click **No**.
- Reuse actions. For example, if you want to add points to a student's score in a game that has several questions, you can set up the action once and then reuse it on each slide.
- Access more action options. For example, you can create calculations from the **Advanced Actions** dialog box.
- Interact with objects on different slides. For example, you can have a button on slide 3 that reveals an object on slide 10.
- Save actions to reuse across multiple slides using different parameters and import/export actions to reuse them in different projects.

In This Chapter

- Working With Variables
- Advanced Actions
  - Standard
  - Conditional
  - Shared
- Managing Advanced Actions

Notes

Working With Variables

Variables, which are stored pieces of information in the project, come in three basic types:

- **System Variables**: System variables are set up by Captivate. They include information about the project (such as the current slide), controls for the project (such as whether the playbar is showing), or quiz information. You cannot set up or delete these variables, but you can use them for conditional logic, display them to students, and even modify some of them to control the project.

Appendix: System Variables, p. 299

- **User Variables**: A user variable is one that you create yourself. You set it up, you define and modify its value, and you decide how it will be used. For example, you can set up a variable to keep score in a game. You can also set up variables that the student controls. For example, you can insert a text box where the student enters his or her name, and then you can use that information later in a certificate.

- **Geolocation**: You can create a user variable for a location's longitude and latitude. You can use this to create location-aware content such as a pop-up box that only appears if the student is in a certain location.

Geolocation, p. 267

Manage Variables

To view variables:

1. Go to the **Project** menu.
2. Select **Variables**.
3. Select **User** or **System** from the **Type** drop-down menu to see a list of each type of variable.

System variables can only be viewed, not modified, in this dialog box. Select one from the list to view its current value and the description.

For user variables, you can delete or change the default value of the variable.

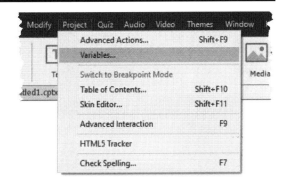

To delete a user variable:

1. Select the variable in the **Variables** dialog box.
2. Click the **Remove** button.

To change the default value of a user variable:

1. Select the variable.
2. Change the value.
3. Click the **Update** button.

To see where a variable is being used:

1. Select the variable.
2. Click the **Usage** button.

To see which variables are not being used:

1. Click the **Unused Items** button.
2. The unused variables are highlighted in gray.

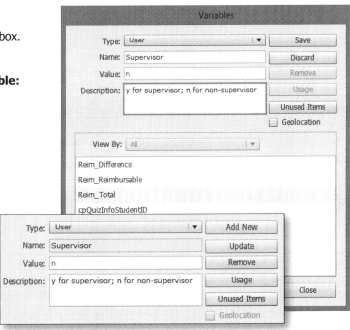

Button options after initially saving the variable.

Add a User Variable

To add a user variable:

1. Go to the **Project** menu.
2. Select **Variables**.
3. Click the **Add New** button.
4. In the **Name** field, enter the name for the variable.
5. In the **Value** field, enter the initial value for the variable.
6. In the **Description** field, add a description about the variable or how it will be used, if needed.
7. Click the **Save** button.
8. Click the **Close** button.

Variable names cannot contain spaces or special characters except underscore.

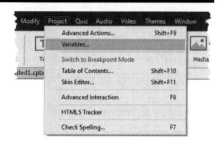

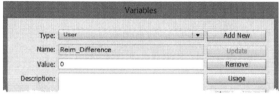

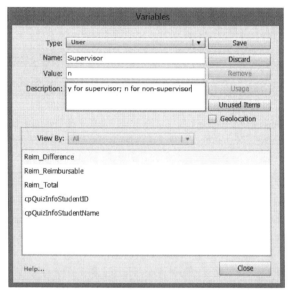

Add a Text-Entry Variable

When you add a text entry field to a project, the student's entry is saved as a variable. You can then use this for conditional logic or to display back to the student. For example, you may have the student enter his or her name.

On the **Style** tab for the text entry box, use the **Variable** drop-down menu to indicate what variable you want to use to capture the student's answer. Either use the default variable created when you added the text box, select an existing variable from the drop-down menu, or click the **[X]** button to create a new variable name.

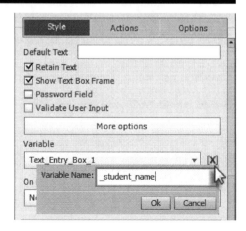

Text Entry Boxes, p. 144

Modify Variables With the Actions Pane

Variables can be modified with simple actions from the **Actions** tab of the various trigger objects. More advanced modifications can be done with advanced actions.

Assign

Use this command to change the value of a variable to an exact value, such as a number or text. For example, you can assign the value for whether or not a student is a supervisor, or reset the score on a game back to 0.

Increment

Use this command to add to a user-defined variable that has a number value. For example, you can add points to a student's score in a game.

Decrement

Use this command to subtract from a user-defined variable that has a number value. For example, you can subtract points from a student's score.

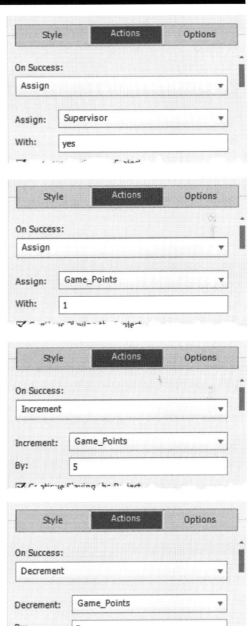

Display a Variable

You can display the value of a variable to the student in a text caption or a shape with text. The variable can be included with other text. The text is updated every time the variable is updated.

For example, you might want to display the student's point value during a game or display a name that the student previously entered in a text box.

To display a variable:

1. Double-click a caption or shape with text.
2. On the **Style** tab, click the **Insert Variables** button. **(A)**
3. Select **User** or **System** from the **Variable Type** drop-down menu, based on the type of variable you want to display.
4. In the **Variables** drop-down menu, select the variable you want.
5. Click the **OK** button.

Options

Click the **Variables** button if you want to go to the **Variables** dialog box to add or make changes to the variables.

The **Maximum length** field shows the maximum number of characters that will be displayed. If the value of the variable is longer than that, the extra characters will be cut off.

 POWER TIP

If you prefer, you can type the variable code into the caption yourself. Type two dollar signs before and after the name of the variable. The variable name you type must be exact, including capitalization.

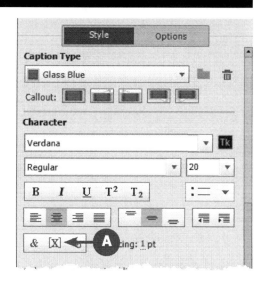

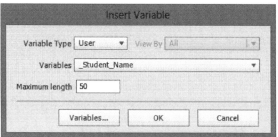

Variable placeholder in edit mode

Congratulations, Diane!

Variable placeholder in published project

Advanced Actions

The **Advanced Actions** dialog box gives you more options than you have in the **Actions** tab in an object's properties, such as grouping actions together or creating conditional actions. You can create a conditional action that only runs if certain conditions are met, or a standard action that runs any time it is executed.

When you create an advanced action, it does not run on its own. You can run that action anywhere in the project (even multiple times) by creating an action that executes it.

1. Create the Action
2. Execute the Action

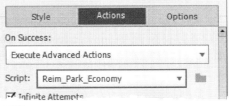

 Execute Advanced Actions, p. 135

Add an Advanced Action

To add an advanced action:

1. Go to the **Project** menu.
2. Select **Advanced Actions**.
3. In the **Action Name** field, enter a name for the action.
4. In the **Actions** list, double-click in the second column.
5. Select the command you want from the drop-down menu.
6. Complete the additional options that may appear in the third column, based on the command you chose.
7. Repeat steps 4-6 for additional commands.
8. Click the **Save as Action** button.
9. Click the **Close** button.

Special Options

- If you'd like to create a new action based on a previously saved action, select that action from the **Create from** drop-down menu.

- Icons indicate if a command is complete. **(A)** A green check means it is complete. A yellow triangle means there is missing or incomplete information, in which case you cannot save the action.

- Click the **Variables** button to add or edit variables.

- Use the icons at the top of the dialog box to manage the entire action. Use the icons above the **Actions** list to modify individual commands.

- The order of your actions may be important. For example, you may want to hide something before you show something in its place. The **Move Up** and **Move Down** buttons let you adjust the order.

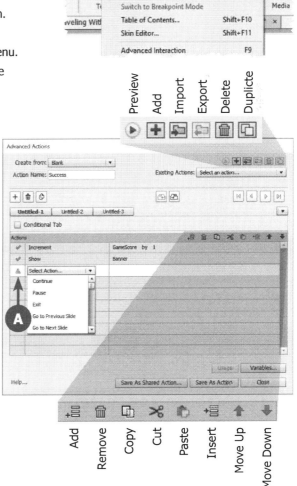

Advanced Action Commands

Many of the action commands available in the **Advanced Action** dialog box are the same as those available in the **Actions** tab. However, some commands are only available here, and some are set up differently here.

The Same
- Continue
- Go to Next Slide
- Go to Previous Slide
- Go to Last Visited Slide

- Return to Quiz
- Jump to Slide
- Open URL or File
- Open Other Project

- Send Mail
- Execute JavaScript
- Apply Effect

Slightly Different

Enable, Disable, Show, Hide, Play Audio, and Stop Triggered Audio

These work *mostly* the same way as they do in the **Actions** tab. In the **Actions** tab, you can only select items on that slide. In the **Advanced Actions** dialog box, you can select any eligible object in the project.

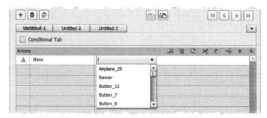

Assign

The **Assign** action still lets you assign a value to a variable. You have some additional choices when you run this action from the **Advanced Actions** dialog box.

Once you select **Assign**, you can then select the variable you want from the drop-down menu in the next column.

Next, a new menu appears letting you choose **variable** or **literal**.

- Select **variable** if you want to change the value of the first **variable** to the value of a different variable.
- Select **literal** if you want to use an exact value, such as a number or text.

Only Available Here

Expression

The **Expression** action lets you create calculations, taking the place of, and providing more options than, **Increment** and **Decrement**.

First, select a variable that will hold the value of the calculation.

Options for building the expression

Then, you can make each part of the equation a variable or a literal value. First, select **variable** or **literal** from the menu. If you select **variable**, you get a list of variables to choose from. If you select **literal**, you get a text entry box to enter the literal value.

Finished expression

Finally, you can select from four calculation types: addition, subtraction, multiplication, or division.

Delay Next Actions By

The **Delay Next Actions By** action lets you delay an action or series of actions by a given amount of time.

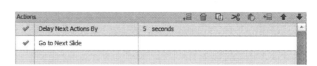

Once you select **Delay Next Action By** you can then enter the amount of time.

Go to next slide action delayed by 5 seconds.

Conditional Actions

With a standard advanced action, all actions run when the advanced action is executed. When a conditional action is executed, the actions only run if or while certain conditions are met. For example, certain information might be shown if the quiz is passed. A conditional action can have three parts.

- **If/While**: This is where you set up the conditions that have to be met in order for the actions to run.
- **Actions**: This is where you set up the individual actions that will run when the conditions are met.
- **Else**: This is where you can set up an alternate set of actions that will run if the conditions are NOT met or when the conditions are no longer met. You can leave this section blank, which means nothing will happen if the conditions are not met.

As with standard advanced actions, you need to first set up the conditional action, and then execute it from the **Actions** tab of an interactive object.

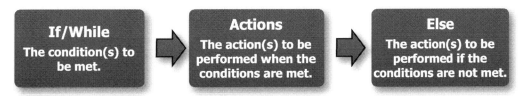

Add a Conditional Advanced Action

To add a conditional action:

1. Go to the **Project** menu.
2. Select **Advanced Actions**.
3. In the **Action Name** field, enter a name for the action.
4. Check the **Conditional Tab** checkbox.
5. In the **IF** section, enter the condition(s) that need to occur in order for the action to run.
6. In the **Actions** section, enter the action(s) that will run when the **IF** conditions *are* met.
7. Click the **ELSE** heading.
8. Enter the action(s) that will run if the **IF** conditions are *not* met.
9. Click the **Save as Action** button.
10. Click the **Close** button.

Refer to the next few pages for details on the **IF**, **Actions**, and **ELSE** sections.

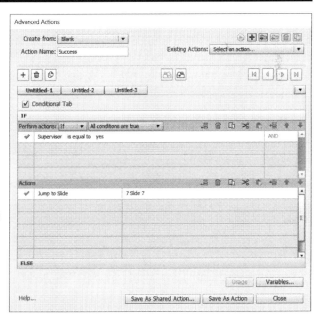

Creating IF/While Conditions

A condition has three parts: the two items being compared and how they should be compared. Double-click a line in the **IF** section, and enter values for the three parts.

1. Select a variable or literal value for the basis of comparison.

2. Select a comparison operator to determine how the two items will be compared, such as greater than, less than, etc.

3. Select what the first value should be compared to, either another variable or a literal value.

While Conditions

If you click the **If** drop-down menu and select **While**, the corresponding actions will happen continuously as long as the conditions are met. This causes the actions to run in a loop until the conditions are no longer met, at which point the **Else** actions (if any) will run.

Multiple Conditions

You can create an advanced action with one or more conditions. If there is only one condition, then you don't need to do anything more. However, if you have multiple conditions, you need to designate how the conditions interact with each other.

For example, you might have a condition about whether an employee is hourly and another about whether an employee is seasonal.

From the **Perform actions** drop-down menu, select one of the following:

All conditions are true: Select this option if all conditions must be met in order for the actions to be run. For example, an employee must be hourly AND seasonal.

Any of the conditions true: Select this option if you only need one of the options to be true for the actions to be run. For example, an employee must either be hourly OR seasonal.

Custom: Select this option if you want to use a combination of AND and OR logic. When you use this option, select **AND** or **OR** for each condition in the third column. For example, the employee must be salaried OR hourly AND seasonal.

Managing Conditions

Conditions can be copied, pasted, moved, etc., just as actions can.

Options for building the conditions

Finished condition

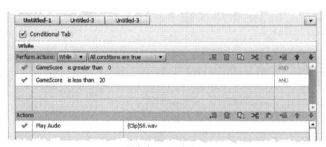

While condition

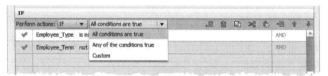

Managing multiple conditions

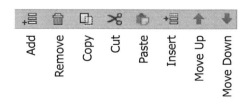

Add   Remove   Copy   Cut   Paste   Insert   Move Up   Move Down

Creating Actions and Else Actions

In the **Actions** section, add one or more actions, just as with standard actions.

To set up the actions that trigger if the conditions are not met, click the **ELSE** heading. Then, add the actions just as with standard actions.

Click the **IF** heading to return to the original view.

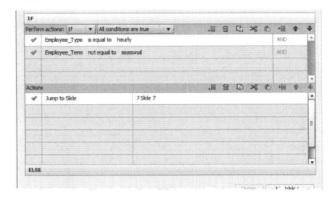

Creating Multiple Decisions

Advanced actions can have multiple decisions, meaning multiple sets of standard or conditional actions. For example, in a game, you can have a standard action that adjusts the points and then a separate set of conditional actions that displays different graphics.

- To select a decision, click the button for that decision. **(A)**
- To rename a decision, double-click the button for that decision, and type the name.
- To add a new decision, click **Add Decision**.
- To delete a decision, select the decision, and then click the **Remove Decision** button.
- To make a copy of a decision, select the decision, and click the **Duplicate Decision** button.
- To change the order of the decisions, select a decision, and click **Move Left** or **Move Right**. **(B)**
- If you have more decision buttons than will fit across the dialog box, use the scrolling buttons to scroll back and forth between them. **(C)**

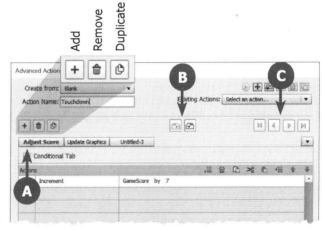

Shared Actions

Actions can be saved as shared actions. When you do this, you can:

- Build new actions based from them, with the shared actions acting like templates.
- Import and export them so they can be used in multiple projects and by multiple developers. When exported, shared actions are saved as **.cpaa** files.
- Reuse the action using different parameters, meaning using different values for some of the arguments.

You can reuse any advanced action multiple times throughout a project. But when you save an action as a shared action, you can configure slide-specific parameters, making the action more reusable.

For example, if you have a course on a time and attendance system, some slides may only be relevant to employees who are supervisors. You can set up an advanced, conditional action to go to slide 3 if the student is a supervisor and slide 6 if the student is not. Later in the course, you might have another situation that needs similar branching. You can't reuse the exact action, because in this new case, you don't want to branch to slides 3 and 6, you want to branch to slides 14 and 18. This is where a shared action can be useful.

If you save the original action as a shared action, it puts placeholders, called parameters, in the saved action. You can then configure those parameters every time you reuse the action—either in the same project or when imported into a different project.

Save as a Shared Action

To save an action as a shared action:

1. Set up your action in the **Advanced Actions** dialog box.

2. Click the **Save As Shared Action** button.

3. In the dialog box, change the name and/or enter a description, if needed.

4. In the **Parameter Description**, describe guidelines for the type of object that should be selected.

5. Click the **Save** button.

6. Click **OK** in the pop-up window that appears.

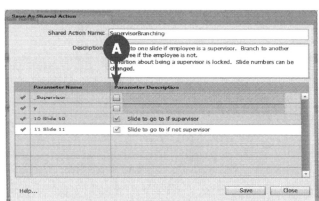

BRIGHT IDEA

Variables and literal values can be turned into parameters. Check the box **(A)** for each variable or literal value you want to turn into a parameter, otherwise they will remain constant when you reuse the variable.

Create a New Action Based on a Shared Action

To create a new action based on a shared action:

1. Go to the **Project** menu.

2. Select **Advanced Actions**.

3. In the **Create from** menu, select the shared action upon which you want to base the new action.

4. Modify and save the action as you normally would.

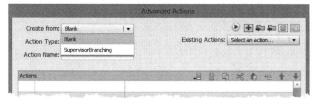

Import and Export Shared Actions

To import a shared action:

1. Go to the **Project** menu.
2. Select **Advanced Actions**.
3. Click the **Import** button. **(A)**
4. Find and select the shared action you want to import.
5. Click the **Open** button.
6. Click the **OK** button.

To export a shared action:

1. Go to the **Project** menu.
2. Select **Advanced Actions**.
3. Click the **Export** button. **(B)**
4. Select the shared action you want to export.
5. Click the **Browse** button.
6. Find and select the location to save it in.
7. Click the **OK** button.
8. Click the **Export** button.
9. Click the **Close** button.

Execute a Shared Action

To execute a shared action:

1. In any action menu, select **Execute Shared Action**.
2. In the **Shared Action** drop-down menu, select the shared action you want.
3. Click the **Action Parameters** button. **{P}**
4. Select the slide-specific elements for the action.
5. Click the **Close** button.

TIME SAVER

Shared actions appear in the library. You can click and drag the action from the library to the object you want to use as a trigger, such as a button. Then the **Shared Action Parameters** dialog box opens so you can configure the action. If the object already has an action, it will be replaced with this shared action.

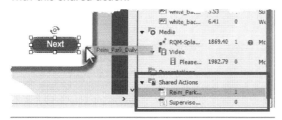

Managing Actions

Managing Advanced Actions

From the **Advanced Actions** dialog box, you can manage existing actions.

- Because of all the panels involved in an advanced action, you can't always see all your parameters at one time. Click **Preview action** to get a dialog box that lists all the parameters, making it easier to document or troubleshoot.

- To view an advanced action, select it from the **Existing Actions** drop-down menu.

- To add an additional advanced action, click the **Create a new action** button.

- To create a new action based on an existing action, select it from the **Create from** menu.

- To delete an advanced action, select it, and then click the **Delete action** button.

- To make a copy of an advanced action, select it, and then click the **Duplicate action** button.

- To modify an advanced action (rename it or add/delete actions and conditions), make the changes, and click **Update Action**, which appears in place of the **Save As Action** button.

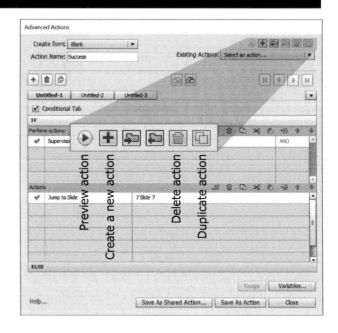

Advanced Interaction Panel

The **Advanced Interaction** panel lets you see all the interactive objects in your project. From this view, you can see many of the key properties of the interactive objects, such as the action, number of attempts, etc. When you click on an object in the pane, the slide appears with the object selected and the object's **Properties** panel showing.

You can access the **Advanced Interaction** panel from the **Project** menu.

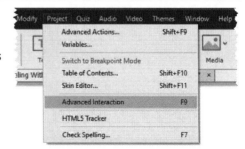

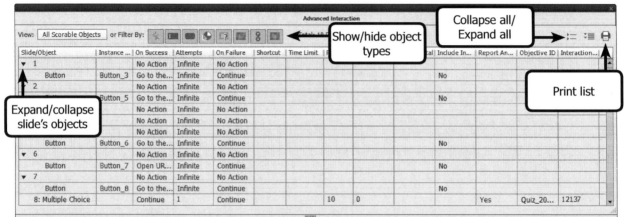

Questions & Quizzes

Introduction

Questions, quizzes, tests, knowledge checks, scenarios, interactions—these course elements often make the difference between *telling* someone something and *teaching* them something. They allow both you and the students to reinforce and apply the content, assess the learning, uncover opportunities for re-teaching, and evaluate the course effectiveness. Captivate offers nine question types you can insert in a graded format and/or survey format.

In this chapter, you will learn how to add questions to your projects, either for pure reinforcement or as part of a graded quiz that reports to a learning management system (LMS). (You'll learn more about the LMS reporting settings in chapter 12.)

In This Chapter

- Creating Questions
- Configuring Questions
- Knowledge Check Slides
- Individual Question Options
- Creating Pretests
- Quiz Master Slides
- Question Pools
- Quiz Results Slides
- Quiz Preferences

Notes

Creating Questions

Add a Question

To add a question to your project:

1. Click the **Slides** drop-down button.
2. Select **Question Slide**.
3. Check the box(s) for the type of question(s) you would like to use.
4. Enter the number of questions you want for that question type.
5. Select **Graded, Survey**, or **Pretest** from the drop-down menu.
6. Click the **OK** button.

 DESIGN TIPS

Question Slide vs. Knowledge Check Slide

You can choose to set up quiz logic to create an overall score for all of the questions added as a question slide. If you have questions you *don't* want to include in the overall score, such as a reinforcement question, use the **Knowledge Check Slide** option instead. Students still get feedback on those questions, but their answers aren't included in a quiz score.

 Knowledge Check Slides, p. 192

Graded vs. Survey vs. Pretest Questions

Use graded questions when there are right and wrong answers. You can indicate which answer is right vs. wrong and provide separate feedback for right vs. wrong answers.

Use a survey question when there isn't a right or wrong answer. All students get the same feedback, regardless of their answer. Use this for opinion questions or questions where students self-grade their answers as compared to the answer you provide.

Use a pretest question to assess the student's knowledge before the course and direct them to certain content based on their results.

 Pretests, p. 207

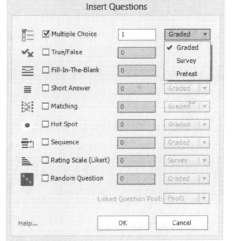

 POWER TIP

In addition to using question slides, you can create your own questions from scratch using buttons or click boxes. Just check the **Include in Quiz** box in the **Reporting** pane for that object.

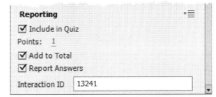

 Click Boxes and Buttons, p. 140-142

Question Types

Multiple Choice Student chooses one or more options among several possible answers. • Can have up to 15 answer choices • Available as graded or survey	**When dealing with an angry customer, it is best to:** ○ A) maintain a calm, soothing voice ◉ B) mirror the client's energy to let him or her know you understand the frustration ○ C) speak to the customer firmly telling him or her to calm down ○ D) ask the customer to take a few minutes to relax
True/False Student decides between two options. • Can change "true" and "false" labels • Available as graded or survey	**As an organization, we believe there are opportunities to learn from clients willing to share their complaints.** ◉ A) True ○ B) False
Fill in the Blank Student types a word into the space provided. • Can be case-sensitive or not • Can allow more than one correct answer • Can be formatted as a multiple-choice question with a drop-down list • Available as graded or survey	**Complete the sentence below by filling in the blank.** The first thing we must do with an angry customer is _____ him or her. **Complete the sentence below by filling in the blank.** The first thing we must do with an angry customer is [▼] him or her. move listen to calm
Short Answer Student types in a longer answer to a question. • Available as graded or survey	**What do you believe are the two or three most important qualities a customer service specialist possesses?**

Question Types (cont'd)

Matching

Student matches items in one column with items in the other.

- Can have up to 8 options per column
- Available as graded or survey

Column 1		Column 2
C	Shannon Fielding	A) VP of Customer Care
A	Jackson Roberts	B) Legal Counsel
B	Maria Velasquez	C) Senior Manager - Customer Care

Hot Spot

Student clicks on one or more designated hot spots on a graphic image.

- Can have up to 10 hot spots
- Available as graded or survey

Where is our largest customer base? Choose the correct city from the list of hotspots.

Sequence

Student arranges a series of items into the proper sequence.

- Can be formatted as a drag-and-drop or drop-down list
- Available as graded or survey

Arrange in sequence

A) Customer is connected to a Customer Care Associate.

B) Customer calls the Customer Care Hotline.

C) Customer is upset and decides to complain.

D) Issue is not resolved via the computerized system.

Arrange in sequence

A) Customer is upset and decides to complain.   ▼

B) Customer calls the Customer Care Hotline.   ▼

C) --Select--   ▼

D) Customer calls the Customer Care Hotline.
Customer is upset and decides to complain.
Customer is connected to a Customer Care Associate.
Issue is not resolved via the computerized system

Rating Scale (Likert)

Students evaluate statements and rate them on a scale.

- Can have up to 5 points on the scale
- Available as survey only

Indicate how strongly you agree or disagree with the following:

	Disagree 1	Somewhat Disagree 2	Neutral 3	Somewhat Agree 4	Agree 5
A) I feel empowered to meet the customers' needs.	○	○	○	○	○
B) I feel competent to handle most customer complaints.	○	○	○	○	○

Configuring Questions

Once you've added your question, you'll need to configure it, changing both the text and the properties. Some options are changed directly on the slide and some are changed on the **Quiz** tab.

The options vary based on question type. The next four pages cover standard properties and options that apply to most question types. The following pages go into question type-specific options.

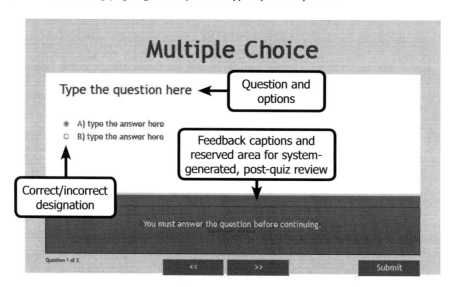

Add Question Content

Your question slide has text placeholders for a title, your question/instructions, and the answer options. To build your question, simply type or paste your text in the placeholders.

To format the text boxes:

1. Select the object(s) you want to format.
2. Click the **Style** tab.
3. Make the changes you want.

 Formatting Caption Text, p. 57

To add more answer options (except T/F):

1. Click the **Quiz** tab.
2. Enter the number you want in the **Answers** field.

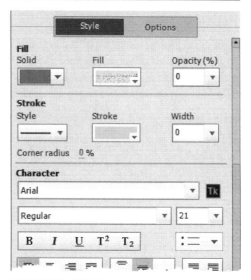

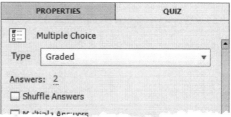

Add Standard Feedback

You can have up to five types of feedback captions, which can be turned on and off via the **Quiz** tab. Change the text, formatting, and location of the feedback caption just like you would any other caption.

Correct (A)

This caption displays when the student answers the question correctly.

Incorrect (B)

This caption displays when the student answers the question incorrectly.

Timeout Caption (C)

If you set a time limit for the question, this caption appears when the time runs out.

Retry Message (D)

If you allow more than one attempt, this caption appears after each failed attempt (except the last one). This option is disabled if you have **Failure Messages** enabled.

Incomplete (E)

If you enable it, this caption appears if the student clicks **Submit** without answering the question.

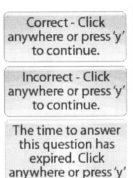

Correct - Click anywhere or press 'y' to continue.

Incorrect - Click anywhere or press 'y' to continue.

The time to answer this question has expired. Click anywhere or press 'y' to continue.

Try again

You must answer the question before continuing.

 Caption Properties, p. 56

Set Number of Attempts

By default, quiz questions are set to allow one attempt. That means if the student does not get the question right the first time, the incorrect logic (captions, actions, points, etc.) runs after that attempt. If you'd like to provide more than one attempt, change the number in the **No. of Attempts** field **(F)**, or check the **Infinite Attempts** box for unlimited attempts.

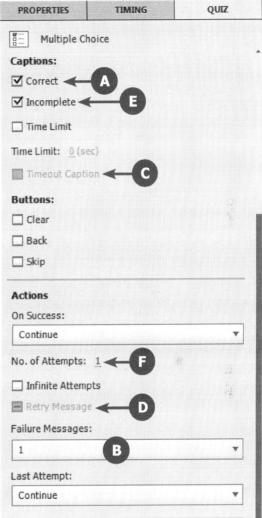

 CAUTION

When configuring questions, some of the features you want will be on the **Properties** panel and some will be on the **Quiz** panel. Be sure you are looking in the right place!

 DESIGN TIPS

- You don't need to make room on your slide for all of these captions. Since most of them will not appear at the same time, they can overlap on your slide to save space.

- Use the **Time Limit** option with care. Limits have accessibility implications for those with physical, cognitive, or developmental disabilities.

- You can use caption styles to help save time with formatting your feedback captions.

 Styles, p. 110

Add Progressive Feedback

If you are giving your students more than one attempt at a question, you can give them more than one level of feedback. For example, if they get a question wrong the first time, you can show an incorrect feedback caption that simply asks them to try again. If they get it wrong again, you can show a different incorrect feedback caption that provides a hint. Then, the third level of feedback can provide the correct answer.

You can have up to three levels of feedback, and you cannot have more feedback levels than you have attempts.

To add progressive feedback to a question:

1. In the **Quiz** panel, enter the number of allowable attempts in the **No. of Attempts** field.

2. In the **Failure Messages** drop-down menu, select the number of failure captions you want.

3. In the work area, add text to each of the failure captions that appear.

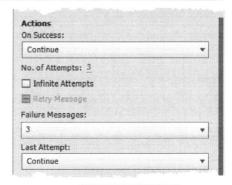

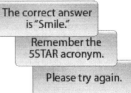

Set Success and Failure Actions

For any graded question type, you can indicate what you want to have happen when the student answers the question correctly (within the specified number of attempts) or incorrectly (after the maximum number of attempts have been used).

By default, both action fields are set to **Continue**. But you can change either one of those actions to create branching (using any of the **Go to** actions), give audio feedback (**Play Audio**), or create advanced game logic (**Execute Advanced Actions**).

To set a success action:

1. On the **Quiz** tab, click the **On Success** drop-down menu.

2. Select the action you want.

To set a failure action:

1. On the **Quiz** tab, click the **Last Attempt** drop-down menu.

2. Select the action you want.

 **CAUTION**

You cannot set a **Last Attempt** action if the question is set to unlimited attempts.

Add Advanced Feedback

Branching Quizzes

If you want more feedback than fits in a feedback caption, you can branch to a different slide with feedback.

To branch to a different slide based on answer:

1. On the **Quiz** tab, add a **Jump to slide** action in the **On Success** and **Last Attempt** fields.

2. In the **On Success** action, select the slide with the correct feedback.

3. In the **Last Attempt** action, select the slide with the incorrect feedback.

 POWER TIP

If your questions branch to other questions based on the student's answer, the student may not take all questions in a quiz, which can affect the quiz score. If you check the **Branch Aware** box in **Quiz Preferences**, Captivate grades the quiz based on the number of questions presented, not the total in the quiz. Learn about quiz preferences on pg. 213.

Option-Specific Feedback

On a multiple-choice question, you can have separate feedback and actions for each option. For example, you can have different feedback if A was chosen instead of B.

To add option-specific feedback:

1. In the work area, select the individual question choice you want to work with.

2. On the **Options** tab in the **Properties** panel, check the **Advanced Answer Option** check box.

3. Add and configure an action, if needed.

4. Check the **Show Feedback Message** box to add a text caption to appear if that option is chosen.

Remediation Back to Content Slides

If students get a question wrong, you can branch back to one or several slides where the content was taught and then return them back to the quiz to retry the question.

To add remediation branching:

1. In the **Last Attempt** field on the question, set a **Jump to slide** action to the first slide with the content.

2. On the last slide with the content, add a **Return to Quiz** action on the slide's next button.

On the content slide, the **Next** button with the **Return to Quiz** action executes a **Continue** action under normal circumstances, but returns students to the quiz if that's where they came from.

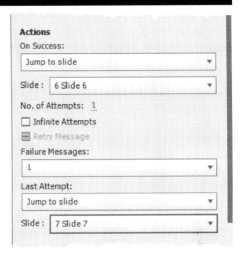

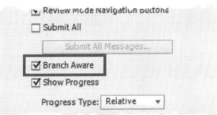

Assign Points to Questions

When you assign points to a question, by default, the students receive all of the points if they get the question right and none of the points if they get the question wrong.

There are several ways to create more advanced point logic. You can have the student lose points for a wrong answer, and for multiple-choice questions, you can provide partial credit if the student selects a "somewhat correct" option.

To add standard points:

1. In the **Quiz** panel, adjust the number in the **Points** field. **(A)**

To deduct points for an incorrect answer:

1. In the **Quiz** panel, adjust the number in the **Penalty** field. **(B)**

To provide points for an incorrect answer:

1. In the **Quiz** panel, check the **Partial Score** box. **(C)**
2. In the work area, select an individual question option.
3. On the **Options** tab of the **Properties** panel, adjust the number in the **Points** field. **(D)**

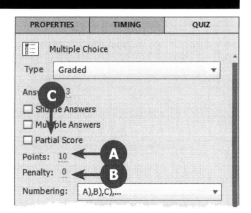

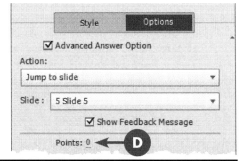

The Review Area

In addition to feedback when the question is answered, you can also provide a post-quiz review. During the review, small icons let the student know what the correct answer is. However, incomplete messages, feedback on short answer questions, and feedback on some question widgets use the review area **(E)** for system-generated feedback when the student goes back and reviews a quiz. You can move and resize the review area to design your page.

From **Quiz Preferences** (**Edit** menu), you can enable or turn the review feature on or off and change the default text for the entire quiz. If you want to change the incomplete message text used for a specific question, select the review area for that question, and then go to the **Properties** panel. You can make edits to the text on the **Options** tab. **(F)**

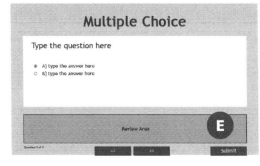

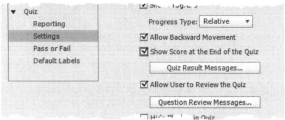

Quiz Preferences p. 213 and 215

CAUTION

- Make sure you do not cover up the review area with any of your slide elements.
- If you resize the review area, check it in preview mode to make sure it is big enough for all the text.

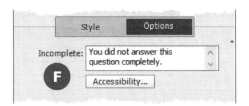

Additional Quiz Properties

In the previous sections on feedback and score, you've learned about most of the properties on the **Quiz** tab. Here are a few more properties that apply to most question types. The following pages cover the properties that are unique to specific question types.

Type (A)

When you added the question, you chose **Graded**, **Survey**, or **Pretest**. You can change that here.

Numbering (B)

Change the type of numbers, letters, and punctuation for the answer options.

Buttons (C)

These buttons appear at the bottom of the slide, giving students options to maneuver through the training. Check or uncheck the boxes based on which buttons you want to include on the slide.

Report Answers (D)

If you check this box, question-specific data will be sent to the learning management system (LMS), rather than just the overall test score.

Interaction ID (E)

If you are sending question-specific data to the LMS, you can enter an interaction number to be sent to the LMS.

Knowledge Check Slides

In addition to regular question slides, you can also create knowledge check slides to test your students. Knowledge check slides look and feel just like regular question slides, but are not included in quiz logic and cannot be reported to a learning management system (LMS).

Add a Knowledge Check Slide

To add a knowledge check slide to your project:

1. Click the **Slides** drop-down button.

2. Select **Knowledge Check Slide**.

3. Check the box for the type of question you would like to use.

4. Enter the number of questions you want for that question.

5. Click the **OK** button.

6. Follow the steps for configuring questions.

Question Types, p. 184
Configuring Questions, p. 186

 CAUTION

Although knowledge check slides look, feel, and operate much like regular question slides, there are a few differences:

- Knowledge check slides can have right and wrong answers with feedback, but the answers cannot be included in quiz scoring logic (results slide).

- Rating scale and random question types are not available for knowledge check slides.

- Knowledge check slides can't be used for survey or pretest questions.

- Unlike a question slide, if a learner passes over a knowledge check slide and then returns to it, the knowledge check slide resets.

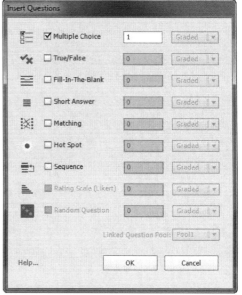

Individual Question Options

The following pages feature elements that are unique to each individual question type.

Multiple-Choice Question Options

Shuffle Answers: Check this box if you want Captivate to shuffle the possible answers so that each student gets the options in a different order. This is great if you don't want your students to "share" answers.

Multiple Answers: Check this box if your question has more than one right answer (e.g., Select all that apply...).

POWER TIP

Remember that with multiple-choice questions, you can have option-specific feedback and scoring.

Add Advanced Feedback, p. 189
Assign Points, p. 190

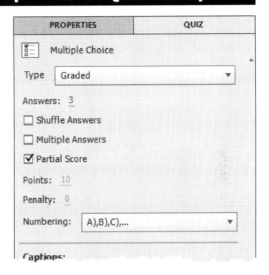

True/False Question Options

True/False questions do not have any properties that are different than the other question types. You can, however, edit the option text boxes right on the slide to change from **true/false** to **yes/no**, **right/wrong**, etc.

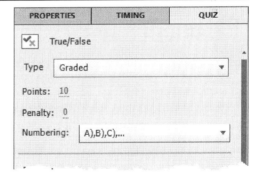

Fill-in-the-Blank Question Options

To set up a fill-in-the-blank question:

1. Type your full statement in the text box provided. **(A)**
2. Select the word/phrase you want the student to fill in.
3. Click the **Mark Blank** button. **(B)**

The part that the student fills in appears as underlined text in edit mode, but appears as a blank in preview mode.

To enter more than one possible correct answer:

1. Double-click your underlined word or phrase. **(C)**
2. Click the **Plus** button in the pop-up window. **(D)**
3. Type any additional correct answers in the box.
4. Repeat steps 2 and 3 for any other answers you want.
5. Click anywhere on the slide to exit the window.

To convert to a drop-down, multiple-choice question:

1. Double-click your underlined word or phrase. **(C)**
2. Click the **User Input** drop-down menu. **(E)**
3. Select **Dropdown List**.
4. Click the **Plus** button. **(D)**
5. Type an answer option.
6. Repeat steps 4 and 5 for additional answer options.
7. Check the box(es) next to the correct answer(s). **(F)**
8. Click anywhere on the slide to exit the window.

BRIGHT IDEAS

- For user input questions, check **Case Sensitive** if you want students to match your capitalization.
- For dropdown list questions, check **Shuffle Answers** if you want to randomize the options.
- Select an option, and click the **Minus** button to delete an answer.
- Use the drop-down menu **(G)** to switch between blanks if you have more than one blank.

CAUTION

- Be careful about user input questions with many correct answers. For example, if the answer is 12:00 p.m., use a dropdown list because of all the correct ways someone could enter that time.
- You can have multiple correct answers on a dropdown list question. It may not be obvious to the students that they can select more than one answer, so either use very clear instructions, or use the multiple-choice question type.

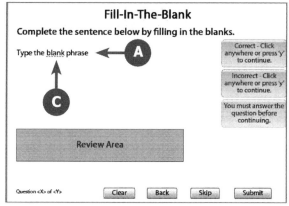

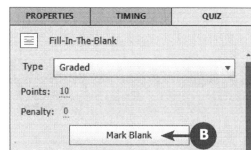

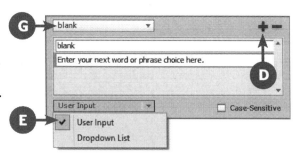

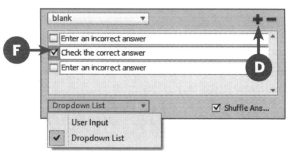

Short Answer Question Options

To enter the correct answer for a graded short answer question:

1. Click the answer text box. **(A)**
2. Enter the correct answer in the dialog box that appears. **(B)**
3. Click the **Plus** button.
4. Type an additional correct answer in the box.
5. Repeat steps 3 and 4 for any other answers you want.
6. Click anywhere on the slide to exit the window.

Options

- Select an answer, and click the **Minus** button to delete that possible answer.
- Check the **Case-Sensitive** box if you want the student to match the capitalization you used.

DESIGN TIPS

- Most short-answer questions are not system-graded because the students are often providing their thoughts and ideas, rather than a specific answer.

- It is best to use a graded short answer test when there is an exact right answer, rather than something subjective. For example, you could use a graded question for "What is our mission statement?" which has only one correct answer, and use a survey question for "How can you put the customer first?" which can have many ways to express the correct answer.

- Even if you have a non-graded survey question, you can still use a single caption with some feedback, or you can take the students to another slide that gives some possible answers for the students to compare their answers to.

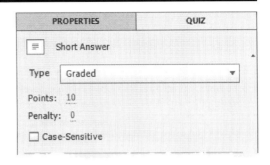

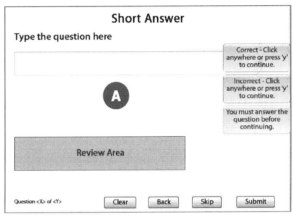

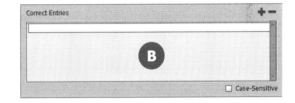

Matching Question Options

To set up a matching question:

1. On the **Quiz** tab, enter the number of options you want in each column. **(A)**

2. Type your options in the text boxes on the slides. **(B)**

3. Select the letter of the correct match from column 2 next to each item in column 1. **(C)**

4. Check **Shuffle Column 1** if you want Captivate to rearrange column 1 to create a different match pattern each time. **(D)**

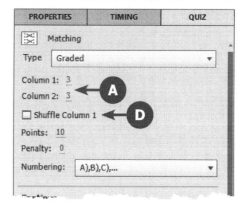

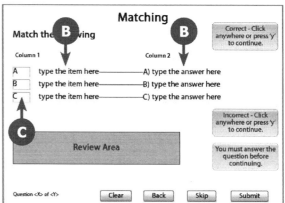

DESIGN TIPS

- If you want distractors (items without a match), then have more items in column 2 than column 1.

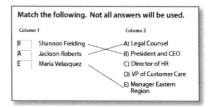

- If you want one item to match to more than one answer, enter the same letter in Column 1.

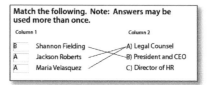

- Be sure to add instructions to let students know about the unmatched or double-matched options.

Hot Spot Question Options

To set up a hot spot question:

1. Place your image(s) on the slide.
2. On the **Quiz** panel, enter the number of hot spots (answers) you want to include. **(A)**
3. Position the hot spot areas on the appropriate places on your slide. **(B)**
4. Select each hot spot on the slide individually.
5. On the **Options** tab in the **Properties** panel for a hot spot, check or uncheck the **Correct Answer** box based on whether or not that hot spot is correct. **(C)**

Quiz Properties Options

Hotspot: When students click on the image, a blue star appears to indicate where they clicked. If you want to change the look of that marker, click the **Browse** button, **(D)** and select a different animation.

Default   *Sample options*

Allow Clicks Only on Hotspots (E): With this box unchecked, students can click anywhere on the slide. With it checked, only clicks in a hotspot count as answers. In the map example, students are only considering the five hot spots. Since they shouldn't be clicking anywhere else, this box could be checked. If you wanted students to consider the whole map, you could add one correct hot spot that was not visible (no stroke or fill) and then check this box. Then, a click anywhere on the map counts as an answer, but only clicks in the one correct hotspot would be correct.

Individual Hot Spot Properties Options

Show hand cursor over hit area: Check this box **(F)** if you want the student's cursor to change to a hand when it is over any hot spot, letting the students know it is a hot spot.

Fill & Stroke: You can make the hot spots either visible or invisible, based on whether or not you use a fill and stroke. Keep them invisible for a more challenging question that makes the student consider all parts of the image. Make them visible if you only want the students to consider certain areas of the image, as in the example shown on the right.

 DESIGN TIP

Be sure to provide clear instructions! For example, let students know if more than one hot spot is correct and that they can undo a selection by clicking the same spot again.

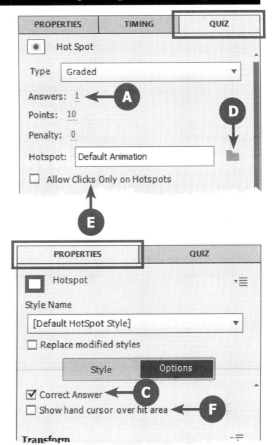

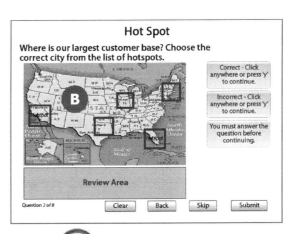

 Fill & Stroke, p. 98

Sequence Question Options

When you set up a sequence question, you enter the items in the proper order, and then Captivate shuffles the options for the student to see in the published project.

To set up a sequence question:

1. In the **Answers** field, enter the number of items you want to use.

2. In the **Answer Type** drop-down menu, select either **Drag Drop** or **Drop Down** based on the question format you want.

3. On the slide, enter the answer items in the provided text fields in the correct order.

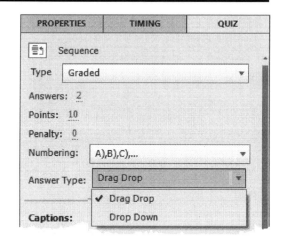

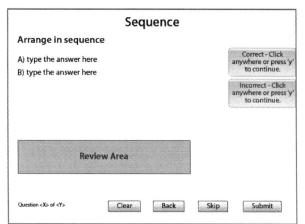

 DESIGN TIP

As with all question types, include clear directions. Students may not realize they are supposed to drag the items around or select them from a drop-down list.

Rating Scale (Likert) Question Options

To set up a rating scale question:

1. In the **Answers** field, enter the number of statements you want the student to evaluate.

2. In the **Rating Scale** drop-down menu, select the number of options you want on the scale (maximum of 5).

3. On the slide, enter the items that the student will evaluate in the text boxes down the left side.

4. Change the rating scale text across the top if you want to use a different scale.

Remember that rating scale questions are only available as survey questions. There are no right or wrong answers, grading, or points.

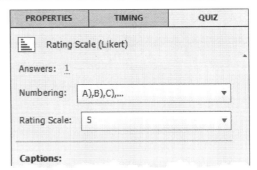

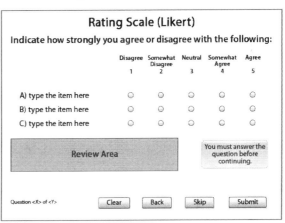

Drag-and-Drop Interaction Wizard

In addition to the questions you can create from question slides, you can also create drag-and-drop interactions with a wizard.

Create a Drag-and-Drop Interaction

To create a drag-and-drop interaction:

1. Add at least two objects to a new slide to be used as drag sources (objects to be dragged) or drop targets (objects to drop them on).
2. Click the **Interactions** drop-down button.
3. Select **Drag and Drop**.
4. On the first page of the wizard **(A)**, click the object(s) that will be the drag source(s).
5. Click the **Next** button.
6. On the second page **(B)**, click the drop target(s).
7. Click the **Next** button.
8. On the third page **(C)**, drag a line from the plus icon on each drag item to the center of its corresponding drop target.
9. Click the **Finish** button which appears where the **Next** button is.
10. Configure the properties. (See next page.)

 TIME SAVER

You can group drag or drop items into types to manage the items as a group. This is useful for many-to-one and one-to-many relationships. Select the items, click the plus button **(D)**, and name the group.

Drag-and-Drop Interaction Properties

Unlike the other question types, properties for this interaction type appear on their own tab. The **Drag and Drop** tab appears automatically, and you can use the **Window** menu to show and hide it.

Many of the properties for drag-and-drop interactions are the same as for any question type. Here are some of the properties that are unique to drag-and-drop interactions.

 Configuring Questions, p. 186

Delete: Click the trash can icon **(A)** to remove the drag-and-drop question logic from the page. All of your on-screen elements will stay on the slide.

Create New Interaction: If you don't already have drag-and-drop logic on a slide, you can click this plus icon **(B)** to create a drag-and-drop question. Whereas using the **Interactions** menu brings up the wizard, this option does not. You would need to set up the question manually.

Select: To manage an individual object in the interaction, select it on the slide or from this drop-down menu. You can also select your groups (custom types) from this menu.

Mark as: Here you can change the designation of an item as a drag source or drop target.

Add to: You manage custom type groups here, including adding the selected item to an existing type, adding new types (plus icon), or deleting types (trash can icon).

Format Tab (If Drop Target Selected)

Effects: If you select **Zoom In**, the drop target gets larger when the student's mouse gets near it.

Object Actions: Click this button to bring up the **Accepted Drag Sources** dialog box **(C)** with extra options for how that drop target accepts drag sources.

- **Drag Source Type**: By default, any drag source can be dropped in any drop target. (It may be wrong, but the student can do it.) Uncheck the box for any object that you don't want dropped in that target. If the student drags an unchecked item into that drop target, it will float back to its original position.

- **Action**: You can designate a separate action for each drag source if it is dropped in that drop target.

- **Count**: If you uncheck **Accept All**, the **Count** field becomes active, where you can set a limit for how many drop sources will be accepted. You can then use the radio buttons to indicate what should happen if the count is exceeded. You can have the extra item return to its place or replace an item that's already in the drop target.

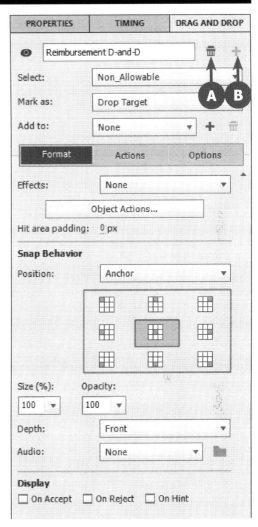

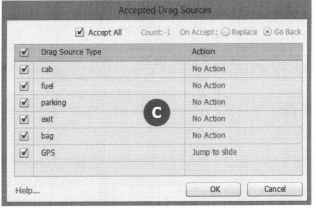

Drag-and-Drop Interaction Properties (cont'd)

Format Tab (If Drop Target Selected, cont'd)

Hit area padding: You can increase this number if you want to make the live area of the drop target larger than the object itself. This means the student's "aim" doesn't have to be precise.

Position: Use this drop-down menu to control how the drag sources are positioned when dropped.

   Anchor: The default option, drag sources are locked to a set point—the point that you select in the thumbnails below the menu. If you have multiple drag sources going to the same drop target, they will overlap.

   Absolute: The drag sources stay exactly where the student drops them.

   Tile: The drag sources are positioned so they don't overlap.

Size: This number controls the size of the drag source after it is dropped. For example, if you set this number to 50%, the drag source will get 50% smaller when dropped into the target.

Opacity: Adjust this number to change the opacity of the drag source when it is dropped in the target. Lowering the number makes the object fade. A value of 0 makes it disappear.

Depth: If your **Position** settings allow drop objects to overlap each other, use this menu to determine whether newly dropped objects appear in front of or in back of the objects already there.

Audio: Use the drop-down menu or the **Browse** button **(A)** if you would like a sound effect to play when an object is dropped in the target.

Display: Use these check boxes to enable captions that appear when objects are dropped on the drop target you have selected. **On Accept** shows a success message. **On Reject** shows a failure message. **On Hint** shows a hint message.

Format Tab (If Drag Source Selected)

Effects: From this menu, you can apply an effect (**Zoom In** or **Glow**) for drag sources while they are being dragged.

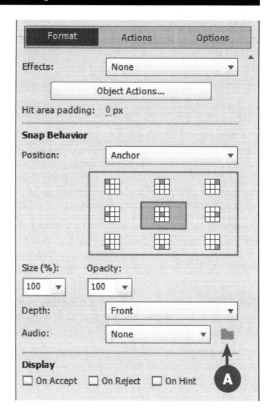

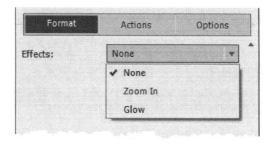

Drag-and-Drop Interaction Properties (cont'd)

Actions Tab

Success/Failure/Attempts: The top half of the **Actions** tab has properties that are found in other question types, such as the action to perform if the student answers correctly vs. incorrectly and the number of attempts.

 Configuring Questions, p. 186

Reset: If you allow more than one attempt, use these radio buttons to designate whether the drag sources should stay where they are (**None**) or snap back to the starting position (**Reset All**).

Pause After X sec: By default, the slide's timeline pauses after 1.5 seconds, giving the students time to interact with your content. You can either change the time for the pause or uncheck the box if you don't want the slide to pause.

Auto Submit Correct Answers: Check this box if you want to evaluate the answers without the student having to click the **Submit** button.

Buttons

Undo: Check this box to put an **Undo** button on the slide so the student can undo his or her last action.

Reset: Check this box to put a **Reset** button on the slide to reset the entire interaction back to the original state.

Reporting: Check the **Include in Quiz** box and configure the options that appear if you want to include the drag-and-drop question in the quiz results.

 Report Answers, p. 191

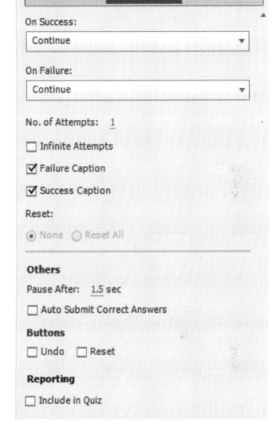

DESIGN TIP

You can find templates for drag-and-drop and other question types from third-party sources online.

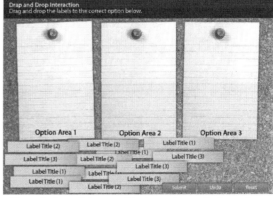

Sample template provided courtesy of eLearning Brothers eLearning Template Library

Drag-and-Drop Interaction Properties (cont'd)

Options Tab

Use Hand cursor: By default, the student's cursor changes from an arrow to a hand when dragging objects. Uncheck this box if you want the cursor to stay as an arrow.

Send Drag Source to original position: By default, if a student drops an object outside any of the targets, the object snaps back to its original position. Uncheck this box if you want the drag source to stay wherever it is dropped, even if it is outside the drop targets.

Play Audio: Check this box to play a default sound effect when a drop target rejects an answer.

Redrag the dropped source: By default, once the student drops an object in one of the targets, the student cannot move it again. Check this box if you want the student to be able to move it again.

Set Correct Answers: Click this button for a dialog box with more options for how to grade the interaction. **(A)**

> **Type**: When **Combination** is selected (the default), the students can drag the objects in any order. If you select **Sequence**, then the objects must be dragged in the order shown in the table.

> **Answer1 table**: Use this table to make modifications to the correct answer pairings you set up when you created the interaction.

>> **Plus button**: Click to add a new row where you can set up a new correct pairing.

>> **Minus button**: Select a row and click the minus button to remove a correct pairing.

>> **Arrow buttons**: If you select **Sequence** from the **Type** menu, use the arrow buttons to put the pairings in the order you want the student to use.

>> **Delete (X) button**: Click this button to delete the entire answer table.

>> **Rows**: In each row, double-click in the **Drop Target** or **Drag Source** column to reveal a drop-down menu where you can select the objects for each correct pairing. Double-click the **Count** cell to change the maximum number of drop sources for the selected drop target.

> **Add New Answer**: Click this button to bring up an extra table where you can set up a completely different set of pairings that would be considered correct.

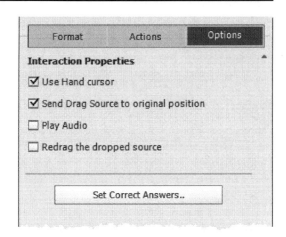

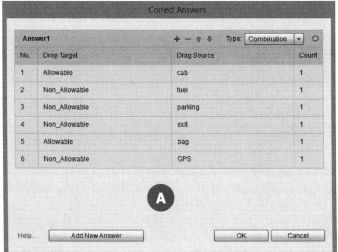

BRIGHT IDEA

Refer to the Adobe Captivate help documentation to review the many hints and cautions around designing a drag-and-drop interaction.

DESIGN TIPS

Drag-and-Drop Object States

When you create a drag-and-drop interaction, you can use the built-in drag-and-drop object states to make the interaction more engaging. For example, you can change the state of an object to show a green checkmark when it's dragged to a correct location or show a red X when it's dragged to an incorrect location.

When you create a drag-and-drop interaction, additional state types become available for the drag source and drop target objects:

Built-in drop source states

- DragOver: The state of an object when a student drags it over a drop target.
- DropAccept: The state of an object when a student drags it to a correct drop target.
- DropReject: The state of an object when a student drags it to an incorrect drop target.
- DragStart: The state of an object when a student starts dragging it.

Built-in drop target state

- DragOver: The state of an object when a student drags an object over it.
- DropAccept: The state of a drop target when a student drops a correct object on it.
- DropReject: The state of a drop target when a student drops an incorrect object on it.
- DropCorrect: The state of a drop target when a student drops a correct object on it and submits the answer.
- DropIncorrect: The state of a drop target when a student drops an incorrect object on it and submits the answer.

 Object States, p. 114

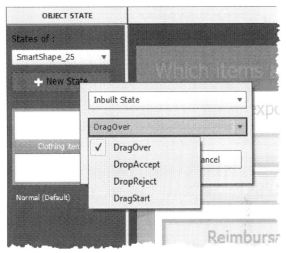

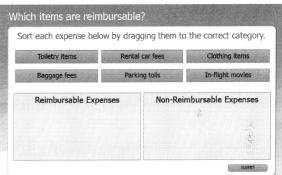

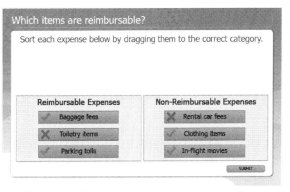

Drag-and-drop interaction showing correct and incorrect states on the drop sources

Importing Questions

GIFT (General Import Format Technology) is a text file format (**.txt**) that uses plain text to create quiz questions. Using a text format instead of the wizard might be faster, especially if you have a lot of questions, and may increase your ability to reuse questions in different systems. (For example, you can import GIFT questions into and export them from Moodle.) You can use the GIFT format to create multiple-choice, true/false, short answer, matching, and numerical question types in Captivate.

Here is the format for a multiple-choice question. Refer to the Adobe Captivate Help documentation for more information on creating GIFT files.

```
::Question Title::
Question
{
~incorrect answer
=correct answer
~incorrect answer
~incorrect answer
}
```

Import GIFT-Format Questions

To import GIFT-format questions:

1. Go to the **Quiz** menu.
2. Select **Import GIFT Format File**.
3. Select the **.txt** file with your questions.
4. Click the **Open** button.

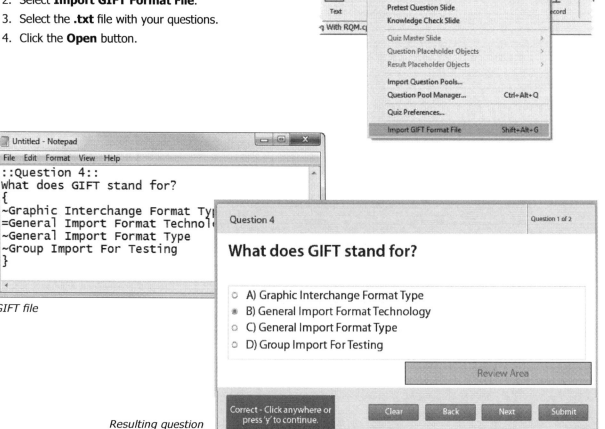

GIFT file

*Resulting question
in Captivate*

Creating Pretests

When building questions, you can designate them to be part of a pretest that includes special pass/fail logic. For example, you can have a pretest where students who achieve an 80% or higher on the pretest can start the course, and those who don't go to a separate module with some foundational information. You can have one pretest per Captivate project, and the pretest scores do not affect the quiz results reported to a learning management system.

Add a Pretest Question

To add a pretest question:

1. Click the **Slides** drop-down button.
2. Select **Question Slide**.
3. Check the box(es) for the question type(s) to add.
4. In the middle column, enter the number of questions you want for that question type.
5. Select **Pretest** from the drop-down menu.
6. Click the **OK** button.
7. Configure your question as described in the first part of this chapter.

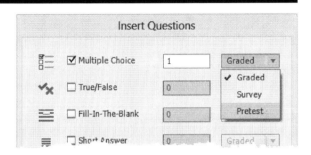

Configure Pretest Logic

To configure pretest logic:

1. Go to the bottom of the **Quiz** panel on any of your pretest slides.
2. Click the **Edit Pretest Action** button.
3. In the **If** section, adjust the passing percentage, if needed.
4. In the **Actions** section, configure the action that you want if the student passes the pretest.
5. Click the **Else** header.
6. Configure the action that you want if the student does not pass the pretest.
7. Click the **Update Action** button.
8. Click the **OK** button in the dialog box.
9. Click the **Close** button.

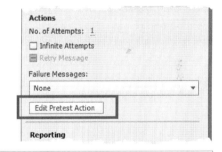

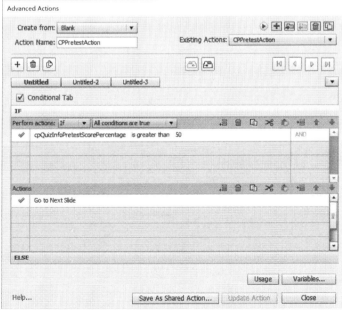

Conditional Actions, p. 175

Quiz Master Slides

When you use a pre-installed theme, it includes master slides for questions. You don't have to do anything special to use or find them—just apply the theme and add the question.

When creating your own theme and master slides, you can create quiz master slides as part of them.

 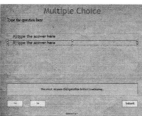 

Master Slides, p. 44
Results Slides, p. 212

Create a Quiz Master Slide

To create a quiz master slide:

1. Go to the **Window** menu.
2. Select **Master Slide**.
3. Go to the **Quiz** menu.
4. Select **Quiz Master Slide**.
5. Select the type of question master you want.
6. Go to the **Quiz** menu.
7. Select **Question Placeholder Objects** or **Result Placeholder Objects**.
8. Select the type of placeholders you want.
9. Format the placeholder objects.
10. Add any static objects, such as text and graphics.

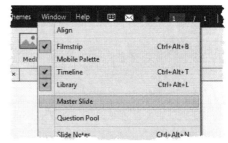

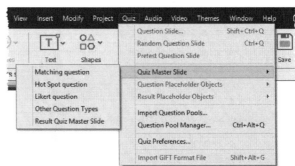

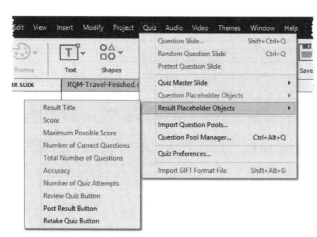

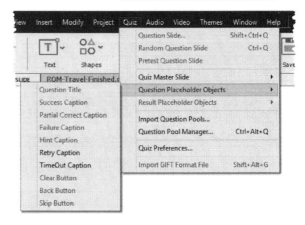

Question Pools

Question pools let you add questions to your project at random, making each user's experience unique. Rather than entering a specific question at a certain point in the project, Captivate selects a question from a group (or pool) of questions that you've created. You can create as many pools as you'd like.

Use question pools when you want to discourage "sharing" of answers or when you want students to get a different set of questions if they need to retry the quiz.

Question pools are separate entities from the actual presentation. If all you do is create a question pool, no questions will appear in your project. You'll need to insert a random question placeholder into your project that pulls questions from the pool.

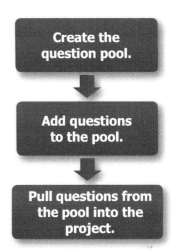

Create the question pool.

Add questions to the pool.

Pull questions from the pool into the project.

Create a Question Pool

To create a new question pool:

1. Go to the **Quiz** menu.
2. Select **Question Pool Manager**.
3. Double-click the name of the pool to rename it, if needed.
4. Click the **Plus** sign in the upper-left corner to create additional pools.
5. Edit the name of the additional pools.
6. Click the **Close** button.

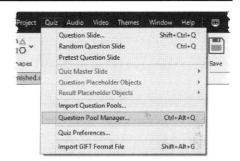

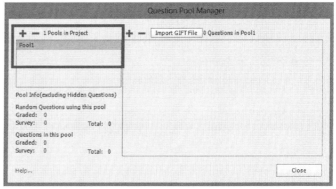

DESIGN TIP

Create a separate pool for each learning objective so you'll know each objective is represented in the quiz.

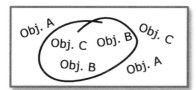

Three questions pulled randomly from one group

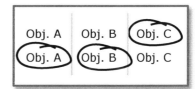

One question pulled randomly from three groups

Add Questions to a Question Pool

To add a question to a pool:

1. Go to the **Quiz** menu.
2. Select **Question Pool Manager**.
3. Select the pool you want to work with. **(A)**
4. Click the **Plus** button on the right. **(B)**
5. In the **Insert Questions** dialog box, select the type and number of questions you want to add.
6. Click the **OK** button in the **Insert Questions** dialog box.
7. Click the **Close** button in the **Question Pool Manager**.

You can add and delete pools and questions from the pool using the **Plus** and **Minus** buttons:

- Add and delete pools **(C)**
- Add and delete questions **(B)**

Rather than build questions with the question wizard, you can click the **Import GIFT File** button for step 4 to add your questions.

 Importing Questions, p. 206

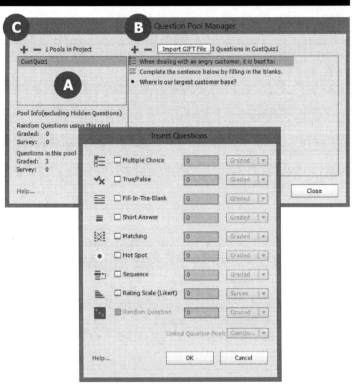

Manage Questions in the Question Pool

Remember that question pool questions are not added to your project, so they cannot be found in your filmstrip. Instead, you can edit the questions from the **Question Pool** panel, found at the bottom of the interface. If the **Question Pool** panel isn't visible, you can go to the **Window** menu to add it.

From the **Question Pool** panel, you can:

- Select a question to show it in the work area so you can work on the question.
- Click the **Add Questions** link to add a new question to that pool.
- Click the drop-down menu to move between the different pools associated with this project.
- Click the **Browse** button **(D)** to bring up the **Question Pool Manager** dialog box.

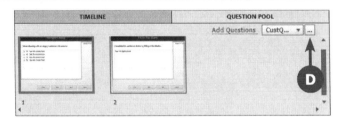

 TIME SAVER

Import question pools from other projects from the **Quiz** menu. Select **Import Question Pools**.

 BRIGHT IDEA

You can move a pool question into another pool or out of the pool to work like a regular question again.

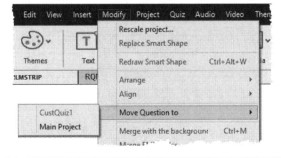

Pull a Question From a Pool to Your Project

Questions in a question pool are not included in your published course unless you specifically pull them in.

To randomly pull questions from your pool into your project:

1. Go to the **Quiz** or **Insert** menu.

2. Select **Question Slide**.

3. In the **Insert Questions** dialog box, check **Random Question**.

4. Enter the number of questions you want to pull from the pool.

5. From the **Linked Question Pool** drop-down menu, select the question pool you want to pull from.

6. Click the **OK** button.

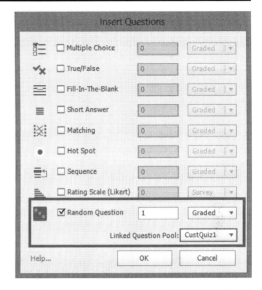

When you add questions to your project from a question pool, they appear as placeholder slides. You cannot edit the questions from the placeholders because they do not represent a single question. They merely represent where one of the questions will end up going in the published project. If you want to edit the question, go to the **Question Pool** panel. (See previous page.)

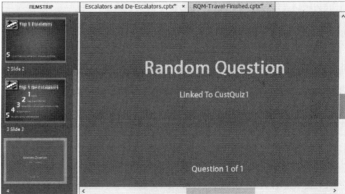

Random Question Properties

When you select the random question slide in the filmstrip, you can see properties in the **Quiz** panel. Most of these properties are the same as for other question slides, such as points and success actions.

In addition, you can change which question pool you want to pull from and add more questions to the pool.

 Configuring Questions, p. 186

Quiz Results Slides

When you add the first quiz question to a project, Captivate adds a quiz results slide, showing the users how they did.

There are many things you can do to a results slide in the same way you would for any slide. You can:

- Hide the slide if you don't want it. For example, if you just want a simple reinforcement question, you may not want a results slide.
- Move it to a different location in the project.
- Apply formatting.
- Add, delete, and move elements, such as text and graphics.

Below you will find some of the editing options that are unique to quiz results slides.

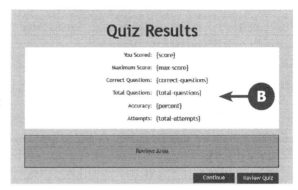

Manage the Quiz Results Slide

To turn scoring data on and off:

1. Click the **Quiz** panel.
2. Check or uncheck the boxes for the features you want.

To add custom scoring elements from variables:

1. Add a text caption or shape to hold the text.
2. In the **Format** pane for that object, click the **Insert Variable** button. **(A)**
3. Find and select the variable you want.

 Display a Variable, p. 172
Quizzing Variables, p. 302

To remove a graded quiz question from the score:

1. Select the slide for the question you want to change.
2. On the **Quiz** tab, uncheck the **Report Answers** box.

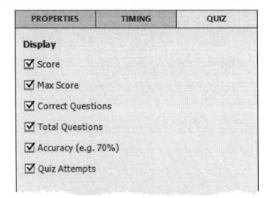

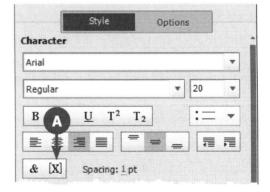

 CAUTION

Be careful about making any changes to the variable placeholders **(B)**. Always preview your work to make sure the variables display properly.

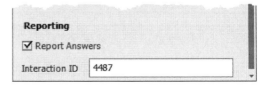

Quiz Preferences

Quiz preferences govern the quiz as a whole. They are found in the **Preferences** dialog box, which can be accessed from the **Edit** menu or the **Quiz** menu.

Change Quiz Preferences

To change the quiz preferences:

1. Go to the **Quiz** menu.

2. Select **Quiz Preferences**.

3. In the **Quiz** section, click each category, and change the settings you want.

4. Click the **OK** button.

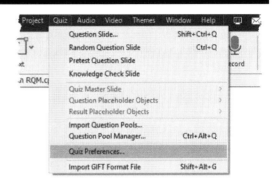

Reporting Category

The **Reporting** category governs how the course interacts with a learning management system or other tracking system. This category is covered in the Publishing chapter.

 Publishing, ch. 12

Settings Category

Name: Enter a name for the quiz, if needed.

Required (A): Indicate whether you want the student to be required to take the quiz:

- **Optional - The user can skip this quiz**

- **Required - The user must take this quiz to continue**: This means the student has to click through all the slides in the quiz—it does not mean the student has to pass or even answer the questions.

- **Pass Required - The user must pass this quiz to continue**

- **Answer All - The user must answer every question to continue**: The student does not have to pass, though.

Objective ID: Use this field to identify the quiz to which a question slide belongs.

Interaction ID Prefix: To help you manage all the data tracked for quiz questions (answer on first attempt, answer on second attempt, etc.), you can assign a prefix that will go at the beginning of all the interaction IDs that are created for this quiz.

 Interaction ID, p. 191

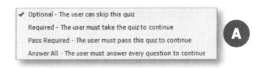

Change Quiz Preferences (cont'd)

Settings Category (cont'd)

Shuffle Answers

This is a global setting for the entire quiz that shuffles the answers for any question type with multiple answers, such as multiple-choice questions. This can be overridden at the question level.

Clear/Back/Skip

These three buttons can be added via the **Quiz** panel on any given question. Here you can set the default for the quiz.

Review Mode Navigation Buttons

Down farther in the settings, you have the option of letting students review the quiz. If you enable this option, the question slides get their own next and back buttons that appear only in review mode. Uncheck this box if you don't want these buttons to appear.

Submit All

If you check this box, students' answers are not graded until the end of the quiz. A **Submit All** button appears on each quiz slide, but does not work until all questions are answered. The quiz result is only sent to a learning management system when the **Submit All** button is clicked on the last question slide. If you select this option, you can click the **Submit All Messages** button to customize the language that the student sees.

Branch Aware

If you have branching in your quiz, a student might not take all of the questions in the quiz. If so, check this box so that the student's grade is calculated based on the number of questions taken instead of the total number of questions.

 Add Advanced Feedback, p. 189

Show Progress

Check this box if you want to include a page count at the bottom of the question slides. Select **Relative** from the **Progress Type** drop-down menu if you want to show the page number and the total number of pages in the quiz. Select **Absolute** if you only want to show the page number.

Allow Backward Movement

Uncheck this box if you want to remove the **Back** button from all the slides in the quiz. You can override this at the question level.

Change Quiz Preferences (cont'd)

Settings Category (cont'd)

Show Score at the End of the Quiz

Uncheck this box if you do not want to include a quiz results slide. Check it again to bring it back.

Quiz Result Messages

Click this button to customize the appearance of a quiz results slide.

Messages: Check the boxes if you want pass and fail messages to appear, and customize the text, if needed.

Score: Check or uncheck the boxes of the slide features you want. These options can also be changed on the **Quiz** tab of the results slide.

 Quiz Results Slides, p. 212

Allow User to Review the Quiz

Check this box if you want to add a **Review Quiz** button to the quiz results slide that lets students go back and review the questions, their answers, and the correct answers, without being able to make any changes.

Question Review Messages

Click this button to customize the text shown to the student during the review. Visual indicators are used to show the students the correct and incorrect answers. To make the course accessible to those using screen readers, you can enter the corresponding text used for the visual symbols.

Hide Playbar in Quiz

If you enable the playbar in your project's skin, you can check this box if you want to hide the playbar on all quiz questions. This prevents the student from moving forward or backward using the playbar.

 Configure Project Skin, p. 244

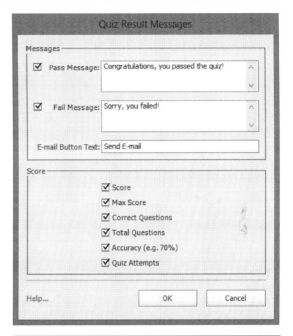

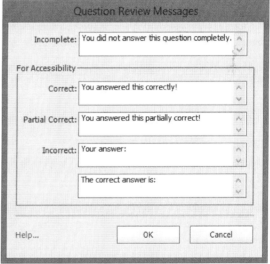

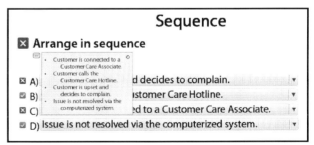

Visual indicators for correct and incorrect answers

Change Quiz Preferences (cont'd)

Pass or Fail Category

Pass/Fail Options: Select the first radio button if you want to grade based on percentage or the second radio button to base it on raw score. Then, enter the passing score for the score type you chose.

If Passing Grade: Select the action that you want to execute if the student achieves the passing score listed above. For example, you may want to branch to a certain slide.

If Failing Grade: Indicate what you want to have happen if the student does not achieve the passing score.

> **Attempts**: Enter the number of attempts you want to give the student, or check the box if you want to allow infinite attempts.
>
> **Show Retake Button**: If you allow more than one attempt, check this box if you want to add a **Retake Quiz** button.
>
> **Action**: Select the action you want to execute if the student does not achieve the passing score.

If the student has not passed the test in the designated number of attempts, the **Retake Quiz** button disappears and the failing grade action is executed.

 Actions, ch. 7

Default Labels Category

This category lets you change all the default styles and messages for the buttons and feedback. For example, if you want to change the message in the success captions when they first appear, you can modify the default here so that you don't have to change the text on each and every slide.

 Styles, p. 110

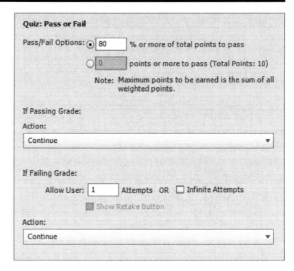

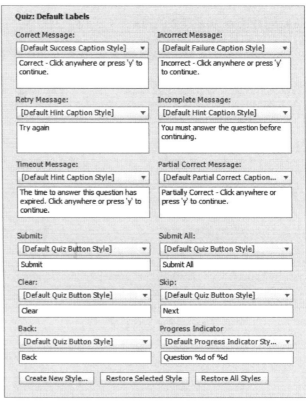

Special Tools & Wizards

Introduction

Adobe Captivate comes with a number of special features designed to save you time and provide more options. In this chapter, you will learn about:

- **Aggregator and Multi-SCORM Projects**: These let you combine multiple projects into one course.

- **Adobe Captivate Draft**: Adobe Captivate Draft is a free app for the iPad that lets you quickly create e-learning content on the go.

- **Templates**: Templates help you save time and achieve a consistent look.

- **Spell Check**: Use this handy tool to check the spelling in captions, slide notes, slide names, text animations, and quizzes.

- **Find and Replace**: With this tool you can search for certain words, any type of object, or any style of any object.

- **The Library**: The library provides one convenient place to manage all the assets in your project.

- **Widgets**: Widgets are configurable **.swf** files that let you extend the capabilities of Captivate.

- **Exporting and Importing to XML**: XML files can let you do things outside of Captivate. For example, you can export to XML, translate your content or do a find/replace to update text, and then import the updated XML back into Captivate.

- **Sharing and Reviewing**: With these features, you can share files and use Adobe Captivate Reviewer to capture and manage feedback from reviewers.

- **Preferences**: You've learned about many preferences so far in the book. In this chapter, you'll learn about the ones that aren't covered in other chapters.

- **Assets**: You can download media assets (some free and some for a fee) to help you design your courses.

In This Chapter

Notes

Aggregator Projects

An aggregator project lets you string together separate Captivate published courses (movies). For example, if you are creating a course on how to use a document management system, you might have five separate screen demonstrations, five practices, and a brief lesson on business rules. Rather than distributing these as individual courses, you can publish them all together as a single, complete course. Aggregator projects can be made up of multiple published **.swf** files created in Captivate.

CAUTION

Aggregator projects can only contain published **.swf** files created in Captivate, not **.swf** files created elsewhere, such as in Flash. All files must be using the same version of ActionScript. You can see the version of ActionScript in the **Publish** dialog box for that project.

Create an Aggregator Project

To create an aggregator project:

1. Publish all the projects you want to include in the aggregator project.
2. Go to the **File** menu.
3. Select **New Project**.
4. Select **Aggregator Project**.
5. Click the **Add Module** button. **(A)**
6. Find and select the published **.swf** to add.
7. Click the **Open** button.
8. Repeat steps 5-7 to add additional files.
9. Configure the settings. (See below.)
10. Click the **Save** button to save the project.

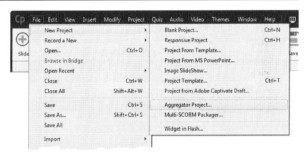

Aggregator Project Settings

Master Movie: One of the courses can be designated as the master. The table of contents settings and project information for that course will be used for the entire aggregator project. Select the course you want to use as the default, and then check this box.

If you want to create course information specific to this aggregator project and not pull it from any of the existing courses, click the **Info** button, and add the course information you want to use.

Movie Titles: Double-click the module title in the list to rename it. If you don't want the title to appear in the published table of contents, select the movie and uncheck the **Include Module Title** check box.

Moving and Deleting Movies: To change the order of the courses, select a course and click the up or down arrow buttons. To delete a course, select it, and then click the **Delete** button. **(B)**

Preview: Click this button to preview what the published project will look like.

Preloader: Click the **Browse** button **(C)** to select an image to show when the published project is loading.

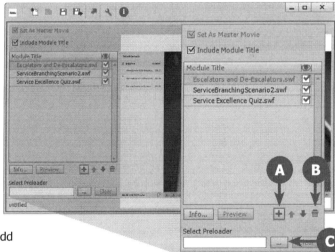

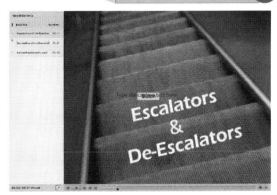

Published project

Publish an Aggregator Project

To publish an aggregator project:

1. Click the **Publish Aggregator Project** button. **(A)**

2. In the dialog box, select the output format you want.

3. Enter a title for the published project.

4. Enter or browse for the location where you want to save the published project.

5. Select the publish settings you want. (See below.)

6. Click the **Publish** button.

Publish Settings

Format: Select from Flash output (**.swf**), Windows-compatible executable file (**.exe**), or Mac-compatible executable file (**.app**).

Publish To Folder: Check this box if you want Captivate to create a separate folder for your published files.

Export To HTML: This option, checked by default, creates an HTML page and a JavaScript file that embeds the **.swf** file into the HTML page. Uncheck it if you only want to publish the **.swf** file. Having the HTML page may be necessary based on how you plan to display the course.

Export PDF: Check this option to create a PDF document that plays the **.swf** file.

ZIP Files: Check this box if you want your published files to be zipped up into a **.zip** compressed folder.

Full Screen: This option includes HTML files that cause the browser window to open up to its maximum size and hide browser elements, such as the toolbar and **Favorites** bar.

Custom Icon: If you choose the **Win Executable** format, you can find and select an icon to associate with the executable file. This icon appears in the user's task bar and next to the file name in Windows Explorer.

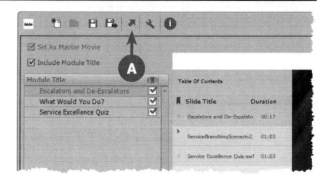

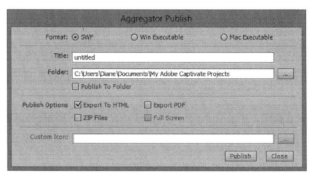

 CAUTION

- Because Aggregator projects are based on Flash output, they will not work on mobile devices or with newer browsers that only support HTML5 output.

- Aggregator projects do not work with learning management systems (LMS). If you need to integrate with an LMS, use the Multi-SCORM Packager.

 Multi-SCORM Packager, p. 222

Aggregator Preferences

There are additional aggregator settings in the **Aggregator Preferences** dialog box, which you can access by clicking the **Publish Settings** button.

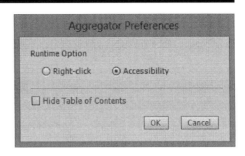

Runtime Option: If you'd like to enable right-click shortcuts for the student in the aggregator menu, select **Right-click**. However, the special logic needed to enable that right-click menu will disable accessibility features. So if you want the menu to be accessible, select **Accessibility** instead.

 Accessibility, p. 289

Hide Table of Contents: Check this box if you want to turn off the table of contents completely in the published project.

Manage Aggregator Files

You can open existing aggregator files from the main Captivate interface, or from the aggregator window if it is already open. Aggregator projects have a file extension of **.aggr**.

To open an existing aggregator file from Captivate:

1. Go to the **File** menu.
2. Select **New Project**.
3. Select **Aggregator Project**.
4. Click the **Open Aggregator Project** button.
5. Find and select the project you want.
6. Click the **Open** button.

If the aggregator window is already open, simply start with step 4.

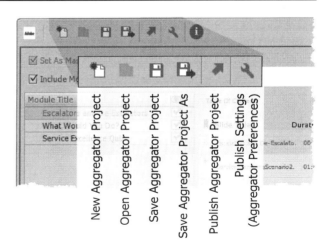

Multi-SCORM Package

The Multi-SCORM Packager lets you combine multiple files into a single shareable courseware object (SCO) to be uploaded to an LMS. The SCO can contain one or more projects from Captivate (**.zip** with SCORM settings), Flash learning interactions (using the LMS Adapter for tracking), Flash quizzes (**.fla**), Adobe Presenter (as a **.zip**), and quizzes made in Dreamweaver with the Coursebuilder extension (converted to SCORM package).

Create a Multi-SCORM Package

To create a new Multi-SCORM Package:

1. Go to the **File** menu.
2. Select **New Project**.
3. Select **Multi-SCORM Packager**.
4. Select the template you want. (See below.)
5. Enter the course manifest details.
6. Click the **OK** button.

(Continued on next page.)

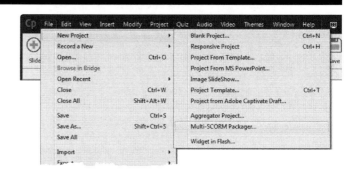

Template Options

You have three options for a course template:

Multiple SCOs

This course can contain any type and number of SCO files. The final score will be an average across all assessments.

Simple Remediation

The course can have many modules; each module with content and a post-test. Each post-test can be given a weight, with the final weighted average being reported to the LMS.

Pre-Test or Post-Test Rollup

The course can have many modules, each module with a pre-test, content, and a post-test. Students get credit for each module if they pass the pre-test. Content and post-tests are only enabled if a student fails the pre-test. Each post-test can be given a weight, with the final weighted average being reported to the LMS.

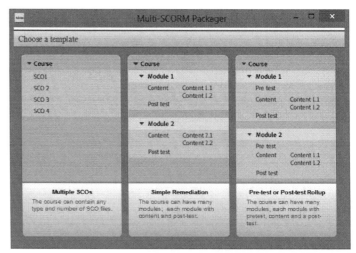

 CAUTION

The Multi-SCORM Packager uses the SCORM 2004 standard (and SCORM 1.2 for the **Multiple SCO** option). Each included file must be published to the same standard. If your LMS requires a different standard, then the packager will not work for you. Test a sample early on to make sure it works with your LMS.

Create a Multi-SCORM Package (cont'd)

(continued from previous page)

7. Click the plus button for the section you want to add content to.

8. Find and select the SCO or PDF file you want to add.

9. Click the **+ Module** button to add additional modules to the template.

10. Click the **Publish Course** button. **(A)**

11. In the dialog box **(B)**, enter the project title and location for publishing.

12. Click the **Publish** button.

Package Options

*   The **PreTest** and **Post-test** sections can only have one file each. Content sections can have multiple files. To rearrange them, select a file and then use the up and down arrows at the bottom of the dialog box. If the modules need to be completed in a set order, check the **Force Content Sequence** box.

*   To change the name of the course or a module, click the pencil icon next to that item.

*   Click the trash can icon at the bottom of the dialog box to delete all content in the selected module.

*   By default, all post-tests are given an equal weight. Click the blue text in the **Weightage** fields if you want to give a quiz more or less weight. **(C)**

*   If you are using the **Multiple SCOs** template, you won't see as many of these options.

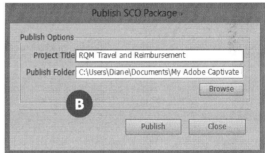

Adobe Captivate Draft Projects

Adobe Captivate Draft is a free app for the iPad that lets you quickly create e-learning content on the go. With the Adobe Captivate Draft app, you can create simple projects using basic objects, shapes, and other interactive objects. You can also insert videos, add web objects, and create true/false, multiple choice, matching, and sequence questions.

With the Adobe Captivate Draft app, you can sync your project to the Adobe Creative Cloud to be reviewed and edited by others. Finally, you can export your project from the app and open it to be edited and published in Adobe Captivate.

Import a Project from the Adobe Captivate Draft App

To import a project from an Adobe Captivate Draft project (.cpdx):

1. On the **Welcome** screen, click the **New** tab.
2. Select **From Adobe Captivate Draft**.
3. Find and select the Adobe Captivate Draft project (**.cpdx**) you want.
4. Click **OK**.

 CAUTION

- Although the Adobe Captivate Draft app includes features to create basic content with objects and shapes, it does not let you work with actions or variables.

- Because the Adobe Captivate Draft app exports and syncs projects to the Creative Cloud, you must have a paid Creative Cloud subscription to download the Adobe Captivate Draft project file (.cpdx).

*True/false question created
in Adobe Captivate Draft*

*True/false question imported
into Adobe Captivate*

Templates

Templates help you create a consistent, professional look for your projects and help you save time in the development process. A Captivate template includes slides, objects, placeholder objects, placeholders for recording slides or question slides, master slides, styles, preferences, and slide notes. Project templates have a **.cptl** extension.

BRIGHT IDEA

Use **Slide Notes** to provide instructions on how to use the template.

For example, if you are creating a series of computer simulations, you can create a template that is set to the right size, has the skin configured the way you want, is set up with all the default styles you want, and has introductory text and closing text placeholders. If you like branching scenarios, you can create a template that has all the pages set up with buttons branching to the different pages. Then, all you have to do is add the content to the pages.

Create a Project Template

To create a project template:

1. Go to the **File** menu.
2. Select **New Project**.
3. Select **Project Template**.
4. In the dialog box, select the size for the project.
5. Click the **OK** button.
6. Add any slides you want.
7. Add standard project elements. (See below.)
8. Go to the **Insert** menu.
9. Select **Placeholder Objects** or **Placeholder Slides**.
10. Select the placeholders you want. **(A)** (See below.)

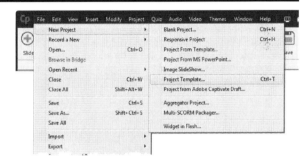

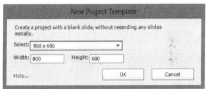

Standard Project Elements

You can add content and configure settings in a template much the same as any project. You can add and delete slides, create slide masters, add objects to slides, set default styles, etc. These slides and objects appear exactly the same way in any project created from the template. For example, if there is a caption at the end of each simulation that says "Click Next to continue," you could add it as a regular caption object with that text.

Placeholder Objects

In addition to standard elements, you can add placeholder objects. Placeholder objects put in a gray placeholder that you can fully format and configure properties for, but contain no actual content. When someone creates a project from the template, they can quickly add the project-specific content to the placeholders. For example, if the text of your closing caption varies from project to project, add it as a placeholder caption instead of a standard caption.

Placeholder Slides

A placeholder slide adds a slide to allow for either screen recording or quiz questions.

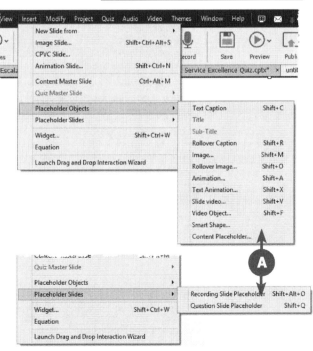

Create a New Project From a Template

To create a new project from a template:

1. Go to the **File** menu.
2. Select **New Project**.
3. Select **Project From Template**.

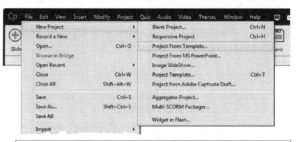

Modifying Standard Elements

When you create a project from a template, you can still add and modify content and settings like you would with any other project. For example, you can delete unwanted slides, add new ones, or change the formatting on objects.

Modifying Placeholder Objects

To add your content to a placeholder, double-click the placeholder. The resulting steps vary based on the type of placeholder. For example, with a caption or rollover caption, the placeholder converts to an editable caption with standard formatting. With an image placeholder, a dialog box appears so you can find and select the image you want.

When you add content from placeholders, they appear with the settings from the template. However, you can override those settings, if you want to. For example, you could change the size of an image or the caption type of a caption.

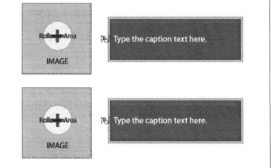

Rollover interaction template with image placeholders and rollover caption placeholders

Adding Questions and Screen Recordings

Double-click the placeholder slide to either add questions or initiate screen recording.

BRIGHT IDEA

How is a template different than a theme?

A *theme* is a set of styles and individual slide templates that can be applied to any project, but it is not a project itself. You need to create a project and add the slides using the options in the theme.

A *template* creates an actual project. When you create a new project from a template, it can have slides already in it—with either actual or placeholder content. For example, you might always have a title slide, an objectives slide, a quiz instructions slide, and a closing slide that are similar.

 Themes, p. 47

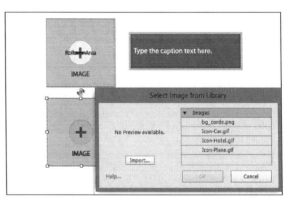

Pop-up window that appears when you double-click an image placeholder

TIME SAVER

You can save an existing project as a template. Just use **Save As**, and select **Captivate Template Files** in the **Save as type** drop-down menu.

Question Slide
Placeholder
Double-click to insert questions

Text-Editing Tools

Check Spelling

The spell check feature in Captivate checks captions, slide notes, slide names, text animations, and quizzes.

To check the spelling in your project:

1. Go to the **Project** menu.
2. Select **Check Spelling**.

Click the **Options** button to change the spell check settings, such as the default language and types of words to ignore.

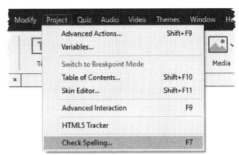

 CAUTION

The spell checker does NOT check alt text added via the **Accessibility** menu.

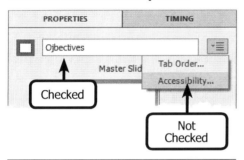

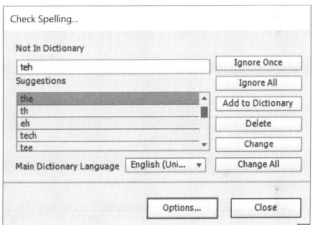

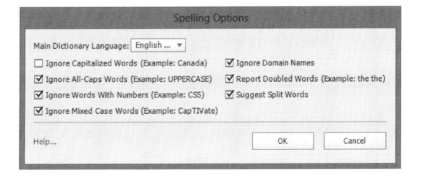

Find and Replace

Find and Replace lets you search for and replace text just like you can in most word processing software. In addition, you can search for certain types of objects, such as rollover captions. This can make it easier to find something in a large project.

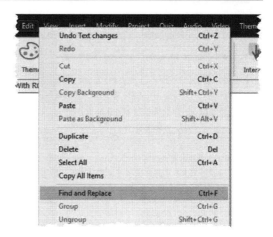

To find text or object types:

1. Go to the **Edit** menu.

2. Select **Find and Replace**.

3. In the **Search In** drop-down menu, select the type of object you want to search in or for, or select **All Object Types**.

4. In the **Style** field, select the styles you want to search in or for, if needed.

5. In the **Find** field, enter the text you want to look for, if needed.

6. In the **Replace** field, enter the text you want to replace the found text with, if needed.

7. Check and uncheck the boxes at the bottom to limit or expand your search.

8. Click one of the four buttons on the right to initiate the search or replacement.

Some fields are only available if your search includes text-related objects.

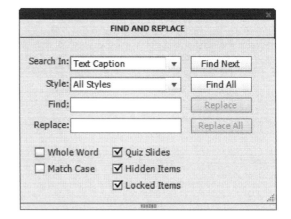

The Library

The library contains all the assets of a project: those currently in use, those added but no longer in use, and those added but not yet used. For example, the library contains:

- The background image and audio of all current slides.
- The background image and audio of all deleted slides.
- Every version of the background image and audio of any slide.
- An image or audio clip you added to the library and then added to a slide.
- An image or audio you added to the library that has not yet been used on a slide.
- Imported content such as PowerPoint presentations or Photoshop files.
- Shared actions

To show the library, click the **Library** button. **(A)**

What can you do with the library?

- Store assets you know you'll need later.
- Revert back to previous versions of an asset.
- Reuse assets over and over again.
- Edit assets.
- Import and export assets.
- Update linked assets, such as a linked PowerPoint or video file.

You can also view important information about your project assets from the library. For example, you can:

Preview the assets: When you select an item in the library, a preview appears in the pane at the top. For audio, video, and animations, click the **Play** button **(B)** to play the media.

Determine if assets are currently in use: The **Use Count** column **(C)** shows you how many times an item is being used in the project. A **0** indicates an unused item.

Sort the assets: Click a column heading to sort the assets by that heading.

Organize into folders: Right-click an item and select **Move to New Folder** to create a new folder with that item. You can drag and drop items into different folders.

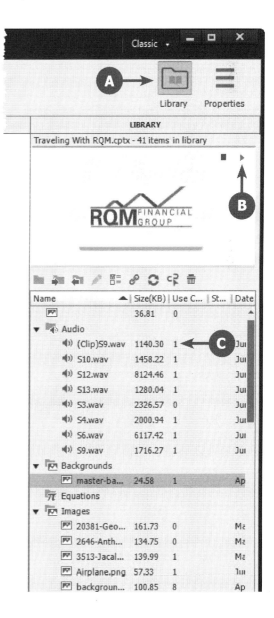

TIME SAVER

You can import a library from another project. Go to the **File** menu, select **Import**, and then **External Library**.

Manage Assets in the Library

You can perform these functions in the library by right-clicking an asset or selecting it and using a button at the top.

To delete an asset:
- Right-click the asset, and select **Delete**. — or —
- Select the asset, and click the **Delete** button.

To delete all unused assets:
- Click the **Select Unused** button, and then click the **Delete** button.

To edit an asset:
- Right-click the asset, and select **Edit with**. — or —
- Select the asset, and click the **Edit** button.

To rename an asset:
- Right-click the asset, and select **Rename**.

To update a linked asset:
- Right-click the asset, and select **Update**. — or —
- Select the asset, and click the **Update** button.

 Update Project Video, p. 94
Update an Imported Slide, p. 37

To use/reuse an asset:
- Drag it to the slide or object you want to add it to.

To export an asset:
- Right-click the asset, and select **Export**. — or —
- Select the asset, and click the **Export** button.

To import an asset into the library:
- Right-click any asset, and select **Import**. — or —
- Click the **Import** button.

To import an asset from another library:
1. Click the **Open Library** button.
2. Find and select the Captivate project with the library you want to use.
3. Click the **Open** button.
4. In the pop-up window, find and select the asset you want to import.
5. Drag the asset to a slide or a folder in the library.

Once you import assets from another project, that project is available from a drop-down menu on the **Open Library** button.

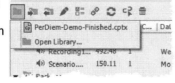

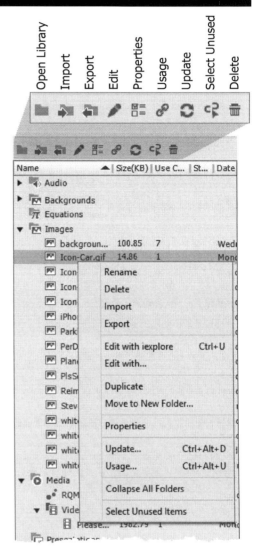

 CAUTION

The library contains all versions of all assets. This can cause problems if:

- You deleted an asset from a slide because there was a problem with it, and then accidentally reused it.

- You had sensitive information that you covered with merged objects, but the original image with that information is still in the library.

- You are concerned about the file size of the **.cptx** file. (Library size does not affect the published course, just the **.cptx** file.)

If these are concerns, it is a good idea to regularly delete unneeded assets.

Widgets

Widgets are Flash objects that can be configured in Captivate without using Flash. Widgets let you enhance and expand the capabilities of Captivate. You can get widgets in one of three ways:

- Use widgets installed with Captivate.
- Download additional widgets from Adobe or third-party sources.
- Create your own in Adobe Flash (not recommended since Adobe has discontinued Flash).

Widgets are configured in two places. With most widgets, a **Widget Properties** dialog box appears when you add the widget. This lets you choose many of the key settings for that widget. In addition, you can configure many of the regular properties in the **Properties** panel. For example, with a button widget, you designate the style and text in the **Widget Properties** dialog box, but you still designate the button actions in the regular **Properties** panel.

Add a Widget

To add a widget:

1. Go to the **Insert** menu.
2. Select **Widget**.
3. Find and select the widget you want.
4. Click the **Open** button.
5. Configure the widget properties. **(A)**
6. Click **OK**.

Pre-installed widgets can be found in the Captivate program files on your hard drive.

The widget properties vary based on the widget being used. To edit the properties after inserting it, click the **Edit** icon in the **Properties** panel. **(B)** The **Properties** panel for a widget is the same as for any animation.

 Animations, p. 69

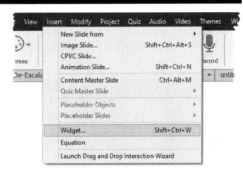

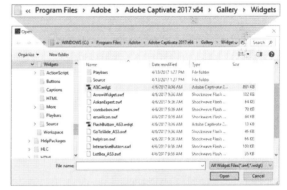

 **CAUTION**

Widgets are Flash based and will not play on mobile devices and newer browsers that only support HTML5 output.

Exporting and Importing XML

Exporting to XML, or extensible markup language, is a way to convert your Captivate project to a text-based form that can be translated, imported into other software applications, or re-imported back into Captivate.

```
<group datatype="plaintext" cp:datatype="x-property" restype="x-cp-slide-label" extype="337">
    <trans-unit id="911-337">
        <source>Standard Fill</source>
    </trans-unit>
</group>
<group datatype="plaintext" cp:datatype="x-property" restype="x-cp-slide-accessibility"
extype="1285">
    <trans-unit id="911-1285">
        <source> </source>
    </trans-unit>
</group>
<group cp:datatype="x-object" restype="x-cp-audio-item" id="1409" extype="275">
    <group cp:datatype="x-object" restype="x-cp-closed-caption-items" id="1410" extype="113">
        <group cp:datatype="x-object" restype="x-cp-closed-caption-item" id="1442"
        extype="114">
            <group datatype="plaintext" cp:datatype="x-property" restype="x-cp-closed-caption-
            name" extype="207">
                <trans-unit id="1442-207">
                    <source>Adding a fill color to your cells can make your spreadsheets more
                    visually interesting. But it can also make them easier to understand. By
                    adding a fill color to header rows or cells with key information, you can
                    make the important elements stand out. </source>
                </trans-unit>
            </group>
        </group>
    </group>
</group>
<group cp:datatype="x-object" restype="x-cp-items" id="912" extype="69">
    <group cp:datatype="x-object" restype="Text Caption" id="1462" extype="19">
        <group cp:datatype="x-paragraph" css-style="line-spacing:1.00;line-indent:0.00">
            <trans-unit id="1462-19-1">
                <source>
                    <g id="1462-19-1-1" css-style="font-family:'Myriad Pro';font-
                    face:'Regular';color:#333333;font-size:18.0pt" ctype="x-cp-font">Select
                    the cells you want to format.</g>
                </source>
```

Export to XML

To export a project to XML:

1. Go to the **File** menu.
2. Select **Export**.
3. Select **To XML**.
4. Find and select the location where you want to save the file.
5. Click the **Save** button.

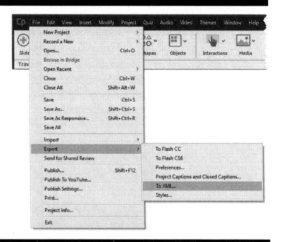

Import From XML

To import a project from XML:

1. Go to the **File** menu.
2. Select **Import**.
3. Select **From XML**.
4. Find and select the file you want to import.
5. Click the **Open** button.

Sharing and Reviewing

Adobe Captivate Reviewer lets you post your course online to capture comments from reviewers, helping you manage the review and editing process more easily. When you send a file for shared review, you can post your course to a server, save it to a network location, or even email the review file (**.crev**). Reviewers can view the project in a special interface that lets them add comments. Your reviewers must first install Adobe AIR and then install Adobe Captivate Reviewer to view the project and add comments. (They do not need Adobe Captivate installed on their computers, though.) You can then accept, reject, or ask for feedback on the comments.

Send for Shared Review

To send for shared review via server/network:

1. Go to the **File** menu.
2. Select **Send for Shared Review**.
3. Enter a name for the file.
4. Click the **Next** button.
5. Enter the locations for the published files and the comments files.
6. Click the **Publish** button.

Once you have done this, let your reviewers know where they can access the **.crev** file, such as on a shared network drive.

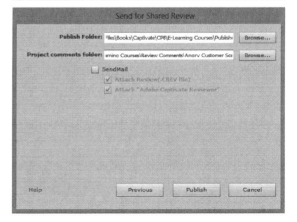

Send for Shared Review (cont'd)

To send for shared review via email:

1. Go to the **File** menu.
2. Select **Send for Shared Review**.
3. Enter a name for the file.
4. Click the **Next** button.
5. Enter the locations for the published files and the comments files.
6. Check the **SendMail** box if you want to generate an invitation email.
7. Check the boxes to include the Captivate review file (**.crev**) and/or the Adobe Captivate Reviewer app.
8. Click the **Email** button.
9. Enter the address, subject line, and message for the email to be sent to the people you are sharing the file with.
10. Click the **SEND** button.

Your reviewers will receive the email and any attachments you selected.

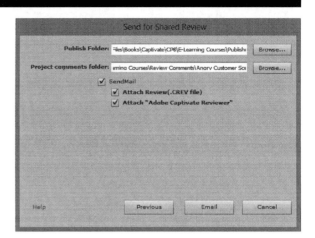

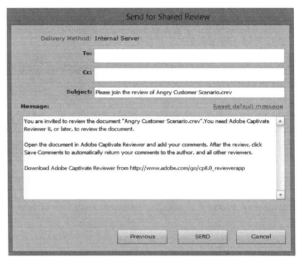

The Adobe Captivate Reviewer toolbar

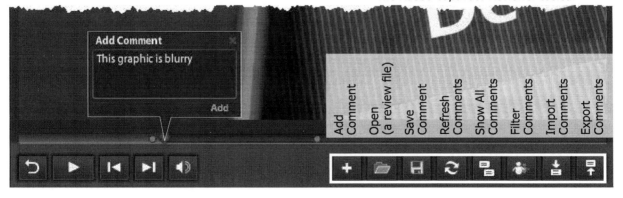

Manage Review Comments

Comments can be managed in the Adobe AIR application or directly in your Captivate project.

To view comments in Captivate:

1. Go to the **Window** menu.
2. Select **Comments**.
3. In the **Comments** panel, click the **Refresh Comments** button.
4. Log in with your Adobe ID, if needed.

There are three ways to look at your comments.

- In the timeline, a dot appears for each comment. Hover over the dot to read the comment. **(A)**

- In the **Comments** pane, you can view all the comments for the project using the **View By** drop-down menu to sort by time, reviewer, or status. **(B)**

- In the filmstrip, a comments icon appears to let you know there is a comment for that slide. **(C)**

The **Comments** pane has a number of buttons to help you manage the comments. For some commands, you need to first check the box next to a comment.

Import Comments: Click this button to incorporate comments that others exported for you.

Export Comments: Click this button to create a back-up file or to share with another user.

Reply: Click this button to type a response to a comment.

Accept: Click this button to change the status to "Accepted." You can include a message here.

Reject: Click this button to change the status to "Rejected." You can include a message here.

Edit Comments: Click this button to edit a comment.

Save Comments: Click this button to save comments.

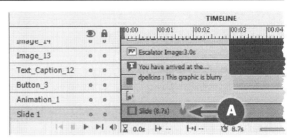

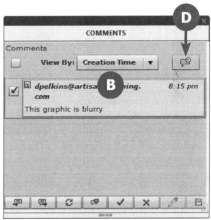

BRIGHT IDEA

Refer to the Adobe Captivate help documentation for more information on how to use the Captivate Reviewer. (Search for **Reviewing Adobe Captivate projects**.)

CAUTION

The **End Review** button **(D)** is not for ending a particular review session. It is for ending the entire review cycle by deleting all of the comments. Only click this button if you are sure you want to delete all of the comments.

Preferences

Preferences, available from the **Edit** menu, has important settings ranging from quality and project defaults to publishing and reporting. In this book, most of the preferences are covered in the chapter relating to that type of preference. The remainder are covered here.

- Recording preferences: chapter 2
- Project preferences: chapter 12
- Quiz preferences: chapter 10

General Settings

Rescale Imported/Pasted Slide: When you copy or import a slide that is a different size than the project is being added to, Captivate keeps the slide elements at their original size. This means they may not fit properly. If you check this box, Captivate rescales the slide objects to fit, which may skew the objects.

Generate Project Backup: Check this box if you want Captivate to create a backup file of your project. It is saved with a **.bak** extension. Change the extension back to **.cptx** to restore the file.

Require Indic Composer: Check this box to author in Indo-European languages, such as Sanskrit, Hindi, Urdu, Bengali, and other languages of India, Pakistan, and Sri Lanka. If it is a right-to-left language, check the box for that as well.

Enable Custom Workspaces: If you check this box, you can rearrange the interface and save your customizations.

Default Locations

>**Publish At**: This is where published projects will be saved, unless you change the location.

>**Project Cache**: Software uses cache to temporarily store data to help speed up processing. This field indicates what location is being used for cache.

>**Clear Cache**: If you are having performance problems, you can clear your cache by clicking here.

>**Comments At**: If you use Adobe Captivate Reviewer, this is where the comments will be saved.

>**Grid Size**: You can use an on-screen grid to help line up objects on a slide. Change this number to make grid lines closer (smaller #) or farther apart (larger #).

Spelling Preferences: Click this button to change spell check preferences.

Confirmation Messages: Captivate displays confirmation messages, such as when you delete a slide. Click this button to turn messages on or off.

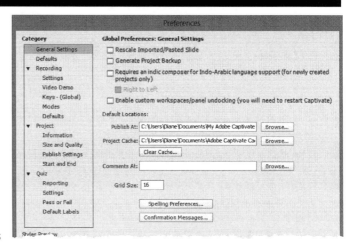

Custom Workspaces, p. 7

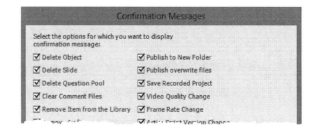

Default Settings

Slide Duration: This the length of slides when they are first added to the project. Change the length (in seconds) if you prefer a different default length.

Snap to Guide Offset: If you choose to snap objects to guides to help with alignment, you can indicte how close the obect has to be to the guide before it snaps to it.

Default Guide Color: Click the color swatch to change the color of any guides you add.

 Guides, p. 107

Background color: By default, all new blank slides have a white background. Change the color here if you want a different default background color.

Preview Next: When you preview a project, one of the options is to preview a small chunk of slides—five by default. **(A)** If you would like that menu option to preview a different number of slides, enter that number here.

Object Defaults: In this section, you can designate the length (in seconds) for how long certain objects appear when they are first added to a project. For example, all text captions are three seconds long when they are first added to the project. If you would like to change the default length, select an object from the first drop-down menu, and enter the length just beneath that. You can also designate a default style for the selected object. Click the **Restore Selected** or **Restore All** buttons to go back to the previously saved settings.

 Styles, p. 110

Autosize Buttons: When you create a text button, the button resizes automatically based on how long the text is. Uncheck this box if you do not want the buttons to resize.

Autosize Captions: When you change the text in a caption, the caption resizes automatically to accommodate the changes in the text. Uncheck this box if you do not want the captions to resize.

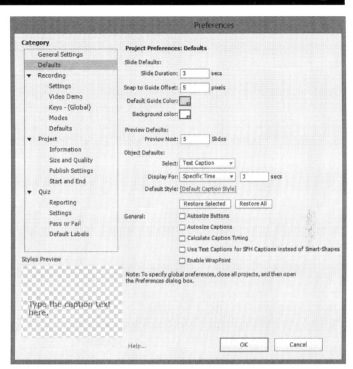

Default Settings (cont'd)

Calculate Caption Timing: By default, captions use the length specified in the **Object Defaults** section when they are added to a project. Check this box if you want the length to be determined by Captivate based on how much text is in the caption. A caption with more text will remain on screen longer, giving the student more time to read it.

Use Text Captions for SFH Captions: When you add interactive objects such as buttons, you can choose to show success, failure, and hint (SFH) messages. By default, these messages are added as shapes with text. If you'd rather have them added as text caption objects instead, check this box.

Enable WrapPoint: In responsive projects, you can enable WrapPoints so that when the screen size reduces to a certain point, objects wrap to the next line instead of just getting smaller. You can designate the wrap point for a slide without making any changes to the preferences here. Check this box if you want to set wrap points for individual fluid boxes.

Once you change this setting, you need to restart Captivate before it takes effect.

 Fluid boxes, p. 274

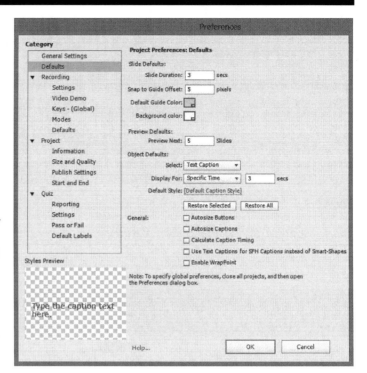

BRIGHT IDEAS

- When working with SFH captions, you can switch back and forth between text captions and shapes via the object's right-click menu.

- If you have a project open when you change the defaults, the changes apply only to that project. If you change them when there are no projects open, they become global preferences for all new projects.

TIME SAVER

You can export preferences from one project/ computer and import them into another project/ computer. On the **File** menu, go to the **Export** or **Import** sub-menu, and select **Preferences**. Preferences are saved as a **.cpr** file.

Assets

Captivate comes with a library of media assets, such as characters, images, videos, templates, and themes. Many of these are free, and others are available for a fee through Adobe Stock.

Download and Insert Assets

To download an asset from Adobe Stock:

1. Click the **Assets** button.
2. Click the **Get Adobe Stock Assets** tab. **(A)**
3. Log into your Adobe Stock account, if needed.
4. Search for the image or video you want.
5. Hover over the shopping cart icon for the asset you want.
6. Select **Buy License & Save to My Library** (or **License and Save to Computer** if you have an Adobe Stock subscription).

To download a free asset from eLearning Brothers:

1. Click the **Assets** button.
2. Click the **Get Free eLearning Assets** tab. **(B)**
3. In the bar at the top, select the type of asset you want.
4. Hover over the asset want.
5. Click the **Download** button.
6. Select the file type you want, if needed.

To insert a previously downoaded asset:

1. Click the **Assets** button.
2. Click the **My Assets** tab. **(C)**
3. Click the button for the type of media you want to add.
4. Select the item you want to add.
5. Click the **Insert** or **Open** button (based on which type of media you chose).

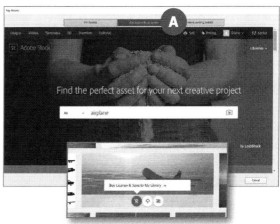

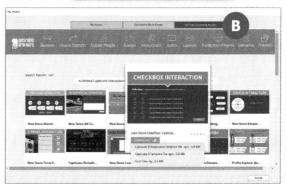

DESIGN TIPS

- With the Adobe Stock collection, you can download a preview to the library to see if you like it before you buy it. Click the middle icon when you hover over an image.

- With the eLearning Brothers library, you can click an asset for a page with more details about that asset.

Notes

Publishing

Introduction

In this chapter, you will learn about the various settings that affect your finished output, such as:

- Whether to include a control toolbar that lets the student control the progress of the finished course.
- Whether to send tracking data to a learning management system (LMS).
- How much to compress the output to accommodate slow connection speeds.

In addition, you'll look at the specific publishing formats:

- Flash (**.swf**)
- HTML5
- Media (**.mp4**)
- Executable (**.exe**)
- Devices (App)
- Adobe Captivate Prime
- Adobe Connect
- Print (Microsoft Word)

In This Chapter

- Rescale a Project
- Project Skins
- Project Settings
- Reporting and Tracking
- Publishing Options

Notes

Output-Related Options

Before you publish your project, you'll want to configure a number of settings that affect your finished output.

Rescale a Project

When you publish your project, the output size is the same as the project size. If you need your published project to be a different size, you need to resize the entire project.

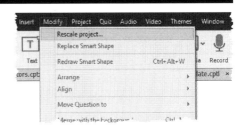

To rescale a project:

1. Go to the **Modify** menu.
2. Select **Rescale project**.
3. Set the new size by width/height dimensions, width/height percentage, or preset sizes from a menu.
4. Set the options for larger or smaller projects.
5. Click the **Finish** button.

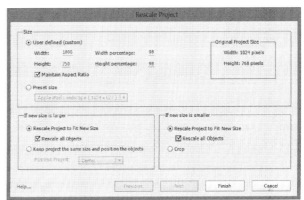

If New Size Is Larger

Rescale Project: Select this option if you want to enlarge the entire background image to fill the new larger slides. Check the box underneath to resize all objects accordingly. Otherwise, they will stay the same size on the larger slide.

Keep project the same size: Select this option if you want to keep the background image and objects at their current size, meaning they will be smaller than the slide. Use the **Position Project** menu to indicate where on the larger slide you want the background and objects to appear (center, top left, etc.).

If New Size Is Smaller

Rescale Project: Select this option if you want to scale down the background image to fit in the new smaller size. Check the box underneath to resize all objects accordingly. Otherwise, they will stay the same size.

Crop: Select this option if you want to keep the background image and objects at 100% of their current size and instead crop off whatever doesn't fit on the new smaller slide. If you select this option, the **Next** button becomes active, letting you indicate what part to keep and what part to crop.

CAUTION

- If you select the crop option, make sure you are not cropping out key areas of the slide.

- Be careful about resizing a project to be larger. You will lose resolution, and the resulting quality may not be what you want.

Configure Project Skin: Playback Controls

The project skin controls three features: the playback controls, a border, and a table of contents.

To select an existing skin:

1. Click the **Project** menu.
2. Select **Skin Editor**.
3. Select an option from the **Skin** drop-down menu.
4. Close the window.

To change the elements of a project skin:

1. Click the **Project** menu.
2. Select **Skin Editor**.
3. Configure the playback control options. (See below.)
4. Click the **Borders** button.
5. Configure the border options. (See next page.)
6. Click the **Table of Contents** button.
7. Configure the table of contents options. (See p. 246.)
8. Close the window.

Playback Control Options

Show Playback Control: Check this box if you want to provide the student with a playbar that controls the course.

Hide Playbar in Quiz: Check this box to hide the playbar on a quiz question slide. This is useful if you don't want students to move forward or back on a quiz slide. (The playbar is always hidden on pre-test slides.)

Playbar Overlay: By default, the playbar appears *under* the course. If you check this box, the playbar is placed *over* the course. This covers up part of the content area, but it keeps the published size the same as the project size.

Show Playbar on Hover: This option is enabled if you select **Playbar Overlay**. With this option, the playbar hides if the student's mouse is inactive for two seconds and then reappears when the mouse is active again.

Playbar: You can select from pre-made playbar colors.

Playbar Two Rows: When you check this box, the buttons appear on one row and the seekbar appears on a bottom row. This is useful for projects that are very small.

Playback Colors: Check this box to use the color swatches to further customize the different elements of the playbar.

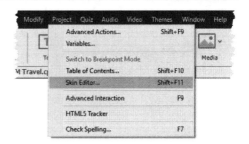

 TIME SAVER

If you customize your skin settings, you can save them to reuse over and over. Click the **Save** button **(A)** to add it to the **Skin** drop-down menu for later use.

Configure Project Skin: Playback Controls (cont'd)

Position: Indicate where in the course you want the playbar to appear: top, left, bottom, or right.

Layout: Indicate the size and more specific position of the playbar, such as stretched across the screen or over to the left or right. Options vary based on what you choose in the **Position** menu.

Button Options: Check the box for each option you want to include on your playbar. (See examples above.)

Alpha: Indicate how opaque or transparent you want the playbar to be. 100% is fully opaque. Lower numbers are semi-transparent.

No Tooltips at Runtime: By default, when a student rolls his or her mouse over a toolbar button, a small tooltip appears, explaining what the button is. Check this box if you don't want the tooltips.

CAUTION

Tooltips are also read by screen readers. If you turn off the tooltips, then your course will not be Section-508 compliant. Be sure to enable the **Closed Caption** button for projects with captioning.

DESIGN TIP

You can find pre-made skins from third-party sources online.

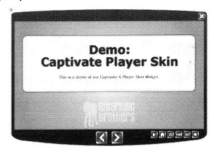

Sample skin courtesy of eLearning Brothers eLearning Template Library.

Accessibility, p. 289

Configure Project Skin: Border Options

Click the **Borders** button **(A)** to configure a border around the published course. The skin you have selected in the **Skin** drop-down menu affects what the default options are.

Show Borders: Check this box if you want to have a border around your project. Then, click the button for each side you want to give a border to. (Click all four for a full border.)

Style: Indicate if you want the border to have square or rounded corners.

Width: Enter the point size for the border width.

Texture: For a patterned border, select from one of almost 100 texture/pattern options, such as brushed metal or wood grain.

Color: Click the swatch to change the color of the border. (The color chosen here does not affect any textures used.)

HTML Background: Click the swatch to change the color of the background area around the project on an HTML page.

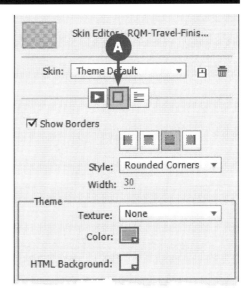

Configure Project Skin: Table of Contents

Click the **Table of Contents** button **(A)** to configure the table of contents (TOC). The skin you have selected in the **Skin** drop-down menu affects what the default options are.

Show TOC: Check this box if you want your published file to have a table of contents that lets the student view a list of slides and possibly move freely around the course.

Title: Double-click a slide title to edit the name as it will appear in the TOC.

Show/Hide TOC Entries: Check or uncheck the box in the show/hide column **(B)** to show or hide that slide in the table of contents.

Buttons

These options change how your slides appear in the table of contents. They do not affect how the slides appear in the project itself.

Folder: Click the **Folder** button to create an entry in the TOC that isn't tied to a slide. This is useful for module headings.

Reset TOC: Click this button to return the entries to their original configuration.

Move TOC Entry Left/Right: Use the left and right arrows to indent or outdent the selected slide.

Move TOC Entry Up/Down: Use the up and down arrows to change the order of the entries. You can also click and drag the slides to rearrange them.

Delete TOC Entry: To delete a topic name, select that line item, and then click the **Delete** button. You cannot delete a slide from your project here, you can only hide them in the TOC.

Project Info

Click the **Info** button to add project information, such as project name, author, and description. This information appears in a pop-up window at the top of the TOC.

 CAUTION

Changes made to your project after you create the table of contents are not automatically updated in the TOC. Instead, come back to this dialog box and click the **Reset TOC** button.

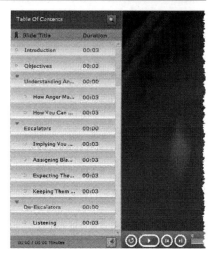

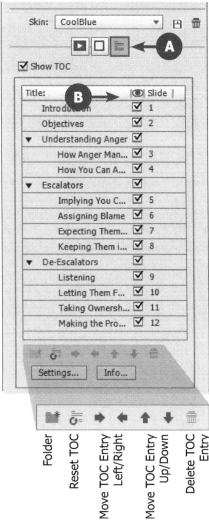

Configure Project Skin: Table of Contents (cont'd)

TOC Settings

Click the **Settings** button (see previous page) to bring up the **TOC Settings** dialog box.

Style: Select **Overlay** to have the TOC appear over the slide with a small show/hide icon that lets the student show or hide it. Select **Separate** if you want the TOC to always appear to the side of the slide.

Position: Indicate if you want the TOC to be on the left or right side of the slide.

Stretch TOC: With this option checked, the TOC is as long as the slide plus the playbar. If it is unchecked, it is only as long as the slide.

Alpha: By default, the TOC is fully opaque. Enter a lower number for semi-transparency.

Runtime Options

Collapse All: When checked, all folders in the TOC will be collapsed when the project plays.

Self-Paced Learning: When checked, students' status flags are not reset when the project is closed, and, upon return, the student may resume where he or she left off previously.

Show Topic Duration: When this box is checked, the slide duration appears next to each slide. Uncheck the box if you don't want the duration.

Enable Navigation: When checked, the student can move around freely using the TOC. Uncheck this if you do not want the student to be able to navigate via the TOC.

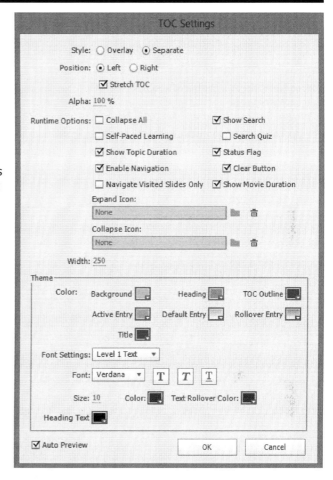

Navigate Visited Slides Only: When checked, students can navigate freely around any slide they have already visited, but can't jump ahead in the course. This option is only available if you have **Enable Navigation** checked.

Show Search: When this box is checked, a search box appears in the TOC. Check the **Search Quiz** box if you want to include quiz slides in the search.

Status Flag: When selected, a check mark appears next to each slide that the user has completed viewing. Check the **Clear Button** box if you want the student to be able to clear his or her status.

Show Movie Duration: When this box is checked, the total time of the course is shown at the bottom of the TOC.

Expand/Collapse Icon: When there are folders, the TOC uses traditional triangle icons for expanding and collapsing the sections. If you want to import your own image, you can do that here.

Width: Enter the width you want for the TOC, in pixels.

Theme: Use these fields to adjust the font and color settings of the various TOC elements, including font choices for up to five levels in the TOC hierarchy.

Auto Preview: Uncheck this option if you do not want to see the changes in the preview panel while you are making them.

Change Project Preferences for Publishing

The **Preferences** dialog box has a number of settings that affect your output. You can:

- Add information about the project, such as the title, author, and description.
- Adjust size and quality settings.
- Indicate which features you want to include, such as audio and mouse click sounds.
- Indicate how you want the published course to start and end.
- Configure options for reporting scores and completion status to a learning management system or other reporting system.

To change the project preferences:

1. Go to the **Edit** menu.
2. Select **Preferences**.
3. Click the category you want to change.
4. Make your changes.
5. Click the **OK** button.

Project Information Settings

Project information provides data about the project, such as the title, author, etc. This can be used as internal information for the developers, included in a table of contents for students to see, or read by screen readers in an accessible project.

Table of Contents, p. 246
Accessibility, p. 289

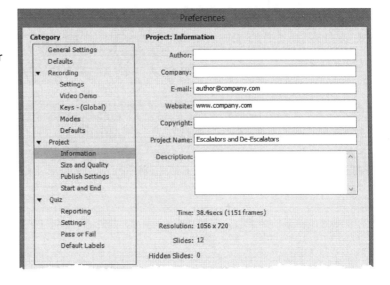

SWF Size and Quality Settings

When publishing your project, you'll want to balance quality with file size. A high-quality output may look good, but may be too large for remote viewers to access easily. Conversely, a small output file may be easy to access but may not look or sound good.

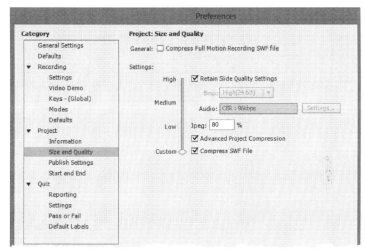

Compress Full Motion Recording SWF file: If you have any full-motion recording in your project, then your course contains video. Check this box if you want to compress that video.

High, Medium, and Low: Set the slider at any of these positions for settings, which provide that level of quality for audio and video.

Custom: Set the slider at this level if you want to set each quality setting individually.

> **Retain Slide Quality Settings**: Check this box if you want to manage quality at the slide level. Or, uncheck it and enter settings for the entire project here.

 Slide Quality, p. 40

Bmp: Select high or low quality for the screenshots that were taken during your capture session.

Audio: Click the **Settings** button to change the audio quality of any voice-over, music, etc.

 Configure Audio Compression, p. 79

Jpeg: Select a compression percentage for any **.jpg** images you placed on your slides.

Advanced Project Compression: If you check this option, Captivate looks for similarities between slides and publishes only the differences as the project goes from slide to slide. Be sure to check your output with this option to make sure everything renders properly.

Compress SWF File: If you select **High**, **Medium**, or **Low**, this box is checked, meaning additional compression is used (other than the options listed above). If you don't want extra compression, uncheck this box.

Publish Settings

Frames Per Second: To create a movie effect, Captivate publishes at 30 frames per second. You may need to change this if you are embedding a **.swf** movie into another file that uses a different rate.

Publish Adobe Connect metadata: Selecting this option makes it easier to integrate your course with Adobe Connect.

Include Mouse: Keep this checked if you want the slide mouse movements from a screen recording to appear in the published course.

Enable Accessibility: Check this box to make your course compatible with screen readers and to enable any other accessibility features you set up.

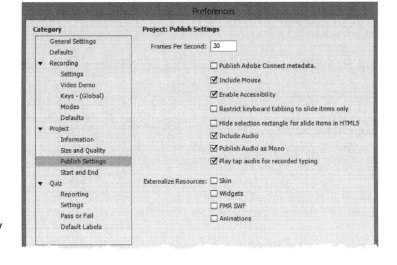

 Accessibility, p. 289

Restrict keyboard tabbing to slide items only: When you check this box, the TOC and playbar are skipped when students use the **Tab** key to navigate a course.

Hide selection rectangle for slide items in HTML5: When students use the **Tab** key to navigate the course, a yellow rectangle appears around the active object. Check this box if you want to hide that rectangle for HTML5 publishing.

Include Audio: Keep this checked if you want to publish any audio that you've added to the project.

Publish Audio as Mono: This setting converts stereo audio to mono audio, resulting in a smaller file size. With voice-over narration, mono audio is a good way to reduce file size without sacrificing audio quality.

Play tap audio for recorded typing: If you captured any typing during a screen recording, keep this box checked for the published file to play keyboard tapping sounds. Uncheck this box if you don't want to hear these sounds.

Externalize Resources: When publishing to Flash output, your course publishes as a single **.swf** file that includes the skin, widgets, full motion video, and added animations. If you prefer to have these objects published as separate files (to be referenced by the **.swf** file), then check the box for that object type. This can help decrease download times for extremely large files.

Start and End Settings

Auto Play: By default, a published course starts playing immediately. Uncheck this box if you don't want it to autostart. If it is not set to autostart, a play button appears on the first frame for the student to click. If you want to select your own play button, click the **Browse** button.

Preloader: The preloader is a small image or animation that plays while the course is downloading. With larger courses or slower connections, preloaders are helpful as they let students know that the course is downloading.

Preloader %: This indicates the percentage of the course that must be downloaded before it starts playing.

Password Protect Project: Use this option if you want students to enter a password before they can view the course. Click the **Options** button to change the system messages regarding the password.

Project Expiry Date: Check this option and enter a date if you want your course to expire after a certain date. An expired course cannot be viewed. This can be useful for limited-time offers or policy/legal information that changes yearly.

Fade In on the First Slide: Check this option to have the first frame of your course fade in.

Project End Options: Use this drop-down menu to designate what action should happen when the course is finished, such as stop, loop back to the beginning, go to a Website, etc.

Fade Out on the Last Slide: Check this option to have the last frame of your course fade out to white.

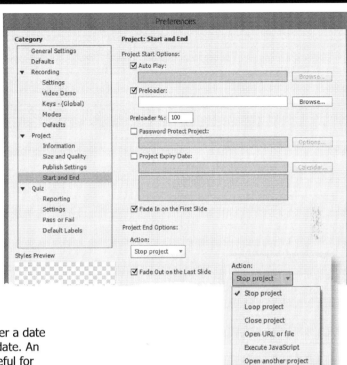

Reporting and Tracking

If you want to publish your course to a learning management system (LMS) and have it track usage on the course, you need to configure the **Reporting** settings in **Preferences** based on the needs of your LMS.

Once the settings are configured, you will need to publish your project using the **Publish to Computer** option with **Zip Files** checked.

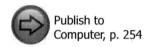

Publish to Computer, p. 254

Quiz Reporting Preferences

Quiz: Check this box to enable reporting. You can use these settings for tracking even if your course does not include a quiz.

LMS: Use this menu to select from a list of LMS types. Choose from **Moodle, Internal Server, Other Standard LMSs, Adobe Connect**, or **Questionmark Perception**.

Standard: Select the LMS standard you want to use for the reporting. This list may not be active based on what you chose in the **LMS** menu. Choose from **SCORM 1.2, SCORM 2004, AICC**, or **xAPI**.

Configure: Click this button to provide details about the course, such as title, description, and length. **(A)** These details will go into the project's manifest file for communication with an LMS. The options will vary based on which standard you have chosen.

Template: This drop-down menu is still included for legacy purposes and is rarely needed.

Status Representation: Indicate if you want to send a status of **Complete** or **Passed/Failed**. Your LMS may require one set or the other.

User Access: With this option, the course is considered completed as soon as it is launched.

Slide views and/or quiz: Select this option if you want to base completion on the amount of slides viewed and/or the status of the quiz. Once selected, check the box for one or both of the options below.

    Slide Views: Enter the percentage or number of slides the student needs to view for the course to be complete.

    Quiz: Select one of the options from the drop-down menu: **Quiz is attempted, Quiz is Passed**, or **Quiz is passed or the quiz attempt limit is reached**.

Quiz Score: Indicate if you want to send the raw score (number of points) or the percent score for the quiz.

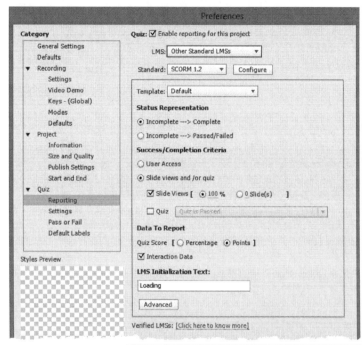

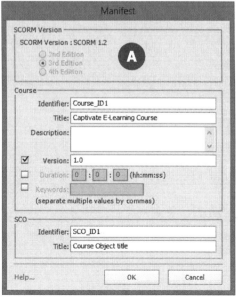

Quiz Reporting Preferences (cont'd)

Interaction Data: Check this box if you want to include data about each individual question in addition to data about the overall quiz results.

LMS Initialization Text: Type the text you'd like to show to the student while the course is opening.

Advanced Button: When you click this button, the **LMS Advanced Settings** dialog box appears.

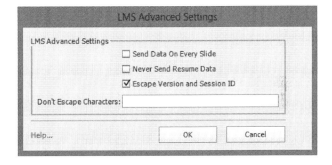

> **Send Data On Every Slide**: By default, Captivate sends tracking data to an LMS when the student leaves the course. Check this box if you want it to be sent on every slide. This can prevent students from losing progress if there is an LMS connection issue.
>
> **Never Send Resume Data**: Most LMSs offer bookmarking, which keeps track of where the students left off and asks them if they want to resume from that location. If you check this box, Captivate will not send information about where the students leave off.
>
> **Escape Version and Session ID**: This option converts the version and session ID to its URL encoded values, which is sometimes necessary for AICC publishing. For example, certain LMSs might have issues if there are special characters in the title name.
>
> **Don't Escape Characters**: If you use the **Escape Version** option, use this field to enter any characters that should not be used.

BRIGHT IDEA

What are SCORM, AICC, and xAPI?

These are industry standards that govern interoperability between a course and an LMS, ensuring that the two can "talk" to each other.

xAPI, also known as Tin Can, is a newer standard, released in 2013. Find out from your LMS provider which standard they use so that you can publish your project accordingly. They may also have suggestions about what other settings work best for their LMS.

When integrating with an LMS for the first time, it is best to conduct a test early on to make sure everything works properly.

CAUTION

- If you have any branching in your course, be careful about requiring 100% slide views, as the student may not ever be presented with all the slides. In these situations, determine the shortest path through the course, and use that as the minimum number of slides.

- Just because you choose to send all interaction data doesn't mean your LMS is able to report on it. Captivate only controls what is sent, not what your LMS chooses to receive and/or display to you.

POWER TIP

The **Internal Server** option on the **LMS** menu is a way to track student data without having an LMS. Instead you can report data to your own internal server using Adobe Captivate Quiz Results Analyzer. Refer to the Captivate help documentation for full technical details.

Publishing

There are several ways to publish your content, based on how you want your users to view your course.

Publish to Computer (HTML5/SWF)

To publish your project to HTML5/SWF:

1. Click the **Publish** drop-down button.
2. Select **Publish to Computer**.
3. In the **Publish as** field, select **HTML5/SWF**.
4. In the **Project Title** field, enter the name for the course.
5. In the **Location** field, click the folder icon to find and select the location for the published files.
6. Select the publishing options you want. (See below.)
7. Click the **Publish** button.

Publishing Options

Zip Files: Check this box if you want Captivate to put your published files in a **.zip** folder. This is useful if you want to upload your files to a file sharing site or load them into an LMS.

Publish to Folder: Check this box if you want Captivate to create a separate folder in the target location for your published files.

Typekit Domains: If you are using Typekit for your fonts, enter the domain(s) where the course will be published. If your course web address is **www.rqm.com/courses/travel/index.html**, you would enter ***.rqm.com**.

Output Format: Click the buttons to indicate if you want to include **SWF** and/or **HTML5** files in your finished output. You can select one or both. The selected options are displayed as dark gray.

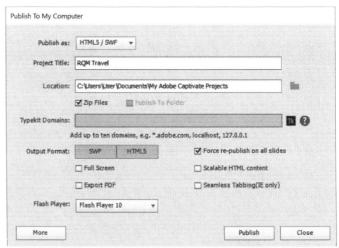

Typekit, p. 57

Fullscreen: This option includes HTML files that cause the browser to open to its maximum size and hide browser elements, such as the toolbar and **Favorites** bar.

Export PDF: Check this box to create a PDF document that plays the project.

Force Re-Publish On All Slides: For any publish after the initial publish, Captivate detects what has changed and re-generates only the slides that have changed. Check this box if you want to republish everything from scratch.

Scalable HTML content: Check this box if you want the contents of HTML5 projects to scale based on the size of the window they are viewed in.

Seamless Tabbing: Check this box if you want students using the **Tab** key for navigation to be able to tab out of the Flash movie and into the surrounding HTML. Leave it unchecked to have all **Tab** navigation stay within the movie.

Flash Player Version: You can select the version of Flash player needed to view the project.

 CAUTION

Adobe is ending support for the Flash Player in 2020. So courses published only to Flash output (SWF) will stop playing at that point (and possibly sooner).

 BRIGHT IDEA

Most of these output options are only available if you select **SWF** output.

Publish to Computer (HTML5/SWF) (cont'd)

More Publishing Options

Click the **More** button in the publishing dialog box for these extra options. In this section, you get a summary of project information including preferences that are set in the **Preferences** dialog box. Any blue item is a clickable link that takes you to where those settings are made.

Audio Settings (A): These settings control audio quality and can also be accessed from the **Audio** menu.

 Audio Settings, p. 79

Display Score (B): This indicates whether the score will be shown to the student at the end of the quiz. This setting can be changed in **Preferences** on the **Quiz > Settings** tab.

 Quiz Settings, p. 214

Mobile Gestures & Geolocation (C): These two options are for mobile-friendly projects.

 Mobile Gestures, p. 270
Geolocation, p. 267

Size & Quality (D): This section tells you what quality/compression settings you have. This setting is found in **Preferences** on the **Size & Quality** tab.

 Size & Quality Settings, p. 249

Accessibility (E): This lets you know if you've turned on the accessibility features to make the course more usable by those with disabilities using assistive technology. This setting is found in **Preferences** on the **Publish Settings** tab.

 Publish Settings, p. 250
Accessibility, p. 289

eLearning Output (F): Here you can see if you've enabled reporting and tracking to an LMS or internal server. This setting is changed in **Preferences** on the **Reporting** tab.

 Reporting & Tracking, p.255

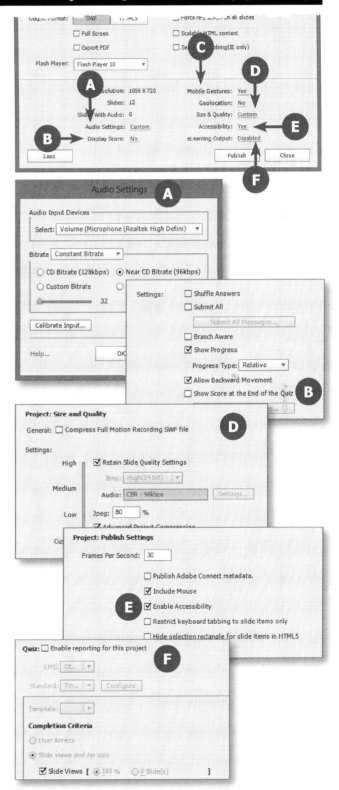

Publish as Video

The video option lets you publish your project as a single .mp4 video file. This can be a handy way to put a simple movie on a Website, for example. This format does not work with interactive elements, such as buttons, click boxes, and quiz questions.

To publish as video:

1. Click the **Publish** drop-down button.
2. Select **Publish to Computer**.
3. In the **Publish as** field, select **Video**.
4. In the **Project Title** field, enter the name for the published movie.
5. In the **Location** field, click the folder icon to select the location for the published files.
6. Select the publishing options you want. (See below.)
7. Click the **Publish** button.

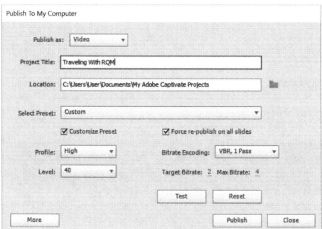

Video Publishing Options

Select Preset: On this menu, you can select the type of format you want. Captivate will apply the appropriate settings for that format.

Customize Preset: If you select **Custom** as your preset, you can change the individual publish settings.

Profile: This menu determines the complexity of the encoding and decoding of the video. Select **Baseline** (low), **Main** (medium), or **High** (high).

Level: This setting affects the complexity of the decoding needed. Choose options between 10 (lowest) and 51 (highest).

Bitrate: Select between **VBR** (variable bitrate) and **CBR** (constant bitrate). **Variable** adjusts the bitrate (amount of information captured) between the value in the **Target** field and the value in the **Max** field, based on what is happening at the time. When less is happening, less information is used. **Constant** uses the **Target** bitrate throughout the whole video.

Test and Reset: Click the **Test** button to determine if your settings are valid. (For example, a high profile and a low level setting might not pass.) Click **Reset** to reset the settings.

Force Re-Publish On All Slides: For any publish after the initial publish, Captivate detects what has changed and re-publishes only the slides that have changed. Check this box if you want to republish everything instead.

Preset	Profile	Level	Bitrate
Video - Apple iPad	Main	31	VBR, 1 Pass Target: 2, Max: 4
Video - Apple iPhone 3	Baseline	30	CBR, Target: 5, Max: 5
Video - Apple iPhone 4 (4S) Apple iPod	Main	31	VBR, 1 Pass Target: 2, Max: 4
YouTube Widescreen HD	High	40	VBR, 1 Pass Target: 2, Max: 4
You Tube Widescreen SD	High	31	VBR, 1 Pass Target: 1, Max: 2
YouTube XGA	High	31	VBR, 1 Pass Target: 2, Max: 4

Publish to You Tube

If you use the **Video** option when publishing, you can upload your movie directly to YouTube.

To publish to YouTube:

1. Publish your project to **Video** format. (See previous page.)
2. In the dialog box that appears when done publishing, click the **Publish to YouTube** button.
3. Follow the on-screen prompts to log in with your YouTube username and password.
4. Enter the requested details about the project.
5. Check the terms and conditions check box.
6. Click the **Upload** button.
7. Wait for the movie to finish uploading.
8. Click the **Close Window** button.

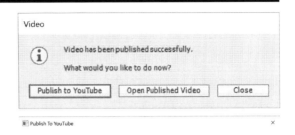

Publish as Executable

The publish as executable option lets you publish your project as a single Windows Executable (**.exe**) or Mac Executable (**.app**) file. This can be a handy if you want to burn your course to a CD or have the course run on a computer like a software application.

To publish as executable:

1. Click the **Publish** drop-down button.
2. Select **Publish to Computer**.
3. In the **Publish as** field, select **Executable**.
4. In the **Publish Type** field, select **Windows Executable (.exe)** or **Mac Executable (.app)**.
5. In the **Project Title** field, enter the name for the published project.
6. In the **Location** field, click the folder icon to select the location for the published files.
7. In the **Icon** field, click the folder icon to locate and select an icon image (**.ico**).
8. Select the publishing options you want. (See below.)
9. Click the **Publish** button.

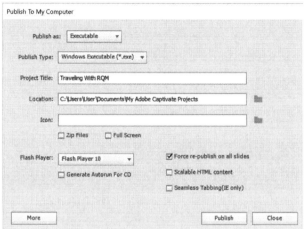

Publishing Options

Zip Files: Check this box if you want Captivate to put your published files in a **.zip** folder. This is useful if you want to upload your files to a file sharing site.

Full Screen: Check this box if you want the published course to automatically play in full screen.

Flash Player Version: You can select the version of Flash player needed to view the project.

Generate Autorun For CD: If you are burning your executable file to CD, check this box to include an autorun file. When your students insert the CD into their computers, the course will automatically begin.

Force Re-Publish On All Slides: For any publish after the initial publish, Captivate detects what has changed and re-publishes only the slides that have changed. Check this box if you want to republish everything instead.

Scalable HTML content: Check this box if you want the contents of HTML5 projects to scale based on the size of the window they are viewed in.

Seamless Tabbing: Check this box if you want students using the **Tab** key for navigation to be able to tab out of the Flash movie and into the surrounding HTML. Leave it unchecked to have all **Tab** navigation stay within the movie.

**DESIGN TIPS**

- What is an icon in this context? It's the symbol that appears next to the name of the file or in your list of open applications.

- You can use programs like SnagIt to create icon files, which use a **.ico** extension.

Publish for Devices (App)

In previous versions of Captivate, you could use a separate program called the App Packager Tool to create an Android- or iOS-native version of your project. This feature is now included in Captivate. While the App Packager Tool has been incorporated into Adobe Captivate, you will also need to use the Adobe PhoneGap service, which is separate.

To publish for devices:

1. Click the **Publish** drop-down button.
2. Select **Publish for Devices (App)**.
3. Enter your PhoneGap login credentials in the **Username** and **Password** fields. (Click the **Register** link to create a PhoneGap account.)
4. Click the **Login** button.
5. Select/enter the publishing options. **(A)**

   (See below.)
6. Click the **Next** button.
7. Click the **iOS** and/or the **Android** check boxes.
8. In the **Cert. Password** and **KeyStore Password** (for Android only) field(s), enter the passwords provided by the Apple and/or Android Development Programs. **(B)**
9. Click the **Publish** button.
10. Click the **Download** button to download the published app file from the PhoneGap service.
11. Submit your app to the Apple App Store for iOS and/or the Google Play Store for Android.

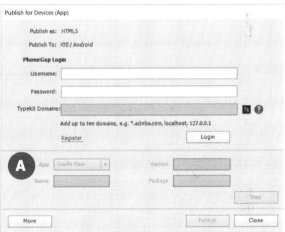

Publishing Options

Typekit Domains: If you are using Typekit for your fonts, enter the domain(s) where the course will be published. If your course web address is **www.rqm.com/courses/travel/index.html**, you would enter ***.rqm.com**.

 Typekit, p. 57

App: Click the **App** drop-down menu to indicate if you are creating a new app or updating an existing one.

Name: Use this field to enter the name of your app.

Version: Use this field to enter the version number of your app.

Package: Use this field to enter a unique package name for your app.

Publish to Adobe Connect

To publish to Adobe Connect:

1. Click the **Publish** drop-down button.
2. Select **Publish to Adobe Connect**.
3. In the **Name** field, enter the name for the published project.
4. In the **URL** field, select the server address you want from the drop-down menu or click the folder icon to enter the address for the Acrobat Connect Server where you will be loading the project.
5. Select the publishing options you want. (See below.)
6. Click the **Publish** button.
7. Follow the prompts in Connect to finish the uploading process.

Publishing Options

Typekit Domains: If you are using Typekit for your fonts, enter the domain(s) where the course will be published. If your course web address is **www.rqm.com/courses/travel/index.html**, you would enter ***.rqm.com**.

 Typekit, p. 57

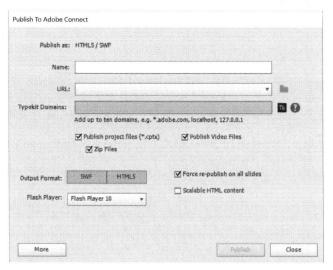

Publish Project Files: If you check this option, the Captivate project file is included. (**.cptx**)

Publish Video Files: If you check this option, any imported video files will be published. (**.flv**)

Zip Files: Check this box if you want Captivate to put your published files in a **.zip** folder. This is useful if you want to upload your files to a file sharing site or load them into an LMS.

Output Format: Click either button to indicate if you want to include **SWF** and/or **HTML5** files in your finished output. You can select one or both. The selected options are displayed as dark gray.

Force Re-Publish On All Slides: For any publish after the initial publish, Captivate detects what has changed and re-generates only the slides that have changed. Check this box if you want to republish everything from scratch.

Scalable HTML Content: Check this box if you want the contents of HTML5 projects to scale based on the size of the window they are viewed in. This option is not recommended for iPad viewing.

Flash Player: You can select the version of Flash player needed to view the project.

Publish to Adobe Captivate Prime

Adobe Captivate Prime is Adobe's online learning management system (LMS). Using this option requires an Adobe Captivate Prime account.

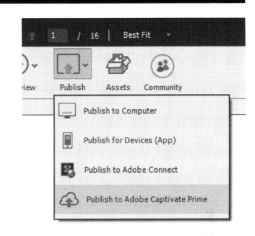

To publish to Adobe Captivate Prime:

1. Click the **Publish** drop-down button.

2. Select **Publish to Adobe Captivate Prime**.

3. In the **Account** drop-down field, select the Adobe Captivate Prime account to publish to. (If you don't see your account listed, select **Setup/Retrieve Captivate Prime Account** to create a new account or retrieve an existing account.)

4. Click the **Publish** button.

5. Continue by setting up the course in Adobe Captivate Prime.

Publishing Options

Typekit Domains: If you are using Typekit for your fonts, enter the domain(s) where the course will be published. If your course web address is **www.rqm.com/courses/travel/index.html**, you would enter ***.rqm.com**.

 Typekit, p. 57

Publishing to Print/Microsoft Word

When you publish to print, you create a Word document that can be used as handouts, storyboards, job aids, etc.

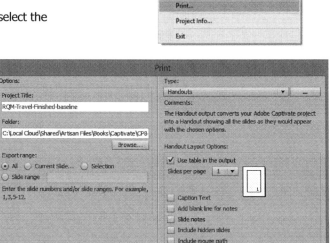

To publish your project to Microsoft Word:

1. Go to the **File** menu.

2. Select **Print**.

3. In the **Project Title** field, enter the name for the published document.

4. In the **Folder** field, click the **Browse** button to select the location for the published file.

5. Select the print options you want. (See below.)

6. Click the **Publish** button.

Print Publishing Options

Export range: Specify which slides you want to include in the output.

Type: Select the format you want from the drop-down menu. The options in the bottom half of the panel vary based on the format you select.

Handouts: Create a format similar to PowerPoint handouts where you specify the number of slides per page and include either the slide notes or blank lines for note taking.

Lesson: Create a document with the background image, text captions, the image of anything covered by a highlight box, as well as the questions and answers for any quizzes.

Step by Step: This format lists all caption text and the portion of the slide background under a highlight box. For screen simulations, use this format to create a job aid that lists all the steps (caption text) and highlighted features (such as the **OK** button). Use the automatic highlight box feature during capture if you want to create a job aid such as this.

Storyboard: Create a document to help you manage production. It includes slide count, preferences, and settings for the whole project, as well as slide-specific information, such as timing, audio, and objects.

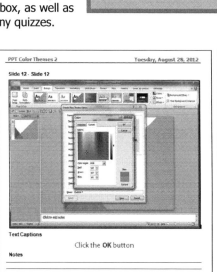

Handouts including caption text and blank lines for notes; table output turned off

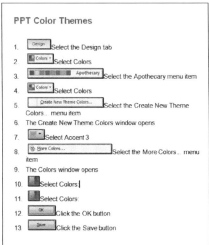

Step by Step output, which includes caption text and the portion of the slide background covered by a highlight box

Sample Output Files

Here are some details about what the output files look like and what to do with them.

SWF Only

Even if you publish to SWF only (and not HTML5), you get both a **.swf** and an **.htm** file. You may get additional files based on some of the content you added or settings you chose (such as **Externalize Resources** in **Preferences**). Typically, you want to post all of the files to a server, and use the **.htm** file as the link for the course. If you don't have other files generated, you may be able to use the **.swf** file alone. For example, you may want to embed it in a Web page or put it into another authoring tool.

SWF and HTML5

When you publish to HTML5, many more files are generated. All of the files must stay together and be loaded together. The **.htm** file is the one that launches the course. If you include the **.swf** publishing option as well, those files will be included. When launched by the student, the course will determine if the student can view the **.swf** version. If so, it will deliver that version. If not, it will deliver the HTML5 version.

SCORM

Typically, you will upload the course to the LMS as a **.zip** file. If you didn't select that option when publishing, you can zip it yourself. Because all the files are zipped, you typically don't need to be concerned about what any of them are. Some LMSs do require that you add custom code to the **imsmanifest.xml** file.

RQM-Travel-Finished-SWF Only.htm	HTML Document
RQM-Travel-Finished-SWF Only.swf	SWF File

SWF option only

adlcp_rootv1p2.xsd	XSD File
browsersniff.js	JS File
captivate.css	Cascading Style S...
ims_xml.xsd	XSD File
imscp_rootv1p1p2.xsd	XSD File
imsmanifest.xml	XML Document
imsmd_rootv1p2p1.xsd	XSD File
metadata.xml	XML Document
RQM-Travel-Finished.htm	HTML Document
RQM-Travel-Finished.swf	SWF File
SCORM_utilities.js	JS File
scormdriver.js	JS File
ScormEnginePackageProperties.xsd	XSD File
standard.js	JS File
Utilities.js	JS File

SWF and HTML5 options

vr	File folder
assets	File folder
dr	File folder
wr	File folder
ar	File folder
callees	File folder
multiscreen.html	HTML Document
RQM-Travel-Finished.htm	HTML Document
RQM-Travel-Finished.swf	SWF File
index.html	HTML Document
project.json	JSON File
standard.js	JS File
captivate.css	Cascading Style S...

SWF option only with SCORM 1.2 reporting

Notes

Mobile Design & Publishing

Introduction

Captivate offers great features that let you publish your content for view on mobile devices, such as phones and tablets, using HTML5.

In this chapter, you will learn about:

- **Geolocation**: If you activate this feature, you can use the student's location to customize the content.
- **Mobile Gestures**: If you activate this feature, students can navigate and control the display of your course using commonly used mobile gestures such as swiping right or left to go forward and backward in the course.
- **Responsive projects:** You can create a project that reconfigures the view based on the type of device used by the student, such as computer vs. tablet vs. phone.
- **Fluid Boxes:** You get heavy control over how your responsive projects reconfigure by using fluid boxes to structure your content.
- **HTML5 Tracker:** With this tool, you can quickly determine if you have included any elements that won't publish properly to HTML5.

Notes

Geolocation

In Adobe Captivate you can create if/then actions that pair up the student's location with location variables you create. For example, you can localize a course by showing certain information if the student who takes the course is in the New York office and other information if the student is in the Boston office. A system variable keeps track of the student's current location (assuming the student is on a GPS-enabled device). You can also create user variables with the target latitude, longitude, and an accuracy threshold. With those variables in place, you can create if/then actions based on the student's location.

Enable Geolocation for a Project

To fully use the geolocation features for a project, you must first enable this feature.

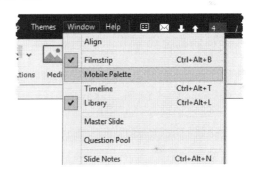

To enable geolocation for a project:
1. Go to the **Window** menu.
2. Select **Mobile Palette**.
3. Check the **Geolocation** box.
4. Click the **OK** button.

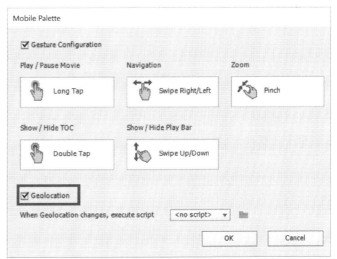

Create a Location-Based Variable

If you want to create if/then statements based on the student's location, you first create a user variable with the location to be used for the condition. For example, if you want a message to pop up when the student is in a certain building, you would set up a variable with the location of that building.

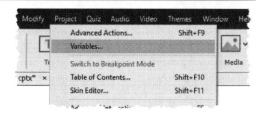

When setting up such a variable, you can also indicate how close the student needs to be to that location for it to be considered true. For example, if you were providing content about different buildings on a corporate or university campus, you could have content pop up if the student is within 30 meters or so. If it is content about different parts of an assembly line, the student might need to be within just a few meters.

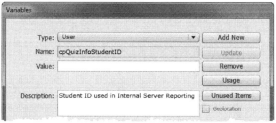

 Variables, p. 169

To create a location-based variable:

1. Go to the **Project** menu.
2. Select **Variables**.
3. Click the **Add New** button.
4. Check the **Geolocation** check box.
5. In the **Name** field, enter a name for the variable.
6. In the **Latitude** and **Longitude** fields, type or paste the latitude and longitude for the location you want.

——— or ———

6. Click the **Choose from Map** icon and select a location from a map. **(A)**
7. In the **Accuracy** field, enter how close (in meters) the student must be to the target location in order to be considered as being in that location.
8. In the **Description** field, enter a description of the location.
9. Click the **Save** button.
10. Click the **Close** button.

 BRIGHT IDEAS

- How do you find out the latitude and longitude of the location you want? If you type in the address in Google Maps, the latitude and longitude appear in the URL.

- How accurate is a phone's GPS? It depends upon several factors including the quality of the phone's system and environmental factors. Many smart phones have accuracy to within a meter, but that kind of accuracy can't always be relied on.

- How many meters in a mile? 1609.344

Create a Conditional Action Using Geolocation

In addition to any user-defined variables, Captivate also has a system variable (**cpInfoGeoLocation**) that keeps the student's location. To create a location-based conditional action, you would create a condition comparing the student's location to your user-defined variable.

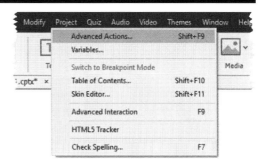

To create a conditional action using geolocation:

1. Go to the **Project** menu.
2. Select **Advanced Actions**.
3. In the **Action Name** field, enter a name for the action.
4. Check the **Conditional Tab** box.
5. In the **IF** section, compare the geolocation variable you created with **cpInfoGeoLocation**.
6. Set up the rest of your action.

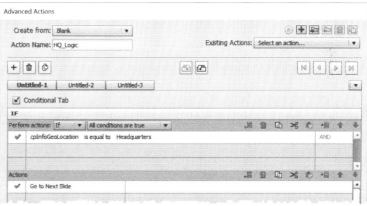

 POWER TIP

In addition to running actions from a button or when a page loads, you can set up an advanced action to run whenever the student's location changes. In the **Mobile Palette** (on the **Window** menu), select your advanced action from the execute script drop-down menu.

 Conditional Actions, p. 175

Emulate Geolocation While Previewing

When you are using geolocation, you might want to test its functionality before publishing your course. You can emulate geolocation while previewing your project.

To emulate geolocation while previewing:

1. Go to the **Preview** drop-down menu.
2. Select **In Browser** or **HTML5 in Browser**.
3. While previewing your project, select a location from the **Emulate Geolocation** drop-down menu.

Mobile Gestures

In addition to using the buttons in your course for navigation and viewing options, you can also enable mobile gestures. These gestures allow your students to use common tablet/phone conventions, such as swiping left and right to move forward and backward in the course. By default, these features are disabled, but it is very easy to enable them.

Enable Mobile Gestures

To enable mobile gestures:

1. Go to the **Window** menu.
2. Select **Mobile Palette**.
3. Check the **Gesture Configuration** box.
4. Click the **OK** button.

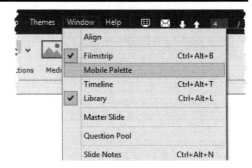

BRIGHT IDEA

How will your students know these gestures are available? If they click the small icon on the launch page, they can see the gesture options.

CAUTION

Make sure the gestures don't conflict with any other navigation or logic in your course. For example, the right/left swiping takes students to the next slide and previous slide *in order*. This circumvents any logic you added that might take them to a different page, via a **Next** button, for example.

Students cannot, however, use gestures to bring up the playbar or TOC if the feature is not enabled on that slide.

Creating Responsive Projects

A responsive project creates pages that reconfigure based on the size of the student's device. If a student is using a phone, the page doesn't just get smaller, it rearranges for optimal viewing. To create a responsive project, there are two steps. First, you have to save the file as a responsive project. Second, you need to set up your pages with fluid boxes that work with the different layouts.

Save Existing Project as a Responsive Project

Saving your project as a responsive project gives you access to the rest of the features in this chapter.

To save an existing project as a responsive project:

1. Go to the **File** menu.
2. Select **Save As Responsive**.
3. Click the **Save** button in the pop-up window.
4. Navigate to the folder where you want to save the file.
5. Type a name for the file.
6. Click the **Save** button.
7. Use the features in the rest of the chapter to optimize your design for different device sizes.

 BRIGHT IDEAS

- Captivate versions 8 and 9 used a different approach to responsive projects, called breakpoints.

- If you open an older project with breakpoints in Captivate 17, you can still use the breakpoints.

- If you want to convert a new Captivate 17 project to the older breakpoints method, you can do that from the **Project** menu.

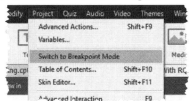

 CAUTION

Not all Captivate features work in responsive projects. When you convert your file, a dialog box appears to let you know if you are using any unsupported features. Click the **Show Unsupported Items** button to open the HTML5 tracker to see what objects won't work in a responsive project.

Create a New Responsive Project

To create a new responsive project:

1. On the **Welcome Screen**, click the **New** tab.
2. Select **Responsive Project**.
3. Click the **Create** button.

————— or —————

1. Go to the **File** menu.
2. Select **New Project**.
3. Select **Responsive Project**.

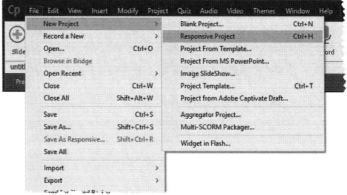

Preview a Responsive Project

When you preview a responsive project, you can see what it will look like on different device sizes.

To preview a project in work mode:

1. Drag the slider **(A)** to the device width you want.

——— or ———

1. Click the **Preview In** drop-down menu.
2. Select the device type you want to preview.

——— or ———

1. Type a width and/or height in the two text boxes next to the menu.

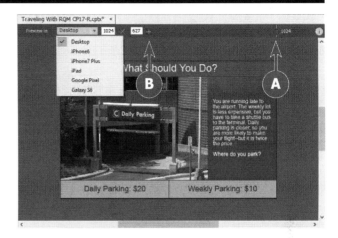

 TIME SAVER

If there's a certain width you need to test often, drag the slider to that width, and then click the plus button that appears **(B)**. This lets you add that width to the drop-down menu.

To preview in a browser:

1. Click the **Preview** drop-down button.
2. Select **Project**.
3. Click and drag the slider **(C)** to the device width you want.

 CAUTION

The browser method is a more reliable indicator of what the slide will look like versus the work mode method. However, neither is an adequate substitute for thorough testing on the devices your students will be using.

 BRIGHT IDEA

If an object gets too small to show completely, a small box appears. **(D)** When students click it, they see the full object (text in this case) in an overlay.

Fluid Boxes

Fluid boxes are "containers" of content that move around based on the device size. You can add boxes in a vertical column, in a horizontal row, and nested inside of each other. If you take the time to plan out your slide, you can structure the boxes in a way that makes sense on any device type. Slides in responsive projects start as a single fluid box.

In this example, three vertical boxes were added to the main parent box. **(A)** Then in the middle box, two horizontal boxes were added and resized to make one bigger than the other. **(B)** Finally, two horizontal boxes were added to the bottom box. **(C)** Boxes 1, 3, and 4 become "parent" boxes that contain "child" boxes. The "child" boxes can contain content.

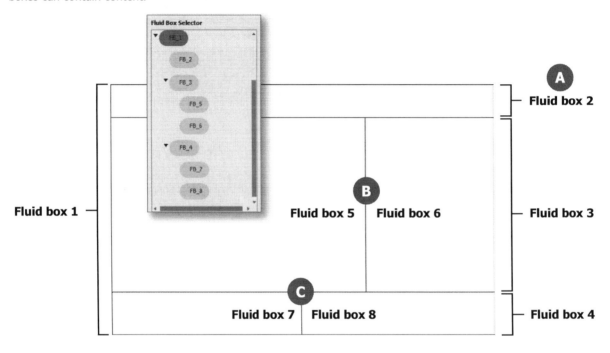

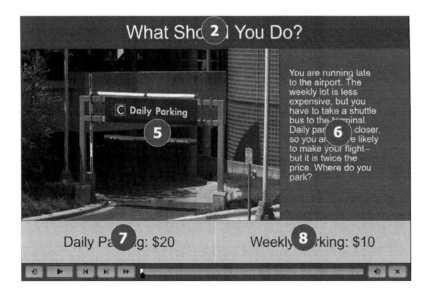

Add Fluid Boxes

To add fluid boxes:

1. Select the slide or the fluid box you want to add fluid boxes to.
2. Click the **Fluid Box** drop-down button.
3. Select **Horizontal** or **Vertical**.
4. Click on the box that represents the number of fluid boxes you want.
5. Click and drag the double blue arrows to position the boxes the way you want. **(A)**

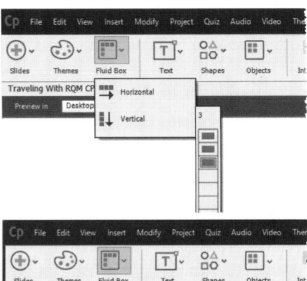

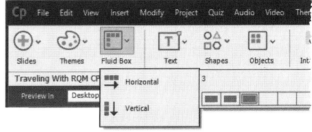

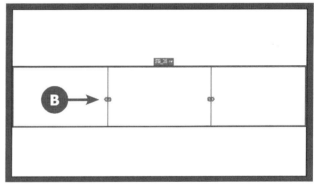

3 horizontal boxes added to the middle vertical box

⏱ TIME SAVERS

- When converting an existing project to a responsive project, you can have Captivate suggest the fluid box structure. Select the slide, and click the **Suggest Fluid Boxes** button in the **Properties** panel.

- Fluid boxes can be set up on master slides.

  Master Slides, p. 44

Manage Fluid Boxes

To select a fluid box:
1. Click the edge of the fluid box.

——— or ———

1. Select any fluid box on the slide.
2. In the **Properties** panel, select the fluid box you want in the **Fluid Box Selector** panel.

To rename a fluid box:
1. Select the fluid box.
2. At the top of the **Properties** pane, type a new name. **(A)**

To resize fluid boxes:
1. Select the fluid box that holds the fluid boxes you want to resize (the parent box).
2. Click and drag the blue arrow handles that appear. (See image previous page.)

To delete a fluid box:
1. Select the fluid box you want to delete.
2. Press the **Delete** key on your keyboard.

To remove all fluid boxes from a slide:
1. Select the slide.
2. In the **Properties** panel, click the **Remove Fluid Boxes** button. **(B)**

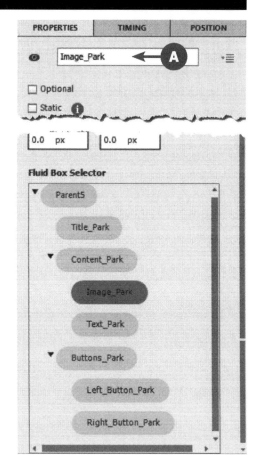

 BRIGHT IDEA

It can be tricky to select a fluid box on the slide once it has content in it. Here are two methods to try.

- Click an object in the fluid box. Hover your mouse to the edge of the fluid box until the edge highlights. Then click the edge.

- Click off to the side of a slide in the work area and then drag your mouse on to the slide to select the outermost fluid box. Then from there, you can use the **Fluid Box Selector** pane to select the fluid box you want to work with.

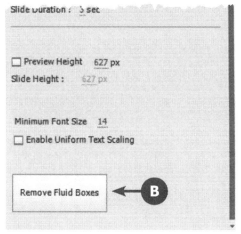

Add Objects to Fluid Boxes

To add an object to a fluid box:

1. Select the fluid box.
2. Insert the object as you normally would.

——— or ———

1. Insert the object as you normally would.
2. Drag the object to a fluid box and release the mouse when the fluid box is highlighted.

To move an object from one fluid box to another:

1. Drag the object to the new fluid box.

To remove an object from all fluid boxes but keep it on the slide:

1. Select the object.
2. In the **Properties** panel, check **Unlock from Fluid Box**.

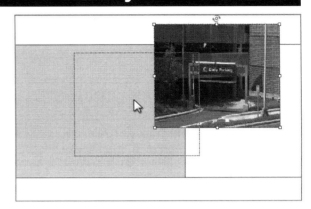

Drag-and-drop method

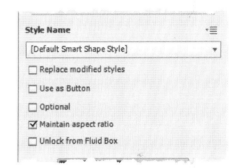

Resize Objects in Fluid Boxes

By default, objects resize automatically to fill as much of the fluid box as possible. If other objects are added, the objects will resize to ensure all objects fit.

You can manually resize objects in a fluid box by dragging the corner resize handles. However, this works differently with fluid boxes than it does on a standard size. You only get resize handles on the bottom and right of the object. If a resize handle is white, you can use it to resize the object. If a resize handle is red, you cannot use it to resize the object.

So why are they sometimes red and sometimes white? That has to do with different property settings. For example, if a fluid box is set to stretch to fit and the object is not set to maintain aspect ratio, the object will fill the box and not allow manual resizing.

Experiment with the various fluid box and object properties covered on the next pages to get the size and position you want.

Same image added to different-sized fluid boxes

Daily Parking: $20	Weekly Parking: $10

Fluid box set to stretch + object set to not maintain aspect ratio = red drag handles that can't be resized.

Responsive Slide Properties

Slides in responsive projects have special properties you won't find in a standard project.

Preview Height

The slider at the top of the work area **(A)** lets you change the preview for different device widths. You can also use the drop-down menu and text boxes **(B)** to change the device width for the preview. If you check the **Preview Height** box, you get a yellow slider handle at the bottom of your slide **(C)** so that you can manually adjust the height of the preview size. You cannot make the preview height larger than the slide height, which is shown for reference.

 DESIGN TIP

If you want to change the slide height, use the **Rescale Project** option on the **Modify** menu.

 Rescale Project, p. 243

Minimum Font Size

Regardless of device size, your text won't ever go below the point size here. To keep the font at least this big, Captivate may make other slide objects smaller or may move the text to a pop-up overlay that students access by clicking the icon that appears. **(D)**

Enable Uniform Text Scaling

If you have text boxes in different fluid boxes, the font size of one box may end up becoming larger or smaller than the font in another box—even if they started out the same size. If you check this box, all fonts will scale in proportion to the original layout.

Suggest Fluid Boxes

If you are converting an existing project to a responsive project, you can have Captivate suggest the fluid box structure.

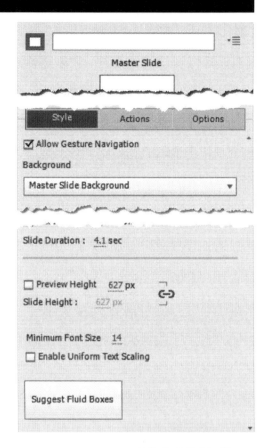

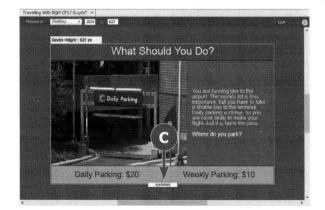
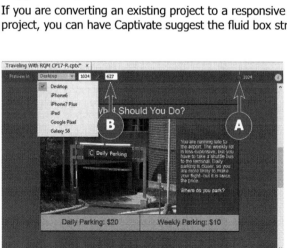

Fluid Box Properties

Optional

Check this box if you want the entire box to disappear on small devices. This is commonly used for images that are more decorative or information that is not critical. This feature only works when using the **Squeeze in a row/column** wrap option.

Static

Check this box if you want the fluid box to keep its exact size and layout regardless of device size. Use this for content with overlapping objects, where the position of the objects in relation to one another is critical to the content, and where you want to have objects in one area fade in and out along the timeline. The box as a whole may change size and position, but the elements within the box will not reposition.

Flow

If you have multiple objects in the fluid box, use this menu to indicate if you want the objects to stack one on top of the other (**Vertical**) or appear side by side (**Horizontal**).

Vertical

Horizontal

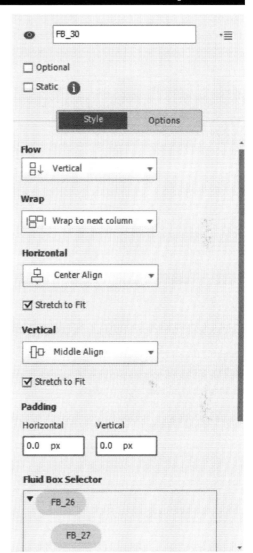

Fluid Box Properties (cont'd)

Wrap

If you have multiple objects in a fluid box, use this menu to indicate what happens to them when the device is narrower. This fluid box with four images is set to horizontal flow.

On a large device, all objects fit. On a smaller device, you can determine how the objects should wrap:

- **Wrap to next row/column**: As the device size gets smaller, individual objects start moving to a next row.

- **Squeeze in a row/column**: Objects get smaller to stay in the same column or row they were already in.

- **One row/column**: Objects wrap in a single line.

- **Symmetrical**: Objects wrap to a new row or column, keeping the same number of objects in each row/column, if possible.

Wrap Percent

When you have the top fluid box selected, there's an extra feature in the **Wrap** field **(A)** that lets you indicate how small the device needs to get before the wrap is implemented. Use the menu to change from the default of 80%.

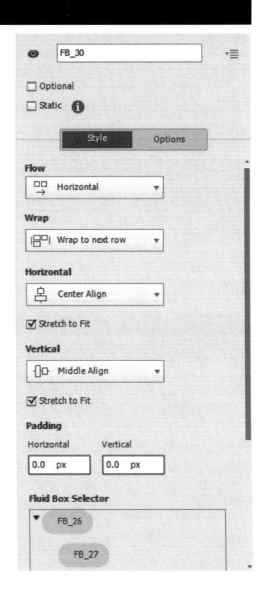

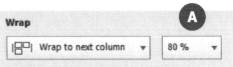

POWER TIP

If you go to **Preferences** on the **Edit** menu and select **Enable WrapPoint** on the **Defaults** tab, you get the **Wrap Percent** for every fluid box, not just the top parent box. When you change it on a child box, it becomes cumulative. So a value of 60% on a child box means 60% of the parent's 80%.

Fluid Box Properties (cont'd)

Horizontal/Vertical

These two menus dictate how multiple objects in a fluid box are aligned, especially when wrapped.

The **Horizontal** menu lets you pick from **Left Align**, **Center Align**, and **Right Align**.

Center alignment (default)   *Left alignment*

The **Vertical** menu lets you pick from **Top Align**, **Middle Align**, and **Bottom Align**.

The next two options appear either on the **Horizontal** or the **Vertical** menu based on what type of flow you selected.

- **Space In Between**: The objects are spaced evenly across the fluid box, with objects going to the edge of the box.

- **Space Around**: The objects are spaced evenly across the fluid box including space between the outermost objects and the edge of the box.

Stretch to Fit

Both fields have a checkbox that is checked by default. When you add an object to a fluid box with this box checked, the object will resize to fill the box. Text captions will stretch in both dimensions, which mean they may change aspect ratio. Images and shapes will stretch as much as they can without changing aspect ratio.

When **Stretch to Fit** is selected, you can only resize objects in certain directions. A white resize handle means you can resize in that direction. A red resize handle means you cannot resize in that direction.

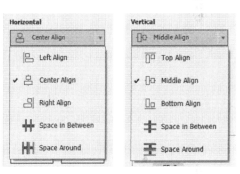

*All three fluid boxes are set to **Stretch to Fit**. The image and the shape keep aspect ratio, so they may not fill the box in both dimensions. The text caption resizes to fill both dimensions.*

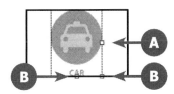

Fluid Box Properties (cont'd)

Padding

Padding puts extra space around all objects, regardless of the wrapping status. You can add space to the left and right of objects in the **Horizontal** field and space to the top and bottom of objects in the **Vertical** field.

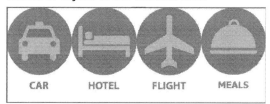

Objects set to top alignment with no padding

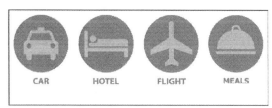

Objects set to top alignment with horizontal and vertical padding

Options Tab

On the **Options** tab, you can set the background for the fluid box.

 Selecting Colors, p. 98–101

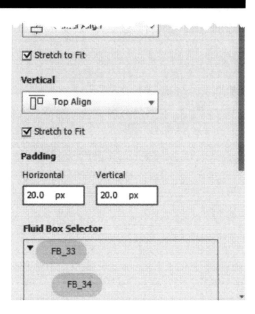

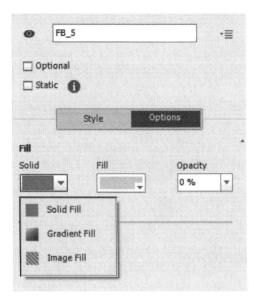

 CAUTION

If you use an image fill, be sure to check the preview to make sure it looks good on the different device sizes. Adjust the settings for tiling, stretching, and maintaining aspect ratio to get the effect you want on different device sizes.

Responsive Object Properties

Objects in responsive projects have additional properties you won't find in a standard project.

Optional

Check this box if you want the object to disappear on small devices. This is commonly used for images that are more decorative or information that is not critical. This feature only works when using the **Squeeze in a row/column** wrap option.

Maintain Aspect Ratio

In other parts of Captivate, this setting lets you resize an object on the slide and keep it in perfect proportion (not stretched in either direction). With fluid boxes, this setting affects how the object looks while editing the slide, and also affects how it resizes when the published course is viewed on different devices. If you uncheck this box and a student is viewing your course on a phone, it is likely that the object may appear compressed horizontally.

By default, images and shapes are set to maintain aspect ratio. Text captions are set to ignore aspect ratio.

Unlock From Fluid Box

If you have an object in a fluid box and want to pull it out, uncheck this box. You might want to do this temporarily to make it easier to format an object. Then, you can uncheck the box to put it back. You may also want to unlock an object that should always stay in the same relative place regardless of device size.

Timing Tab

If you set an object to appear for the rest of the project, it will be pulled out of any fluid box it is in and cannot be added back. This is because fluid boxes live on each slide, so an object in a fluid box on one slide can't continue on to the next slide.

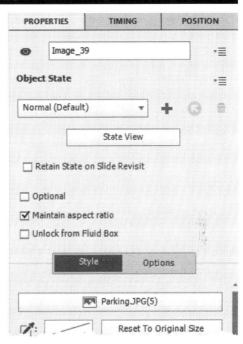

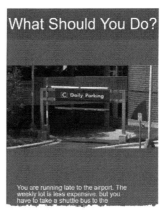

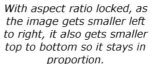

With aspect ratio locked, as the image gets smaller left to right, it also gets smaller top to bottom so it stays in proportion.

With aspect ratio unlocked, as the image gets smaller left to right, it stays the same top to bottom, putting it out of proportion.

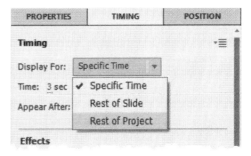

Responsive Object Properties (cont'd)

Position Tab

When you have an object that is unlocked from fluid boxes, you can indicate where you want it to appear. For example, you might have a hint or job aid icon that you always want in the top-right corner.

Object Position

In this section, you can indicate where you want the object to appear:

- **Percent:** Adjusts the object based on a percentage of the slide, such as being 50% of the way down the screen or being 10% of the width of the screen.

- **Px (pixels):** Adjusts the object at an absolute distance, such as 20 pixels from the top or 50 pixels wide.

- **% Relative:** Adjusts the object based on a percentage of the slide in relation to another object on the slide. For example, if you have a highlight box over a diagram, you would want the two objects to change location or size in relation to each other. This way, the highlight box will always be over the right spot. Select both objects, and then select **% Relative** in the position or size areas.

Object Size

Here you can set the preferred size of an object. As with the position, you can measure it as a percent, in pixels, or relative to something else. If you choose **Auto**, then that dimension will adjust automatically based on the other dimension.

Advanced

If you expand the **Advanced** section, you can set a minimum or maximum size for an object. For example, if you have a diagram with a fair amount of detail, you may need to make sure it stays at least a minimum size so that the detail can still be seen.

Align Center

If you check either of these boxes, your object will be aligned to the center of the slide, horizontally, vertically, or both. These settings override what you have in the **Object Position** field.

Smart Position

If you check this box, you see indicators **(A)** showing you what the object is anchored to. By default, that's the top and left of the screen. You can click and drag the indicators to anchor the object to another object instead of to the slide.

Lock Size and Position

If you check this box, you cannot manually move or resize that object. The object will still automatically adjust size and position for each layout, but you cannot manually change it.

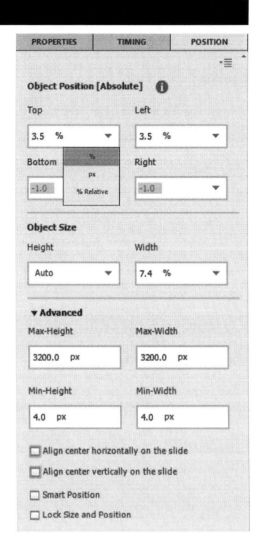

Software Simulations and Responsive Projects

You can add software simulation slides to a responsive project. Rather than shrinking the screen captures to fit on a mobile phone (making them difficult to see clearly), the screen captures are cropped to show just the relevant part of the slide. You can adjust these settings if you want to.

 Software Simulations, p. 21

To change which part of the screen shows:
1. Drag the blue rectangle **(A)** to the part of the slide that should always be showing.

To show the entire screen capture:
1. In the slide's **Properties** panel, uncheck **Use portion of background image**.

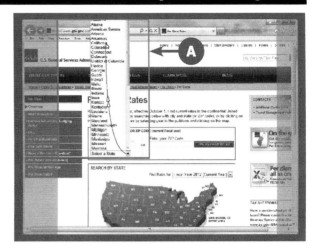

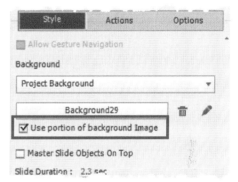

CAUTION

If you uncheck **Use portion of background Image**, the image will be resized to fit completely in the device size, which may cause the image to skew.

BRIGHT IDEA

In the different preview modes, the white area indicates what will show and the shaded area shows what will be cut off.

HTML5 Tracker

Whether you are using a regular project or a responsive project, if you are publishing to HTML5 for mobile devices, you'll want to make sure your course works as expected on all target devices. Captivate comes with an HTML5 tracker that checks your projects for any elements that might not work in HTML5 output.

Run the HTML5 Tracker

To run the HTML5 Tracker:
1. Go to the **Project** menu.
2. Select **HTML5 Tracker**.
3. Click a line item to be taken to that item.

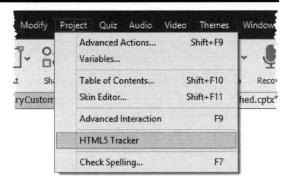

 DESIGN TIP

Here are a few elements to avoid in an HTML5 project:

- Text animations (including the **Replace with Text Animation** feature in a screen simulation)
- Imported **.swf** animations
- Mouse click animations other than the default
- Slide transitions
- Audio attached to invisible objects
- Rollover captions, images, smart shapes, and slidelets

Check the Adobe Captivate online help for the most current list of unsupported objects, issues, and workarounds for HTML5 objects.

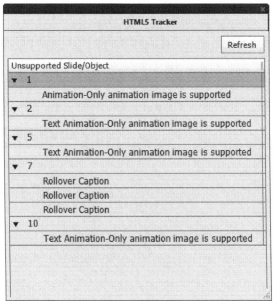

 CAUTION

Many of the object types show up in the issues list are Flash based. In 2020, Adobe will stop supporting the Flash Player altogether. At that point, most browsers will completely stop playing any Flash content. Be very cautious about including Flash content in your courses as those courses could become obsolete very quickly.

Appendix A

In addition to the cool tools found here in the Appendix, be sure to check out the additional tools on this book's companion website:

www.elearninguncovered.com.

Notes

Accessibility

Accessibility in e-learning refers to making courses compatible with various assistive technology devices used by people with disabilities. There are three main classes of disability that affect e-learning: visual, auditory, and motor.

Impairment	Common Assistive Devices	Considerations for E-Learning
Visual Low vision No vision Color blindness	Screen readers that read information about what is happening on-screen to the user Refreshable braille displays that create dynamic braille descriptions of what is happening on screen Screen magnifiers that enlarge all or part of what is happening on screen	In order for screen readers and braille displays to describe what is happening on screen, they need to be "told" what is happening. Therefore, you'll need to add descriptive text (alt text) to course elements for these devices to read. Be sure there are no elements that require recognition of color. Color can be used, as long as it is not the only way to tell what something means. For example, you can include a green check and a red X to indicate right or wrong, because the check and the X alone can convey the meaning. But a red and a green dot would not work, since the student would need to distinguish between the colors to determine meaning. Use strong value contrast (light vs. dark) so those with low vision or color blindness can recognize on-screen elements. For example, a light blue caption on a light background may be hard to read for those with vision challenges. Vision is required in order to use a mouse properly. Visually impaired students generally do not use a mouse, instead relying on keyboard navigation through their screen reader. Therefore, course elements must be keyboard-accessible.
Auditory Hard of hearing Deafness	Closed captioning systems	For individuals with auditory impairments, it is necessary to provide a transcript of any important audio elements in the course. For static content, this can be done with a static transcript text box. For multimedia content timed to audio, the closed captioning should also be timed to audio.
Motor Limited dexterity No manual skills	Alternate navigation devices such as keyboards, joysticks, trackballs, and even breathing devices	For those with limited mobility, be sure that any interactive element (such as a button) is large enough for someone with rough motor skills to use. Make sure all course elements are keyboard-accessible. If a course is keyboard-accessible, then it will work with most other mobility-assistive devices.

Another factor to consider is cognitive impairments such as learning disabilities or dyslexia. Courses are more accessible to those with cognitive impairments when there are no time constraints. For example, you can include play/pause/rewind controls and avoid timed elements, such as a timed test.

Accessibility Requirements and Guidelines

There are two main reasons to make your courses accessible:

1. You want your courses to be available for those in your target audience who may have a disability.
2. You may be required by law.

Internationally, the World Wide Web Consortium (W3C) provides web content accessibility guidelines (WCAG). In addition, many countries have their own standards and requirements. In the United States, Section 508 of the Workforce Rehabilitation Act of 1973 (and later amended) requires that information technology (including e-learning) used by the federal government be accessible to those with disabilities. Many other levels of government and private organizations choose to adopt that standard on their own. Go to **www.section508.gov** for more detailed information on the standards and the requirements.

Creating an Accessible Course

The following pages contain some of the major Captivate features that are used (or should be avoided) to comply with the Section 508/WCAG requirements for e-learning.

Enabling Accessibility

In order for the accessibility features in Captivate to work, you need to enable accessibility for the project in the **Preferences** dialog box, found on the **Edit** menu.

 Change Publish Settings, p. 250

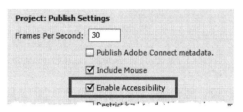

Project Information

Add information such as the title, author, and description in the **Preferences** dialog box.

 Project Information Settings, p. 248

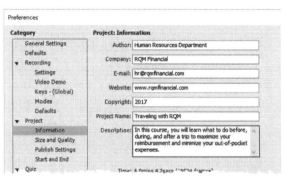

Alt Text

Any visual element with meaning, such as an image or diagram, needs to have a text description so that a screen reader can "describe" it to the learner. Be sure to include enough detail so that the learner can get any information and context that is important for learning while avoiding unnecessary details.

You do not need to add alt text for any text-based objects in Captivate (text box, shape with text, etc.). Screen readers automatically read any text element.

In Captivate, you can add alt text to the slide and to individual objects. By default, the alt text is whatever is in the object name field. **(A)** If you click the **Accessibilty** option on the menu shown, you can use a dialog box where you can enter more detailed text instead. Alt text for a slide works the same way, using the slide's **Properties** panel.

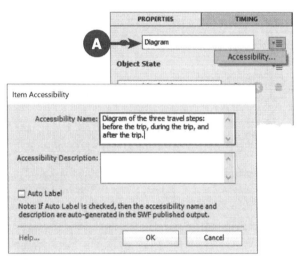

 Slide Properties, p. 39
Object Properties, p. 97

Keyboard Navigation

An accessible course needs to be navigable with a keyboard. This helps individuals with mobility and vision impairments. Even if the learner can't use a keyboard, that person's assistive technology can perform the keyboard functions.

Captivate is set up to make the courses keyboard accessible. Even in a regular browser, you can use the **Tab** key to move between elements, use the **Enter** key to activate a button, and use the arrow keys to move down the menu.

However, some features in Captivate are NOT keyboard accessible. For example, in a quiz, you can only use multiple choice, true/false, and rating scale question types.

 # CAUTION

- This section is not intended to be a stand-alone guide, but rather to be used in conjunction with other educational resources (such as www.section508.gov) and thorough accessibility testing.

- Be sure to only use features that are accessible. Adobe does not provide a list of which features are/are not accessible, so be sure to test everything throughly.

Creating an Accessible Course (cont'd)

Tab Order

Objects being read by a screen reader or tabbed to via a keyboard should be read in a logical order. For example, you wouldn't want a **Next** button to come before a **Submit** button. In a Captivate course, screen readers read objects from the top layer to the bottom layer (front-to-back order). You can click the **Tab Order** button in the slide's **Properties** panel to manually override the tab order of any *interactive* elements on a slide.

 Tab Order, p. 39

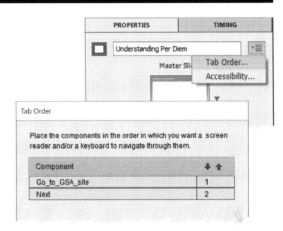

Removal from Tab Order/Screen Readers

To help learners stay focused on what's important, you can remove non-critical objects from tab order. If someone is tabbing through the course, the removed objects will be completely skipped. This is the best choice for items such as colored backgrounds or lines that separate sections of a screen.

For any object you want to remove from tab order, go to the **Accessibility** dialog box for that object, uncheck the **AutoLabel** field, and leave the text fields blank.

 Object Properties, p. 97

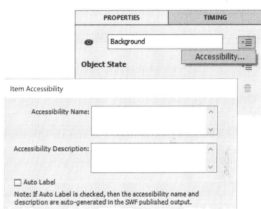

Closed Captions

You can add a closed captioning to any slide with audio or video. You add your text in the **Slide Notes** panel, and then use a dialog box to synchronize the captions to the audio or video. When using closed captioning, be sure to enable the **CC** button on the playbar.

 Closed Captioning, p. 88
Playback Controls, p. 244

 BRIGHT IDEA

Accessibility is subjective, with much debate about what is both usable and compliant. It's important that you evaluate guidance from the government, accessibility groups, and your own organization (legal, H.R., I.T., etc.) to determine what accessibility means for your organization.

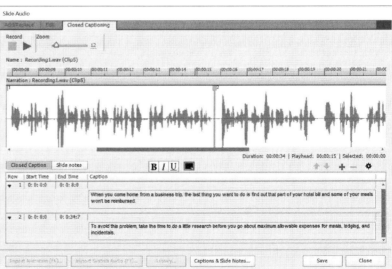

Building an Accessible Course (cont'd)

Tables

To be fully accessible, tables need to have behind-the-scenes information so a screen reader can announce what row or column the student is in at any time. Captivate does not come with this feature. So if you use any tables (either an imported graphic or the table learning interaction), be sure to provide an alternate version that is fully accessible, such as a PDF that is set up with the appropriate data.

Media Controls

In an accessible course, it is important that the learner has control over any media elements. For example, if a learner is using a screen reader, that software "reads" the on-screen elements out loud. If you have audio that plays automatically, it will be talking the same time the screen reader is trying to talk.

In an accessible course, Captivate has features you can use to give the learner more control. For example, you can let learners activate accessibility preferences (stored in a variable). Then on slides with media that plays automatically, you can add an action that pauses the audio or the slide if the accessibility preference is activated.

Actions, ch. 7
Variables, ch. 9

Time Limits

Accessible courses give students the option to turn off or extend any time limits, such as a timed quiz. (There are a few exceptions to this rule.) Consider carefully about whether time limits are truly important in your course, and if so, how you can best provide accessibility options.

Software Simulations

If you are teaching computer procedures, consider very carefully what the best design will be for students using assistive devices. For example, is the software you are teaching accessible? And, would someone using assistive technology be using the software the same way as someone who is not? Consider creating separate courses based on how the student will be accessing the software being taught.

Software simulations can be visually cluttered. Consider the use of highlight boxes, high-contrast captions, and a double-sized mouse cursor to assist students with low vision.

Software Simulations, p. 21

Publishing

Only the Flash output of Captivate is accessible.

	Reimbursable	Requires permission	Never reimbursable
Domestic Flights			
Coach	X		
Coach premium		X	
Business class			X
First class			X
International Flights			
Coach	X		
Coach premium	X		

*Knowing this is an **X** is not enough. A student using a screen reader would need to know it is in the **Domestic Flights** > **First Class** row and the **Never reimbursable** column.*

 DESIGN TIPS

Your design choices affect your course's accessibility For example:

- Make sure you have good color contrast, especially with text.

- Avoid using language that requires a certain sense, such as "Click to see the answer," "in the example below," or "listen to what she has to say."

- Be careful about synchronizing elements to audio. It can be challenging to use the keyboard to get to every item if they are appearing and disappearing.

- Don't include any elements that flicker or flash, as they could cause seizures.

- Consider the accessibility of any content you bring into Captivate, such as a pre-made interaction or a PDF attachment.

- Really think about your alt text. Provide any information that is useful and leave out any information that's extraneous. With buttons and interactive elements, make sure the alt text makes it clear what will happen when the student clicks that element.

- Screen readers register slides better if there are interactive elements that let the student move from slide to slide (i.e., a **Next** button), rather than having the slides play continuously. If slides do advance automatically, make sure there is enough time to tab to everything.

- Avoid looping objects that can cause the page to load over and over again.

Mac and PC Interface Tools

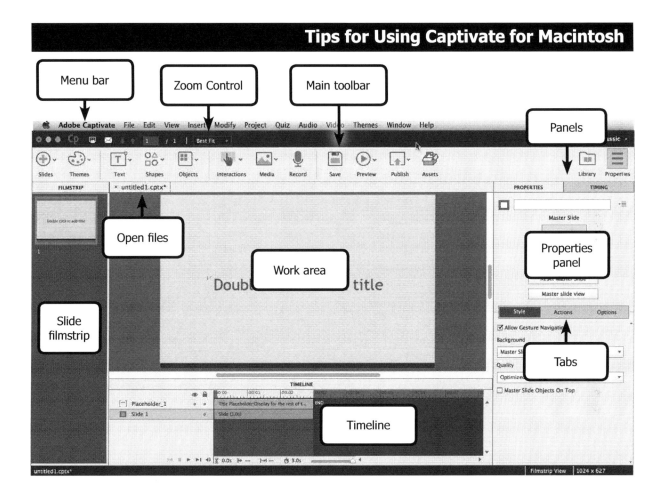

Interface & Navigation

The Mac interface is very similar to the PC interface. Key differences include:

- In most dialog boxes for the PC, **OK** (or similar) is on the left and **Cancel** is on the right. They are usually reversed on the Mac.
- Right-click commands on the PC are control-click commands on a Mac.
- The **Preferences** dialog box is on the **Adobe Captivate** menu instead of the **Edit** menu on a Mac.

Many of the keyboard shortcuts are the same between Mac and PC. The one major exception is that you would use the **Command** key on a Mac instead of the **Control** key on a PC. See page 298 for commonly-used shortcuts.

Please note: This is not intended to be a comprehensive list of differences between Captivate for Mac and Captivate for PC. While most of the capabilities between the two will be the same, you may encounter some differences.

Captivate for Mac Menus

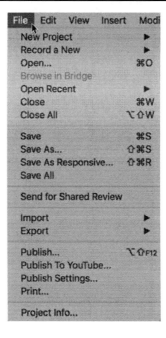

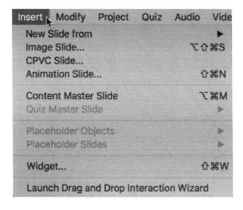

Captivate for Mac Menus

Project Quiz Audio Video

Advanced Actions...	⇧⌘F9
Variables...	
Switch to Breakpoint Mode	
Table of Contents...	⇧⌘F10
Skin Editor...	⇧⌘F11
Advanced Interaction	⌘F9
HTML5 Tracker	
Check Spelling...	F7

Quiz Audio Video Themes Window

Question Slide...	⇧Q
Random Question Slide	⌥⇧R
Pretest Question Slide	
Knowledge Check Slide	
Quiz Master Slide	▶
Question Placeholder Objects	▶
Result Placeholder Objects	▶
Import Question Pools...	
Question Pool Manager...	⌥⇧Q
Quiz Preferences...	
Import GIFT Format File	⌥⇧G

Audio Video Themes Window

Import to	▶
Record to	▶
Edit	▶
Remove	▶
Audio Management...	⌥⇧A
Speech Management...	⌥⇧S
Settings...	

Video Themes Window

Insert Video...	⌥⌘V
Edit Video Timing...	
Video Management...	

Themes Window Help

Save Theme	
Save Theme As...	
Recording Defaults	
Master Slide	
Object Style Manager...	⇧F7
Table of Contents...	⇧⌘F10
Skin Editor...	⇧⌘F11

Window Help

Align	
✓ Filmstrip	⌥⌘B
Mobile Palette	
Timeline	⌥⌘T
✓ Library	⌥⌘L
Master Slide	
Question Pool	
Slide Notes	⌥⌘N
Project Info	
Progress Indicator	
Branching View	⌥⇧⌘B
Skin Editor	⇧⌘F11
Drag and Drop	
Advanced Interaction	⌘F9
HTML5 Tracker	
Comments	⌥⌘X
Swatch Manager	
Find and Replace	⌘F
Effects	▶
Workspace	▶

Help

Search	
Adobe Captivate Help	F1
Adobe Captivate Draft Help	
Adobe Product Improvement Program...	
Adobe Captivate Blog	
Complete/Update Adobe ID Profile...	
Sign Out (pjaising@adobe.com)	
Updates...	
Access Adobe Resources...	

Captivate for PC Menus

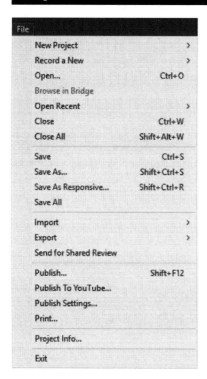

File

New Project	>
Record a New	>
Open...	Ctrl+O
Browse in Bridge	
Open Recent	>
Close	Ctrl+W
Close All	Shift+Alt+W
Save	Ctrl+S
Save As...	Shift+Ctrl+S
Save As Responsive...	Shift+Ctrl+R
Save All	
Import	>
Export	>
Send for Shared Review	
Publish...	Shift+F12
Publish To YouTube...	
Publish Settings...	
Print...	
Project Info...	
Exit	

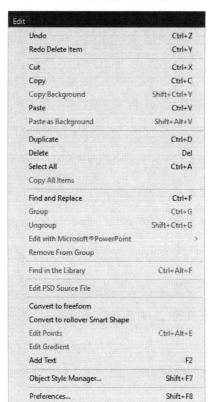

Edit

Undo	Ctrl+Z
Redo Delete Item	Ctrl+Y
Cut	Ctrl+X
Copy	Ctrl+C
Copy Background	Shift+Ctrl+Y
Paste	Ctrl+V
Paste as Background	Shift+Alt+V
Duplicate	Ctrl+D
Delete	Del
Select All	Ctrl+A
Copy All Items	
Find and Replace	Ctrl+F
Group	Ctrl+G
Ungroup	Shift+Ctrl+G
Edit with Microsoft®PowerPoint	>
Remove From Group	
Find in the Library	Ctrl+Alt+F
Edit PSD Source File	
Convert to freeform	
Convert to rollover Smart Shape	
Edit Points	Ctrl+Alt+E
Edit Gradient	
Add Text	F2
Object Style Manager...	Shift+F7
Preferences...	Shift+F8

View

Zoom In	Ctrl+=
Zoom Out	Ctrl+-
Magnification	>
Hide Comments	
Hide Slide	Shift+Ctrl+H
Lock Slide	Ctrl+K
Lock	Ctrl+Alt+K
Hide	Ctrl+Alt+H
Show Grid	
Snap to Grid	
Snap to Object	
✓ Show Drawing/Smart Guides	
Show Rulers	Ctrl+Alt+R
Hide Guides	Ctrl+;
Clear Guides	
Lock Guides	
Snap to Guide	
Create Multiple Guides	
New Guide	

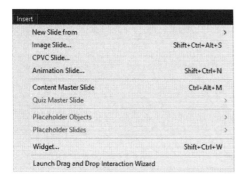

Insert

New Slide from	>
Image Slide...	Shift+Ctrl+Alt+S
CPVC Slide...	
Animation Slide...	Shift+Ctrl+N
Content Master Slide	Ctrl+Alt+M
Quiz Master Slide	>
Placeholder Objects	>
Placeholder Slides	>
Widget...	Shift+Ctrl+W
Launch Drag and Drop Interaction Wizard	

Modify

Rescale project...	
Replace Smart Shape	
Redraw Smart Shape	Ctrl+Alt+W
Save Smart Shape	
Arrange	▸
Align	▸
Move Question to	▸
Merge FMR Slides	
Merge with the background	Ctrl+M
Sync with Playhead	Ctrl+L
Show for the rest of the slide	Ctrl+E
Increase Indent	Ctrl+I
Decrease Indent	Shift+Ctrl+I
Auto-adjust Rollover Area	Ctrl+Alt+R
Update from Source	
Mouse	▸
Group	▸

Project

Advanced Actions...	Shift+F9
Variables...	
Switch to Breakpoint Mode	
Table of Contents...	Shift+F10
Skin Editor...	Shift+F11
Advanced Interaction	F9
HTML5 Tracker	
Check Spelling...	F7

Captivate for PC Menus (cont'd)

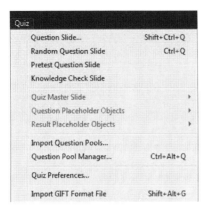

Quiz

Question Slide...	Shift+Ctrl+Q
Random Question Slide	Ctrl+Q
Pretest Question Slide	
Knowledge Check Slide	
Quiz Master Slide	▸
Question Placeholder Objects	▸
Result Placeholder Objects	▸
Import Question Pools...	
Question Pool Manager...	Ctrl+Alt+Q
Quiz Preferences...	
Import GIFT Format File	Shift+Alt+G

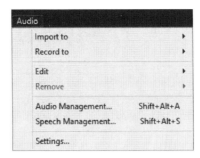

Audio

Import to	▸
Record to	▸
Edit	▸
Remove	▸
Audio Management...	Shift+Alt+A
Speech Management...	Shift+Alt+S
Settings...	

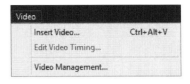

Video

Insert Video...	Ctrl+Alt+V
Edit Video Timing...	
Video Management...	

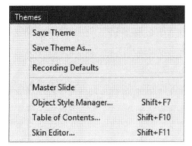

Themes

Save Theme	
Save Theme As...	
Recording Defaults	
Master Slide	
Object Style Manager...	Shift+F7
Table of Contents...	Shift+F10
Skin Editor...	Shift+F11

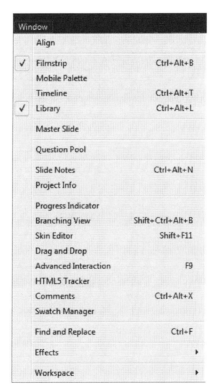

Window

Align	
✓ Filmstrip	Ctrl+Alt+B
Mobile Palette	
Timeline	Ctrl+Alt+T
✓ Library	Ctrl+Alt+L
Master Slide	
Question Pool	
Slide Notes	Ctrl+Alt+N
Project Info	
Progress Indicator	
Branching View	Shift+Ctrl+Alt+B
Skin Editor	Shift+F11
Drag and Drop	
Advanced Interaction	F9
HTML5 Tracker	
Comments	Ctrl+Alt+X
Swatch Manager	
Find and Replace	Ctrl+F
Effects	▸
Workspace	▸

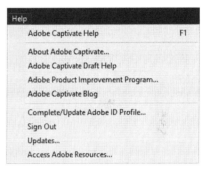

Help

Adobe Captivate Help	F1
About Adobe Captivate...	
Adobe Captivate Draft Help	
Adobe Product Improvement Program...	
Adobe Captivate Blog	
Complete/Update Adobe ID Profile...	
Sign Out	
Updates...	
Access Adobe Resources...	

Useful Keyboard Shortcuts

There are over one hundred keyboard shortcuts in Captivate, all of which can be found in the Adobe Captivate Help documentation. Here is a list of the shortcuts that the authors find most useful to memorize.

Insert

	PC	Mac
New Slide	Shift + Ctrl + V	Shift + Cmd + V
Blank Slide	Shift + Ctrl + J	Shift + Cmd + J
Question Slide	Shift + Ctrl + Q	Shift + Q
Text Caption	Shift + Ctrl + C	Shift + Cmd + C
Mouse	Shift + Ctrl + U	Shift + Cmd + U

Editing

	PC	Mac
Undo	Ctrl + Z	Cmd + Z
Redo	Ctrl + Y	Cmd + Y
Cut	Ctrl + X	Cmd + X
Copy	Ctrl + C	Cmd + C
Paste	Ctrl + V	Cmd + V
Duplicate	Ctrl + D	Cmd + D

File Management

	PC	Mac
Save	Ctrl + S	Cmd + S
Publish	Shift + F12	Option + Shift + F12

Formatting

	PC	Mac
Bold	Ctrl + B	Cmd + B
Underline	Ctrl + U	Cmd + U
Italics	Ctrl + I	Cmd + I

Timing

	PC	Mac
Sync Object to Playhead	Ctrl + L	Cmd + L
Show for Rest of Slide	Ctrl + E	Cmd + E
Start Next Slide (in Edit Slides Audio)	Ctrl + S	

Play/Preview

	PC	Mac
Play Slide	F3	F3
Preview Project	F4	F4
Preview From This Slide	F8	Cmd + F8
Preview Next 5 Slides	F10	
Preview In Web Browser	F12	Cmd + F12
Preview in HTML5	F11	Cmd + F11
Toggle Play/Pause	Space	Space

View

	PC	Mac
Zoom In	Ctrl + =	Cmd + =
Zoom Out	Ctrl + -	Cmd + -

Default recording shortcuts for PC

General:
To Stop Recording: End
To Pause/Resume Recording: Pause

Manual Recording:
To Capture a Screenshot: Print Screen

Full Motion Recording:
To Start Full Motion Recording: F9
To Stop Full Motion Recording: F10

Panning:
For Automatic Panning: F4
For Manual Panning: F3
To Stop Panning: F7
To snap recording window to mouse: F11

To toggle mouse capture in Video Demo: F12
To insert an UNDO Marker: Ctrl+Shift+Z

Default recording shortcuts for Mac

General:
To Stop Recording: Cmd-Enter
To Pause/Resume Recording: Cmd-F2

Manual Recording:
To Capture a Screenshot: Cmd-F6

Full Motion Recording:
To Start Full Motion Recording: Cmd-F9
To Stop Full Motion Recording: Cmd-F10

Panning:
For Automatic Panning: Cmd-F4
For Manual Panning: Cmd-F3
To Stop Panning: Cmd-F7
To snap recording window to mouse: Cmd-F11

To toggle mouse capture in Video Demo: Cmd-F12
To insert an UNDO Marker: Shift-Cmd-Z

System Variables

Movie Control Variables

In **Advanced Actions**, you can assign the value of these variables for custom navigation and interface elements.

Variable	Definition	Default	Comments
cpCmndCC	Enable/disable closed captioning. Set value to 1 to display closed captions.	0	Rather than just adding a closed captioning button to the Playback Control bar, you can add your own buttons or logic by setting this variable to 1 vs. 0.
cpCmndExit	Use this variable (set to 1) to exit the movie.	0	Rather than just adding an exit button to the Playback Control bar, you can add your own button or logic by setting this variable to 1.
cpCmndGotoFrame	Specify a frame number for the movie to jump to and then pause.	-1	These let you create navigation to a specific point in a slide. One option pauses the movie when the student arrives; the other plays the movie. Temporarily display the **cpInfoCurrentFrame** variable at the point where you want to jump so that you can determine the frame number.
cpCmndGotoFrame-AndResume	Specify a frame number for the movie to jump to and then play.	-1	
cpCmndGotoSlide	Assign the slide number that the movie should move to before pausing.	-1	This works the same as a **Jump to Slide** action. You can use it as part of an advanced action or when integrating with Flash or JavaScript.
cpCmndMute	Mute the audio. Set to 1 to mute and 0 to unmute.	0	Rather than just adding an audio on/off button to the playbar, you can add your own buttons or logic by setting this variable to 1 vs. 0.
cpCmndNextSlide	Set the value to 1 to jump to the next slide.	0	This works the same as a **Go to the Next Slide** action. Use it with Flash or JavaScript.
cpCmndPause	Set the value to 1 to pause the movie.	0	Rather than just adding a pause button to the Playback Control bar, you can add your own buttons or logic by setting this variable to 1.
cpCmndPlaybarMoved	Set to 1 if the playbar has moved.	0	Use this to find out if students use the playbar to move around (other than **Play/Pause**)
cpCmndPrevious	Set the value to 1 to jump to the previous slide.	0	This works the same as a **Go to the Previous Slide** action.
cpCmndResume	Set the value to 1 to resume play of the movie.	0	If the movie is paused, create a button or logic to unpause it by setting this variable to 1.
cpCmndShowPlaybar	Set to 1 to show the playbar or 0 to hide the playbar.	1	Use this variable to create show/hide controls for the playbar, or to hide the playbar on certain slides, such as the final quiz.
cpCmndTOCVisible	Set to 1 to show the TOC or 0 to hide the TOC.	0	Use this variable to create show/hide controls for the table of contents, or to hide the TOC on certain slides.
cpCmndVolume	Control the movie's volume, from 0 to 100.	100	You can change volume throughout the movie or create a control that lets the student do it.
cpLockTOC	Enable/disable user interaction on the TOC. Set to 1 to disable.	0	If you want the table of contents to be for information only and not for navigation, you can lock it so that it isn't interactive. Or you can lock it just for certain slides, such as quiz slides.

Movie Information Variables

Variable	Definition	Default	Comments
CaptivateVersion	Current version of Captivate.	v9.0.0	This might be useful if you are working in Flash or JavaScript and want the behavior to be different based on which version of Captivate you are using.
cpInfoCurrentFrame	Returns the current frame number.	1	Use this to identify the frame you want when using the **cpCmndGotoFrameAndResume** and **cpCmndGotoFrame** variables.
cpInfoCurrentSlide	Current slide number. Index begins with 1.	1	Use this to display a page counter to the student.
cpInfoCurrentSlideLabel	Name of the Current Slide.	slide	Use this to create a caption that displays the slide label as a heading for the slide.
cpInfoCurrentSlideType	Type of the slide that plays now. This can be Normal Slide, Question Slide, or Random Question Slide.	Normal	Use this information for if/then logic based on slide type. For example, enable TOC navigation on normal slides but disable it on quiz slides.
cpInfoElapsedTimeMS	Time elapsed (in milliseconds) since the movie started playing.	0	This information might be useful if you are working in Flash or JavaScript.
cpInfoFPS	The frame rate of the movie in frames per second.	1	
cpInfoFrameCount	Returns the total number of frames in the project.	1	
cpInfoHasPlaybar	Provides information about the visibility of the playbar. Returns 1 if the playbar is visible, else 0.	1	Use this to create a toggle to show or hide the toolbar. Add a show action if this is 0 and a hide action if this is 1.
cpInfoIsStandalone	This value would be set to 1 when published as .exe or .app. Otherwise, it is set to 0.	1	This information might be useful if you are working in Flash or JavaScript.
cpInfoLastVisitedSlide	The slide last visited.	0	Use these variables as conditions based on navigation. For example, you might want to show something different on slide 6 if they are coming from the home page versus coming from slide 5.
cpInfoPrevSlide	The previous slide.	-1	
cpInfoSlideCount	The total number of slides in the project.	1	Use for a page counter showing x of xx pages.

Movie Metadata Variables

Variable	Definition	Default	Comments
cpInfoAuthor	Name of the Author.	author	These variables pull information from the **Project Information** tab in **Preferences**.
cpInfoCompany	Name of the Company.	company	
cpInfoCopyright	Copyright Info.	copyright	
cpInfoCourseID	ID of the Course.	-1	These variables are no longer used by Captivate.
cpInfoCourseName	Name of the Course.	Course Name	
cpInfoDescription	Description of the Project.	project description	These variables pull information from the **Project Information** tab in **Preferences**.
cpInfoEmail	E-mail Address.	author@company.com	
cpInfoProjectName	Name of the Adobe Captivate Project.		
cpInfoWebsite	URL of the company website, starting with www.	www.company.com	

System Information Variables

Use the date information to display on a certificate or to create your own expiration feature. Comments below reflect what would show on: Saturday, Aug. 11, 2012 at 8:02 p.m.

Variable	Definition	Default	Comments
cpInfoCurrentDate	Day of the month.	Format: dd	11 (11th day of the month)
cpInfoCurrentDateString	Current date in the format mm/dd/yyyy.	Format: mm/dd/yyyy	8/11/2012
cpInfoCurrentDateStringDDMMYYYY	Current date in the format dd/mm/yyyy	Format: dd/mm/yyyy	11/8/2012
cpInfoCurrentDay	Current day of the week.	Format: 1	7 (7th day of the week)
cpInfoCurrentHour	Current Hour: Hour set on user's computer.	Format: hh	20 (military time for 8:00 p.m.)
cpInfoCurrentLocaleDateString	Current Date from locale settings on user's computer.	Format: full text	Saturday, August 11, 2012
cpInfoCurrentMinutes	Current Minutes: Minutes set on user's computer.	Format: mm	2 (2 minutes after the hour)
cpInfoCurrentMonth	Current Month: Month set on user's computer.	Format: mm	08 (8th month of the year)
cpInfoCurrentTime	Current Time in the format hh:mm:ss.	Format: hh:mm:ss	20:02:36
cpInfoCurrentYear	Current Year: Year set on user's computer.	Format: yyyy	2012
cpInfoEpochMS	Time elapsed, in milliseconds, since January 01, 1970.	0	1344729953402
cpInfoMobileOS	Indicates type of mobile OS.	0	Desktop, iOS, Android, etc.

Quizzing Variables

Variable	Definition	Default	Comments
cpInQuizScope	If the student is currently in a quiz.	0	The quizzing variables cannot be set with an **Assign** action, but can be used for conditional logic or displayed to the student.
cpInReviewMode	Indicates whether the user is in Review mode or not.	0	
cpInfoPercentage	Scoring in percentage.	0	For example, you can:
cpQuizInfoAnswerChoice	Student's answer to the current question.		• Create custom certificates displaying information about the total quiz.
cpQuizInfoAttempts	Number of times the quiz has been attempted.	0	• Display question-by-question information, such as the number of points at stake or the number of points earned.
cpQuizInfoLastSlidePointScored	Score for last quiz slide.	0	
cpQuizInfoMaxAttempts OnCurrentQuestion	Maximum attempts allowed on a question.	0	
cpQuizInfoNegativePoints onCurrentQuestionSlide	Negative points for the current slide.	0	• Set up conditional logic based on the points earned or the type of question.
cpQuizInfoPassFail	Quiz result.	0	• Set up conditional logic based on the quiz score as a whole.
cpQuizInfoPointsPerQuestionSlide	Points for the question slide.	0	
cpQuizInfoPointsscored	Points scored in the project.	0	
cpQuizInfoPreTest MaxScore	Maximum score for the pretest questions.	0	
cpQuizInfoPreTest TotalCorrectAnswers	Number of correctly answered pretest questions.	0	
cpQuizInfoPreTest TotalQuestions	Number of pretest questions in the project.	0	
cpQuizInfoPretestPointsscored	Points scored in the Pretest.	0	
cpQuizInfoPretestScorePercentage	Percentage scored in the Pretest.	0	
cpQuizInfoQuestionPartialScoreOn	If partial scoring is turned on for a question. 1 equals yes; 0 equals no.	0	
cpQuizInfoQuestionSlideTiming	Time limit in seconds for the current question.	0	
cpQuizInfoQuestionSlideType	Question slide type, such as multiple-choice or true/false.	choice	
cpQuizInfoQuizPassPercent	Percentage needed to pass the quiz.	80	
cpQuizInfoQuizPassPoints	Points needed to pass the quiz.	0	
cpQuizInfoTotalCorrectAnswers	Number of correct answers.	0	
cpQuizInfoTotalProjectPoints	Total project points possible, including those that are excluded from reporting.	0	

Quizzing Variables (cont'd)

Variable	Definition	Default	Comments
cpQuizInfoTotalQuestions PerProject	Number of questions in the entire project.	0	See previous page.
cpQuizInfoTotalQuizPoints	Total quiz points possible, including those that are excluded from reporting.	0	
cpQuizInfoTotalUnanswered Questions	Number of unanswered questions.	0	

Mobile Variables

If your project has geolocation enabled (**Mobile Palette** on the **Windows** menu), then you'll get the following system variable.

Variable	Definition	Default	Comments
cpInfoGeoLocation	Returns the student's physical location.	N/A	Use this variable for location-aware content, such as displaying a certain text box based on where the student is viewing the course.

Notes

Index I

Index

Put your new skills to work by visiting the companion site at:

www.elearninguncovered.com

➤ Access practice files.

➤ Download free resources.

➤ Subscribe to our blog.

➤ Ask about bulk purchases.

➤ Explore the other books in the series.

Made in the USA
San Bernardino, CA
19 April 2018